STAGES OF
READING
DEVELOPMENT

STAGES OF
READING
DEVELOPMENT

SECOND EDITION

Jeanne S. Chall

Harcourt Brace College Publishers

Fort Worth   Philadelphia   San Diego   New York   Orlando   Austin   San Antonio

Toronto   Montreal   London   Sydney   Tokyo

Publisher	Ted Buchholz
Editor in Chief	Christopher P. Klein
Senior Acquisitions Editor	Jo-Anne Weaver
Project Editor	Laura Hanna
Production Manager	Lois West
Art Director	Sue Hart

Requests for permission to make copies of any part of the work should be mailed to: Permissions Department, Harcourt Brace & Company, 6277 Sea Harbor Drive, Orlando, Florida, 32887-6777.

Address for editorial correspondence: Harcourt Brace College Publishers, 301 Commerce Street, Suite 3700, Fort Worth, Texas 76102.
Address for orders: Harcourt Brace & Company, 6277 Sea Harbor Drive, Orlando, Florida, 32887. 1-800-782-4479, or 1-800-433-0001 (in Florida).

Library of Congress Catalog Card Number: 95-79647

ISBN: 0-15-503081-7

Printed in the United States of America

5 6 7 8 9 0 1 2 3 4   039   9 8 7 6 5 4 3 2 1

To the memory of my father

CONTENTS

CONTENTS

INTRODUCTION

THE SECOND EDITION of *Stages of Reading Development* is an update of the original, published in 1983. This introduction presents new evidence from research and theory on the validity of the Stages and assesses its effects on teacher training and on the development of reading curricula for students with normal reading development and for those with special needs.

THE STAGES: RESEARCH AND THEORY

A number of research studies on reading published during the past decade have reported that reading development tends to follow the Stages as reported in Chall's *Stages of Reading Development* (1983), and several have confirmed the reality of the reading stages.

Linnea Ehri (1985), in an invited address presented at the American Educational Research Association, "Learning to Read and Spell," used an adaptation of Chall's reading development scheme to remind her listeners of the general course of reading and spelling acquisition.

More recently, Louise Spear-Swerling and Robert J. Sternberg (1994), in their theoretical model of reading disability, note that they view reading acquisition as a developmental process in which the nature of reading changes with development, "similar to Chall's stages." They note further: "Our view of normal reading acquisition is similar in many ways to Chall (1983). Like Chall, we view reading acquisition as a developmental process involving qualitatively distinct phases ... " (p. 93).

THE REALITY OF STAGES 0 AND 1

Evidence on the reality of Stage 0 (Prereading) and Stage 1 (De-coding) comes from a research synthesis of the effectiveness of different reading approaches in the early grades—language experience, whole language, and basal readers (Stahl and Miller, 1989). Overall, the synthesis showed that both whole language, and language experience tended to produce the same or slightly higher results in kindergarten than Basal Reading approaches. However, by the end of the first grade, those children who had been exposed to basal reader instruction and its phonics instruction did better. Stahl and Miller interpreted the results in terms of Chall's Stages, noting that since Stage 0 depends primarily on a global and contextual approach to text (reading without decoding), the language experience and whole language approaches may have an advantage. But by Stage 1, when reading an alphabetic language requires knowledge of sound-letter relations, the advantage shifts to approaches that foster the learning of these relationships—in this case, the basal reader approach which presented more systematic instruction in sound-symbol relations.

The Stahl and Miller findings of the developmental nature of reading, with different components having different effects at different times, are similar to what I found in 1967. Indeed, it was this differential that made it possible for me to understand conflicting evidence on the effects of phonics on reading achievement. A comparison by grades showed that programs weak in phonics produced results that were either better, or as good as, those that taught phonics in the beginning of grade 1. However, by the end of grade 1 and beyond, the advantages went to those who had instruction in phonics (Chall, 1967, 1983a, 1983b).

Studies from Australia found that more than 80 percent of the reading comprehension of second and third graders was accounted for by phonemic awareness and decoding strategies (Freebody and Byrne, 1988).

A recent study of Reading Recovery gives additional evidence on the reality of Stage 1 as a decoding Stage (Iverson and Tunmer, 1993). The regular Reading Recovery Program was compared to one that gave more systematic instruction in phonological decoding but was otherwise the same. Thus, two groups of children in grade one were given Reading Recovery—with one exception. One received the regular Reading Recovery word analysis, which is less formal, less structured, and is based on the child's errors.

The other received systematic, explicit phonics. The group that received the more structured, systematic phonics was significantly ahead of the group that used Reading Recovery's more incidental, informal approach.

They further found that the children selected for Reading Recovery (the bottom 10 to 20 percent of first graders) were particularly deficient in phonological processing skills and that their progress in the program was strongly related to the development of these skills. Thus, for children in Stage 1 (grade 1 and beginning grade 2), systematic instruction in decoding seems to produce better results than incidental instruction, particularly for the lowest 10 to 20 percent who are deficient in phonological processing.

STAGE 2, CONFIRMATION AND FLUENCY

Confirmation and Fluency (Chall's Stage 2) has received considerable current interest. Stahl has been studying the reading of sec ond graders to highlight the effects of fluency.

Working with four second-grade teachers, a program was designed to increase fluency by increasing the amount of reading that children did in school and at home. Stories were sent home to be read by parents and then read by the children in class. All classes had a free-reading period and a home reading program.

The fluency practice was eminently successful. The children made average gains during the school year of 2.2 grade levels on an informal reading inventory. "Furthermore, only three of the 85 children in the project failed to reach a second grade level by the end of the project" (Stahl, Eubach, & Cramond, 1995).

TRANSITION FROM STAGE 2 TO 3

A program to give extensive practice in the transition from "learning to read" (Stages 1 and 2) to "reading to learn the new" (Stage 3) was designed by Shany and Biemiller (in press) for poor readers from low-income families. The investigators used a program with increased reading practice in order to help the children make the transition from Stage 2 to 3.

Their conclusion was: "Consistent with the expectations from Chall (1983a) Chall, Jacobs, and Baldwin (1990), Smith (1978), and Stanovich, (1984, 1986), increased reading experience led to increased reading competence" (Shany and Biemiller, in press, p. 24).

STAGES 3, 4, AND 5

Various studies have found that Stages 3, 4, and 5 differ from each other and from Stages 0, 1, and 2. For example, Paris and his associates found that the same training programs are not necessarily successful with students at different stages of development. For example, a reading comprehension program to develop metacognitive abilities was not as successful with third graders as it was with fifth graders (Paris and Jacobs, 1984). The investigators explained the difference in terms of the Stages of Reading Development. Since most third graders, they noted, were still at Stage 2 (the confirmation/fluency stage) they were not yet able to benefit from a Stage 3 activity. Most fifth graders, however, were on Stage 3 (reading to learn the new), and therefore were able to benefit from the more advanced metacognitive practice.

Haller, Child, and Walberg (1988) also found differences in the effects of metacognitive instruction related to students' Stage levels. In a synthesis of 20 studies on the effectiveness of metacognitive instruction, the investigators found that it was effective in the seventh and eighth grades (Stage 3), but not earlier, in grades 1 to 3 (Stages 1 and 2).

> Effects were largest for the seventh and eighth grades, close to the age when Piaget described formal logical operations as reaching full maturity. . . . Metacognitive instruction seems to have had the least influence on students in the fourth, fifth, and sixth grades. Chall (1983b) suggested that fourth grade is a transition point when the conceptual demands of instruction significantly increase. She noted that even students able to read stories may inadequately comprehend content selections. This may be due, in part, to a shifting curriculum emphasis from learning to read to reading to learn and, as classroom observations show (Durkin 1978–79), little instruction time is allotted to comprehension.

> (Haller, Child, & Walberg, [1988] pp. 7–8)

CORRELATIONAL STUDIES

Validation data for the subtests of the Roswell and Chall, Diagnostic Assessments of Reading (DAR, 1992) give further evidence for the reality of the Stages. The 6 DAR subtests (word recognition, oral reading, word analysis, word meaning, spelling and silent reading comprehension) correlated differently with each other at the different stages. For example, at Stage 1 (grade 1 and beginning grade 2), the correlation between word meaning (tested orally) and word recognition (of isolated words) is quite low on the DAR. At Stage 2 (grades 2 and 3), however, the correlation increases. By Stage 3 (grades 3 to 8), the correlation of word meaning and word recognition becomes quite substantial. Thus we see again that Stages 1 and 2 represent a different developmental stage in the acquisition of reading than Stages 3 and beyond. Achievement in Stages 1 and 2 depends strongly on word recognition and phonology. By Stage 3, language and cognition take on greater importance.

On the whole, the highest correlations were among subtests that measured word recognition and decoding—word recognition, spelling, word analysis, and oral reading; and those subtests that measured word meaning and silent reading comprehension. (See, for example, R. L. Thorndike, 1973-74.)

The correlations by separate grades also revealed that the word recognition/decoding scores had the lowest correlations with word meaning scores in the early grades (Stages 1 and 2). However, by Stage 3 and above (grade 4 and above), silent reading comprehension correlated substantially with all the reading measures—and especially with word meaning—suggesting the increasing importance of language and meaning.

In the early grades, word meaning scores had lower correlations with reading achievement (oral reading and silent reading comprehension) than did the word recognition and decoding scores—confirming again the distinction between early reading (Stages 1 and 2) and more mature reading (Stages 3, 4, and 5).

Similar findings were reported by others. (See, for example, Perfetti [1985], Stanovich [1986], and Juel [1988], who reported that word recognition and decoding were of first importance in early reading.) Beyond the primary grades, many have reported that word meanings and cognition are more highly correlated with each other and with reading achievement. (See E. L. Thorndike, 1917; Davis, 1972; R. L. Thorndike, 1973-74; Chall and Stahl, 1985.)

These findings are similar to those reported by Chall (1967 and 1983a) in *Learning to Read: The Great Debate*. A synthesis of 20 studies published from 1938 to 1963 found that in the lower grades, letter and/or phonic knowledge correlated higher with reading comprehension than language and mental ability. However, in grades 3 and beyond, word meanings and mental ability were the greater predictors of reading achievement. (See also Stanovich, Nathan, & Vala-Rossi, 1986.)

The changing nature of the correlations of reading achievement with cognition and word meanings as compared with word recognition and decoding fits the qualitative changes in reading as depicted in the Stages scheme. According to the Reading Stages scheme, in Stage 1 (grade 1 and beginning grade 2), decoding and word recognition are the essential learning tasks. In Stage 3 and beyond, when most readers have mastered decoding (grade 4 and above), word meaning and cognition are of critical importance. (See Chall, Jacobs, and Baldwin, 1990; Carroll, 1977 and 1993.)

THE RELATION BETWEEN ORAL LANGUAGE AND READING

Two early studies of the relation between students' oral language proficiency and their reading achievement give further evidence on the reality of the Stages. Loban (1963) and Strickland (1962) found non-significant correlations between oral language and reading achievement in the primary grades. By the sixth grade, however, the correlations were significant, suggesting that language becomes a stronger factor as reading develops.

Biemiller (1994) reports essentially the same trends as those found by Strickland and Loban thirty years earlier. He studied changes with age in decoding, oral comprehension, and reading comprehension among first to sixth graders and found that reading comprehension is closely related to word identification among younger and slower readers; while it is closely related to oral comprehension and age among older and faster readers. Slower readers develop similar to younger readers where word recognition is also critical. For older and faster readers who have mastered word identification, reading can reach the more advanced oral comprehension level.

Curtis (1980) reported higher scores in the early grades on listening than on reading comprehension. Listening comprehension was nearly twice that of reading comprehension in grade 2. By grade 5, however, listening and reading comprehension became more similar. The correlations between listening and reading comprehension were essentially zero in grade 2, but rose to .74 in grade 5. This also suggests the primary importance of decoding in Stage 1, and the shift to a stronger influence of language in grade 5 (Stage 3).

Sticht's (1974) earlier review of the research comparing listening comprehension (auding) to reading comprehension also found listening comprehension higher than reading comprehension until about grade 7. Above a seventh-grade reading level, the listening and reading scores tended to be similar.

Thus, the Curtis and Sticht findings give further confirmation to the findings from the correlational studies (see earlier) that for the early grades (Stages 1 and 2), word recognition and decoding are the stronger influences on and predictors of reading achievement. However, comprehension of oral language and word meanings (tested orally) become the stronger influence and predictors of reading at Stages 3 and higher (grades 4 and above). (See also Chall, Jacobs and Baldwin, 1990; Chall and Jacobs, in press.)

Biemiller calls this phenomenon the concept of "developmentally limited variables—variables which have significance for the acquisition of reading skill during a few years of development but which cease to be important to reading as the learner becomes highly skilled." They also note that Perfetti (1985) similarly proposed "a threshold beyond which increments in verbal efficiency (word recognition and decoding) have little bearing on comprehension performance" (p. 9).

Biemiller and Siegel acknowledge the similarity between the concept of "developmentally limited variables" and Chall's *Stages of Reading Development* (1983b).

> In conclusion, this study points to two quite different phases in learning to read, with quite different implications for instruction. In the earlier phase, mastery of word identification skills is the main concern. In the later phase, a variety of experiential and naturalistic factors (indexed here by oral comprehension and "grade") play a large role in the development of reading comprehension, while further increases in word identification skills have little further impact on individual differences in reading competence. The transition from one phase to the other is presumably gradual. This conclusion is similar to Chall's (1983b) stages of reading development and the general experience of elementary school teachers.
>
> (Biemiller & Siegel, in press, p. 31)

STAGES OF READING DEVELOPMENT AND LOW-SES CHILDREN

The Stages model was used in an intensive study of the reading development of children of low-income families to help explain their deceleration in reading achievement (Chall, Jacobs, and Baldwin, 1990). Thirty students from low-income families in grades 2, 4, and 6 (followed up in grades 3, 5, and 7 and later in grades 7 to 11) were studied to determine the course of their reading, writing, and language development and whether it differs from that of the greater population of children. It was thought that studying the way these children advance through the Stages, as compared to children in the general population, would give some insights into their unique strengths and weaknesses.

The Reading Stage model suggested some hypotheses to explain why their reading achievement diverged from that of the larger child population—particularly after the primary grades. A "fourth-grade slump" had been noted by researchers and teachers. The occurrence of such a slump at about the fourth grade may arise because low-SES children may not possess the skills and abilities needed to do Stage 3 reading—that is, reading for information in texts that are increasingly complex linguistically and conceptually. Is it possible that low-income children are more able to meet the demands of reading in the primary grades when the task is learning to recognize and sound out words, most of which may be familiar to them in speech and listening?

To examine this, we needed to assess a full range of the children's reading abilities as well as their writing and language achievement. Therefore, an early edition of the DAR, which assesses six components of reading and language, was used. This allowed us to assess the components, how they developed, and how they were related grade to grade. Through these analyses we sought to identify those components of literacy and language that are critical for the early and the later stages of reading of children from low-income families.

FINDINGS

We found a general decelerative trend in reading that started around fourth grade among the low-income children. The start of the slump and its intensity varied by the children's reading ability and by the reading components tested. The below-average readers started to decelerate earlier, and they experienced a more intensive slump through the sixth and seventh grades. The above-average readers started to decelerate later, and their slump was less intense.

Word meanings decelerated earliest (at grade 4) among both good and poor readers. The next to decelerate were word recognition and spelling. Oral and silent reading comprehension held up the longest. Thus, we found what seemed to be a fourth-grade slump—particularly among the below-average readers and on tests that did not rely on context. Fluency also varied considerably for the above- and below-average readers. Most of the above-average readers, at each grade, read fluently. But no more than 40 percent of the below-average readers were rated fluent in any one grade. Thus, at grades 2 and 3 (when, theoretically, most readers begin to become fluent) (see Chall, 1983b), most of the below-average readers, even in the higher grades, were rated dysfluent.

On a follow-up study five years later, the patterns of test scores were similar to those when the students were in the intermediate and upper elementary grades. On most tests, the reading scores were below the test norms, and the discrepancies grew larger in each succeeding grade.

As in the earlier grades, the pattern of deceleration differed somewhat for the different reading and language components. The components that decelerated earlier and faster were those that were not surrounded by context, for example, word meaning, word recognition, and spelling. The tests that decelerated later and slower were those that permitted the use of context—oral reading and silent reading comprehension. Thus, in grades 7 and 9, reading comprehension was the strongest component. By grade 11, however, it also had decelerated considerably—to the 25th percentile.

When the students were in elementary school, their scores on reading comprehension and oral reading held up longer than other tests that did not rely on context—word meaning, spelling, word recognition—probably because they compensated for their lack of precise knowledge of word recognition and word meanings by relying on context. A similar scenario seems appropriate for the students in the seventh to eleventh grades. In grades 7 and 9, their relatively high scores on reading comprehension were possible as long as their word meaning and word recognition scores were not too low. However, when there was too great a gap between the students' word recognition and word meanings, and the difficulty of the texts they read, their use of context was no longer sufficient to meet the challenge.

As predicted by the Stages model, different components of reading seem to be needed at different times. When they are lacking, later development seems to be at risk. (See also Stanovich, 1986.) The trends in scores for the seventh to eleventh graders, as well as the trends when they were younger, suggest that we cannot be sanguine when the students do well in silent reading comprehension but have difficulty in word meaning and word recognition. Their scores in high school indicate that if they are weak in word meanings, particularly in academic vocabularies, and in recognizing and spelling less common words, they will decelerate later in reading comprehension.

The general trend of decreasing reading gains with increasing years in school is reminiscent of earlier research. The landmark study of Coleman and his associates (1966) reported that the verbal achievement of children from lower-income families was lower than that for the general population and that the discrepancies increased in succeeding years in school. The National Assessments of Educational Progress reported similar trends more than 20 years later. While disadvantaged urban students at age 9 were already performing below the overall national average, at age 17 they were four to five years behind (Applebee, Langer, and Mullis, 1988).

The deceleration among low-income children with increasing years in school is clearer when we divide the six stages into two major categories—Stages 0, 1, and 2 (beginning reading, kindergarten through third grade) and Stages 3, 4, and 5 (mature reading, fourth grade through college). Essentially, the major learning task for reading in kindergarten through grade 3 is recognition and decoding of words in print—words that the child already knows when they are heard or spoken but not recognized. Typically, average children can use, and comprehend when heard, about 5,000 or 6,000 words when they enter grade 1 (Chall, 1983b); but it takes most children about three years to learn to recognize them in print. It is significant that most children in the primary grades (1 to 3), even those with limited English, are more advanced in language and thinking than in reading skills. For most children, the new task in the early grades is to learn to recognize the words they already know when they hear them, and to learn the letters, their sounds, and the relationships between them. As accuracy and speed of word recognition and decoding, and fluency improve, so do scores on oral and silent reading comprehension tests.

The fact that, in grades 2 and 3, our sample of low-SES children scored on grade level on the tests of word recognition, oral reading, and spelling indicates that they were making good progress in these beginning reading tasks. These skills are usually learned in school, and the school did indeed provide a strong instructional program in beginning reading for them.

These children were also on grade level in word meaning when they were in the second and third grades. The words they were asked to define tended to be common, familiar, concrete words and the low-SES children did as well or better than other children in the same grades. This is particularly important because some theories have attributed the low literacy achievement of poor children to language deficiencies in the early grades (Chall, Jacobs, and Baldwin, 1990). We found no real differences in word meaning in the early grades when the words tested were common, high-frequency words. We did, however, find differences beginning at about grade 4, when words were less common.

Reading Stages 3 to 5 (grade levels 4 through college) increasingly focus on the reading of unfamiliar texts and on the use of reading as a tool for learning. At these advanced stages the reading materials become more complex, technical, abstract, and are beyond the everyday experiences of most children. Thus, beginning about fourth grade, readers must cope with increasingly complex demands upon language and cognition as well as on reading skills. Whereas the major hurdles prior to grade 4 are learning to recognize in print thousands of words whose meanings are already known, the hurdle of grade 4 and beyond is learning the meanings of less common, technical, abstract words, and understanding more difficult texts.

Why do low-SES students with strong beginnings in reading skills and in word meanings in Stages 1 and 2 slump at about Stage 3? First, as noted earlier, the reading task changes—from a focus on reading familiar texts where the main task is one of recognizing, decoding, and comprehending familiar texts to comprehending harder texts that use more difficult, abstract, specialized, and technical words. The concepts and organization of reading materials also become more difficult, more abstract, and more complex— and understanding them also requires more sophisticated levels of background knowledge and cognition. In addition, beginning with Stage 3 reading, students are expected to begin to use reading as a tool for learning and analyzing new ideas, facts, and opinions. The transition from the reading task of the primary grades (Stages 1 and 2) to that of the intermediate grades (Stage 3) also requires more advanced word recognition, greater facility in decoding, and greater fluency in reading printed text to make a smooth shift to concentrating on meanings and ideas. This is perhaps one of the most important transitions made in reading, and difficulties in making it have long characterized those who have reading problems. (See Chall, 1967, 1983a, and 1983b; Orton, 1937; LaBerge and Samuels, 1976; Roswell and Chall, 1992, 1994.)

PREVENTING THE FOURTH-GRADE SLUMP

Students seem to need three kinds of strengths in order to progress to Stage 3: sufficient knowledge of the meanings of more academic and abstract words, sufficient reasoning ability to understand the more difficult texts, and facility with reading skills—word recognition and decoding, and fluency (see Carroll, 1977). Thus, in grade 4 (Stage 3), the below-average readers who were behind in word meanings, word recognition, and fluency experienced the earlier and more intensive deceleration. The above-average readers were in a better position. Although they had fallen below national norms on word meanings, they remained strong in word recognition, spelling, and fluency. Therefore, it may be hypothesized that above-average readers compensated for their weakness in word meanings with strong reading skills in word recognition and fluency.

A SCENARIO FOR THE CUMULATIVE DEFICITS

Can the Reading Stages help explain the good start of these children when they were in the primary grades and the slump they experienced in the intermediate and higher grades? It should be recalled that the low-income children in our study were about in the middle range of reading ability—half at stanines 2 and 3 (the below-average readers) and half at stanines 5 and 6 (the above-average readers). We did not include children in stanine 1, who might have had serious reading problems or learning disabilities; we did not include those who were not proficient in English. Children in stanines 7, 8, and 9 also were excluded so as not to bias the sample toward exceptional children.

Our explanation for the trends in their achievement is based on two theoretical views: First, Carroll's view (1977) that reading comprehension depends on three major factors—language, cognition, and reading skills; second, the Stages model. The following scenario views the reading Stages model in terms of Carroll's theoretical view.

According to the Stages model, word recognition, decoding, and fluency are the major tasks of reading in Stages 1 and 2 (grades 1 to 3). Although language and cognition are also important at these stages, they do not usually present a major hurdle for early reading achievement because most beginners already have enough language and cognitive abilities for the books they are expected to read. (Perfetti, 1985; Stanovich, 1986; Freebody and Byrne, 1988; Chall, 1967 and 1983a.)

As noted earlier, reading in the early grades correlates higher with word recognition and decoding than with word meaning. For example, in kindergarten the highest correlation with reading is knowledge of names of the alphabet letters (Chall, 1967 and 1983a). High correlations with early reading achievement have been found also for rhyming, sound discrimination, auditory segmentation, and blending, now referred to as phonemic awareness. Thus, in the earliest grades, word recognition and phonemic abilities are most critical for success with the reading task—more than word meaning and cognition.

A general shift takes place when reading has reached about a fourth-grade reading level, when language and cognition become the stronger correlates of reading. It is a time when the curriculum devotes more time to the study of science, social studies, and literature. It is a time also when more advanced language and cognitive abilities are required. The instructional materials reflect this change, containing more difficult concepts, vocabulary, syntax, and text organization. (See Chall and Dale, 1995.)

Standardized reading tests reflect these changes as well, with text passages of familiar experiences in the tests for grades 1 to 3 and selections from science, social studies, and literature in tests for grades 4 and above (Auerbach, 1971). Also, from fourth grade through high school, the research literature generally indicates higher and stronger correlations of reading with cognition and language than with word recognition and phonics. (See Biemiller and Siegel, in press.)

Judging from their scores in grades 2 and 3, we can hypothesize that the low-income children in our sample had the cognitive and linguistic abilities to learn to read in these grades. Their performance was equal to national norms, and there were few differences between good and poor readers.

At about grade 4 (Stage 3), when the reading materials require higher cognitive and linguistic abilities, the children's reading began to slip. The biggest slump was on word meanings, particularly on abstract, literary, and less common words. Word recognition and spelling also declined, but not as drastically as word meaning. The lower scores in word recognition and spelling could also have been influenced by the lower scores in word meaning, for when the meanings of words are not known, they are harder to identify and spell. The last, and lowest, declines were in oral and silent reading comprehension—tasks that provided the students with contexts that permitted intelligent guessing.

A key question is why the above-average and below-average readers who were on grade level in grades 2 and 3 began to pull apart in grade 4 and grow further apart in grades 5 to 7? In the primary grades, both groups had similar strengths in language, cognition, and reading skills. In intermediate grades, both slumped at about the same time and with about equal intensity on word meanings. In oral and silent reading, above-average readers stayed on grade level or above until about grade 6, while the below-average readers were already testing below grade level in grade 4. The following is offered as a likely explanation.

Although knowledge of word meanings is essential in intermediate grades and higher, it is possible when reading tasks provide context (as in oral and silent reading tests) for students to make intelligent guesses. The above-average readers could do this better than the below-average readers in grades 4 to 6 because they had two strengths to help them—greater strengths in word recognition and in fluency. Although they were not superior to the below-average readers in word meanings, their greater abilities in identifying longer and harder words and their greater fluency in reading connected texts resulted in higher performance when reading difficult texts.

It is possible that, through grade 6 or 7, accurate recognition, decoding, and fluency can compensate for the lack of word meanings. This is possible especially on oral and silent reading tests that permit students to use language and cognitive abilities to guess from context. However, after the sixth or seventh grades, when the material becomes even more difficult, guessing from context does not seem to work as well because they have to guess the meanings of too many unknown words.

Why would low-income children decelerate first and most intensively in word meanings? The words they did not know were less familiar, less common words usually acquired through being read to, through the students' reading, through the study of various content subjects, and through direct instruction. Although we did not compare our population with a middle-class group of the same age, one could speculate that our population probably owned and read fewer books (see NAEP, 1985); and they were read to less than middle-class children (Chomsky, 1972).

Thus, it would appear that the language and literacy environment of our population was sufficient for reading achievement in primary grades (Stages 1 and 2) but not for reading in intermediate and upper elementary grades (Stage 3).

THE STAGES AND ADULT DYSLEXICS

A recent study by Fink (1992) of adult dyslexics adds some interesting information with regard to the reality of the Stages model. Fink interviewed 12 dyslexic adults about their reading histories; she did not test them or ask for test scores.

From the retrospective reports, all 12 seemed to have had no difficulty with Stage 0; they had the language, intelligence, and curiosity to learn to read. But all had extreme difficulty with Stage 1—word recognition and decoding. Some were given intensive, individual help by teachers, parents, aunts, and/or private tutors, with varying amounts of success. Some received such help over many years. But, in spite of their extreme difficulty with decoding (one of the 12 still has extreme difficulty decoding words), they learned to do Stage 5 reading, according to Fink, because they read, as young children, books that were of great interest to them.

Fink's interpretation was that these adults went through alternative pathways in learning to read. Her adult sample, she wrote, bypassed their weaknesses (for example, word recognition and decoding) and learned to read by reading what interested them.

It should be noted that some of her subjects continued to have difficulty with decoding even as adults, many also had difficulty with fluency, were slow readers, and did not feel comfortable with reading until late in life. At least one still had to read everything twice—once to decode and once to comprehend.

Most of the 12 adult dyslexics interviewed were highly intelligent (one was a Nobel-Prize-winning immunologist) and as such were able to make good use of context. They moved on into Stage 3 and above, according to Fink, not because they mastered Stages 1 and 2 (decoding and fluency), but because they engaged early in reading on topics of interest to them.

It is curious that no mention is made of the differences in reading development by special groups discussed in *Stages of Reading Development* (for example, slow language development, difficulties with print, emotional difficulties, adult illiterates and functional literates, bilingualism, and reading of the deaf.) In fact, most, if not all of the 12, fit the "difficulties with print" special group.

Fink notes that factors other than reading of books of high interest enabled her subjects to move to more advanced reading stages; for example, family support, encouragement, and tutoring. In fact, the 12 adults in the study received considerable remedial instruction as children, even during the time they were reading books for instruction and pleasure. One wonders how much this special tutoring contributed to the adult dyslexics' progress.

USES OF THE STAGES MODEL IN PRACTICE AND IN TEACHER EDUCATION

Soon after its publication in 1983, the Stages were used in schools to plan reading curricula. This may have been stimulated by a desire of many schools to move away from the highly detailed skills hierarchies approach popular in the late 1970s. By the 1980s many sought a more open, qualitative approach to curriculum planning. The Stages seemed to provide such an approach.

From the beginning, authors of methods textbooks on the teaching of reading cited the Stages in their definitions and overviews of reading. (See, for example, Harris and Sipay, 1990.) I also have received many requests for permission to reprint portions of the book—particularly tables that summarize basic data on the Stages—for use in methods textbooks, in courses on teaching reading, and in workshops for teachers.

The recent paper by Ehri and Williams, "Learning to Read and Learning to Teach Reading are Both Developmental Processes" (in press), focuses on developmental aspects that should be used to prepare teacher education students for the task of teaching reading and for providing needed remedial instruction. They cite Chall's *Stages of Reading Development* (1983) and indicate how students "learning to read follow a predictable course of development so developmental issues need to be understood," and that "The appropriateness of methods depends upon which reading procedures are being taught at which points in development, as multiple methods rather than a single method must become part of a teacher's repertoire."

Because most practical uses of the Stages have been in teacher training, I asked Sara Brody, a former doctoral student, now an assistant professor of reading and learning disabilities, to describe how she has used the Stages for such purposes.

Her letter of September 6, 1993, is reproduced with her permission:

> *Stages of Reading Development* has served as a text in a course, Language and Reading Development, that I teach at Riviera College. I use Stages to provide background, and to present a framework within which to understand instructional needs and strategies. Along with Stages, I use journal articles that illustrate specific effective strategies for teaching the skills of any particular stage.
>
> At the beginning of the course, I sketch an overview of reading based on the Stages. Next, I teach sequentially (stage-by-stage) the nature of students' reading needs along with methods that could be used to meet those needs. Students learn about phonemic awareness, basic decoding skills, practicing for automaticity in decoding, then reading for meaning. The Stages are used to explain how instruction concerning each component fits into the larger picture of reading. The Stages help illustrate that a component under study is a crucial aspect, but not the whole, of reading. Students indicate that the *Reading Stages* offer a helpful guideline concerning when to teach various strategies.
>
> Currently, I am writing a text for the Language and Reading Development course. In the first chapter of the text, I reference and

draw on the *Reading Stages* extensively to explain a developmental view of reading maturation. In addition, I describe a composite model of mature reading. While presenting the model, I explain why the components of each of the stages must be mastered if mature reading is to occur. The chapters that follow discuss the nature of various components of reading instruction in great detail. In the chapters, these components are often described in terms of how they fit into the reading stages. Throughout the text, Stages are referred to as a resource that provides an in-depth understanding of reading maturation and its relationship to physiological, psychological, and cognitive development. In addition, many references are made to the Stages as a convenient yardstick for planning and interpreting assessments and instructional recommendations.

I use the Stages framework extensively since my students respond to it very positively. They indicate that, with the Stages scheme, 'it finally all makes sense.' The Stages framework also 'puts all the battles in the field of reading into perspective' and helps them 'understand the individual needs of their students' when they are faced with classes of very diverse reading abilities.

(Sara Brody, personal communication, August, 1993)

Another report on uses of the Stages in teacher training comes from Esther Geva (1993) of the Ontario Institute for Studies in Education. In her discussion of *The Reading Crisis: Why Poor Children Fall Behind* and *Stages of Reading Development* at a recent conference in Toronto, she highlighted the relevance of both books for teaching and teacher training.

Among the points she noted were the following:

- The need to pay attention to the students' developing skills.
- Children, including those at risk, benefit from instruction with challenging texts.
- Fluency among fourth graders can be developed through periods of reading to the teacher. This results not only in improvement of fluency but also of word meaning and reading comprehension.
- Teacher training should focus on both reading in and out of school. "Once they have learned how to decode and have built up a reasonable repertoire of sight vocabulary, children need to be given carefully crafted homework and reading

assignments so they *can* continue to acquire new vocabulary and new knowledge" (p. 9).

- At-risk children from poor families need assistance to deal with unfamiliar vocabulary to increase their lexicon. They need tools for decoding new words, but if those were not appropriately developed through a blend of structured techniques during the "learning to read" stage, they should receive instruction later to benefit from reading texts in the subject areas.

With regard to the relevance of the Stages model from a multilingual-multiethnic population, Geva noted "I don't have a reason to believe that the fundamental steps in such a theory should be different, though they may be acquired at a different pace" (p. 12). Based on her research, she noted first and second language word recognition skills were highly correlated and children whose phonological skills are well developed in their first language will do well not only in learning to read their first language, but also in another language. In addition, the correlations between oral proficiency in the second language and word recognition skills are low. "In other words, when we talk of L2 language (second language) proficiency and basic decoding skills we talk of separate skills" (p. 12). (Compare with correlations for English; see pp. 6–11.)

Geva continues: ". . . just as with L1 (first language), we need to address both domains—teach the prerequisite word-based skills, and enhance the development of grammar and vocabulary, which are essential for text comprehension" (p. 13).

The need for making such distinctions, she notes, requires training on the part of teachers, and the Stages help teachers understand the need for such distinctions and how to make them.

Geva concludes with an overview of the meaning of the Stages model for teacher training, for teaching, and for professional understanding.

So what should be our conclusion? . . . that college teachers should become familiar with various reading theories, and learn to view reading, writing, and language development as a complex set of abilities and skills that change with development. The reading tasks set by the school curriculum vary from stage to stage, as do the abilities and skills needed to meet these task requirements.

Consequently, teachers need to learn also that the home and school factors influencing reading achievement may change with development.

What Chall has shown us is that reading is not a unitary skill, that word recognition, word meaning and reading comprehension are distinct aspects of literacy, which need to be fostered in different ways, in the earlier years of schooling and in later grades.

(Esther Geva, 1993)

Dale M. Willows, Department of Instruction and Special Education of the Ontario Institute for Studies in Education, uses the following transparencies for her teacher training courses and workshops when she discusses *Stages of Reading Development:*

The value of the Stages framework as an organizer for planning classroom programs and for assessing and remedying difficulties.

The need for different types of texts and activities at different stages of reading development.

The role of the prereading (emergent literacy) stage and the importance of not confusing it with Stage 1.

The need for phonics instruction in Stages 1 and 2.

The need for vocabulary control in reading material used by children in Stages 1 and 2.

The importance of considering the relation between listening and reading efficiency at different stages of reading development.

The value of reading to children at different stages of reading development.

The crucial need for the confirmation/fluency stage in the automization of word recognition.

The need to select appropriate reading material to facilitate the students' movement from one reading stage to the next.

The place for narrative and expository text in the reading program and the need to teach children how to read expository text in Stage 3.

The need to teach. The role of the teacher and how it must change at different reading stages.

The reading-to-learn stages and the changing demands on the reader.

In her 1991 article in *Exceptionality Education Canada*, Willows applied the Stages (Stages 0 to 3) model to the needs of most children in the elementary grades for reading, spelling, and writing, and for children with problems in learning print skills. She also analyzed whole language practices in relation to the needs of readers as characterized in the Stages and confirmed by research.

OTHER READING STAGE MODELS

In 1985, the National Assessment of Educational Progress (NAEP) published a five-level Proficiency Scale to make more meaningful the scores obtained by students and adults on the NAEP reading tests.* The NAEP scale uses both quantitative and qualitative measures—from the Rudimentary Level, the easiest, to the Advanced Level, the most difficult. The qualitative descriptions of each level present additional information on the "complexity of the material . . . familiarity with the subject matter, and the kinds of questions asked at each proficiency level" (p. 14).

Table 1 presents these five proficiency levels from the *Reading Report Card* (NAEP, 1985), p. 15.

Table 1
PROFICIENCY SCALES FROM THE READING REPORT CARD
NATIONAL ASSESSMENT OF EDUCATIONAL PROGRESS, 1985

Rudimentary (150)
　　Readers who have acquired rudimentary reading skills and strategies can follow brief written directions. They can also select words, phrases, or sentences to describe a simple picture and can interpret simple written clues to identify a common object. *Performance at this level suggests the ability to carry out simple, discrete reading tasks.*

*The 1992 NAEP uses a three-level scale—Basic, Proficient, and Advanced—for different reading purposes (literary experience, reading to gain information, and reading to perform a task). Separate descriptions of the three achievement levels for Basic, Proficient, and Advanced are given separately by grade 4, 8, and 12.

Basic (200)

Readers who have learned basic comprehension skills and strategies can locate and identify facts from simple informational paragraphs, stories, and news articles. In addition, they can combine ideas and make inferences based on short, uncomplicated passages. *Performance at this level suggests the ability to understand specific or sequentially related information.*

Intermediate (250)

Readers with the ability to use intermediate skills and strategies can search for, locate, and organize the information they find in relatively lengthy passages and can recognize paraphrases of what they have read. They also can make inferences and reach generalizations about main ideas and author's purpose from passages dealing with literature, science, and social studies. *Performance at this level suggests the ability to search for specific information, interrelate the ideas, and make suggestions.*

Adept (300)

Readers with adept reading comprehension skills and strategies can understand complicated literary and informational passages, including material about topics they study at school. They also can analyze and integrate less familiar material and provide reactions to and explanations of the text as a whole. *Performance at this level suggests the ability to find, understand, summarize, and explain relatively complicated information.*

Advanced (350)

Readers who use advanced reading skills and strategies can extend and restructure the ideas presented in specialized and complex texts. Examples include scientific materials, literary essays, historical documents, and materials similar to those found in professional and technical working environments. They also are able to understand the links between ideas even when those links are not explicitly stated and to make appropriate generalizations even when the texts lack clear introductions or explanations. *Performance at this level suggests the ability to synthesize and learn from specialized reading materials.*

If we omit Chall's Stage 0, it would appear that the NAEP five-level Proficiency Scale is quite similar to the five remaining Stages. The qualitative descriptions of the five NAEP proficiency levels focus on changes in cognitive demands of reading comprehension, similar to qualitative descriptions of Chall's Stages (see Chall, 1983b). The NAEP levels, however, do not refer to school grades or to standardized reading equivalents. (See John Carroll [1987] for estimated readability levels.) Further, they do not refer to basic word skills—word recognition and decoding.

NAEP's Intermediate level and Chall's Stage 3 are quite similar, since both characterize a level of reading beyond the most elementary—a level at which one can begin to use reading for learning the unfamiliar and the new. Chall's Stages 4 and 5 and the NAEP levels 4 (Adept) and 5 (Advanced) are also quite similar, with both emphasizing reading that goes beyond the literal.

THE NAEP 1992 READING REPORT CARD FOR THE NATION AND THE STATES

This report card includes data on classroom instructional practices that were related to students' reading achievement. This is highly relevant for the Stages scheme. However, the instructional information was obtained only for the fourth grade: "Teachers of the fourth graders in the national and state assessments were asked to characterize their reading instruction by describing the amount of emphasis they placed on various approaches to teaching reading—literature-based reading, integration of reading and writing, whole language, and phonics" (p. 30).

It should be noted that according to the Stages scheme, instruction in phonics would be appropriate at Stage 1 (grade 1 and beginning grade 2) and, where still needed, in Stage 2 (grades 2 and 3). For grade 4, it would be appropriate for those who are lagging behind, particularly in acquiring the alphabetic principle. The other approaches—literature-based reading, integration of reading and writing, and whole language—fit primary, intermediate, and even later grades.

The NAEP findings were that, with the exception of phonics, about half the fourth graders (40 to 54 percent) were receiving instructional emphases on each of these approaches. The emphasis on phonics was considerably less. "Both the comparatively small percentage of fourth graders receiving heavy emphasis in phonics (11 percent), and their lower average proficiency compared to fourth graders receiving little or no such emphasis, indicate that the tendency to use the phonics approach with young readers may carry over into remedial situations with less proficient fourth graders" (p. 30).

Thus, a heavy emphasis on teaching phonics in fourth grade signals that the students to whom it is taught are functioning below their expected level. Most research and practice have found that phonics instruction is best given in the first few grades. Therefore, an interpretation that a heavy phonics emphasis produces lower scores would be questionable. Rather, the more appropriate interpretation would be that a heavy phonics emphasis in grade 4 is the result, not the cause, of low achievement.

To gather useful data on the effects of phonics, compared to the other approaches, it would have helped to ask the same questions of first-, second-, and/or third-grade teachers.

A SPECIAL NOTE ON THE MEANING OF THE STAGES

It is not uncommon in presenting developmental schemes that some people interpret them differently from the author. Thus, the first few stages have at times been viewed by some readers as being concerned with decoding only. This is unfortunate since it was not my intention. In fact, the first stage, Stage 0, is viewed as a process of guessing and predicting that relies mainly on language and cognition. Stage 1, which I labeled initial reading or decoding, is characterized by the acquisition of the alphabetic principle— the learning of sound-to-letter relations that makes it possible to identify printed words and comprehend text. Along with decoding, readers grow in Stage 1 in the ability to identify words and to read and understand connected text.

The process of comprehension is practiced in all of the stages, from the earliest to the most advanced. However, to highlight the meaning of each stage, its uniqueness was emphasized, particularly the stage's advancement over earlier stages. The labels were selected to show development.

Viewing the early stages as decoding only may stem from the tendency in our long history of reading research and practice to separate decoding from comprehension and to assume that decoding did not include comprehension and that comprehension did not include decoding.

CONCLUSION

The more recent literature from research, theory, and practice points to the value of viewing reading developmentally as going through qualitative changes as it becomes more and more advanced and proficient. The recent research literature tends to confirm the Stages scheme proposed by Chall (1979 and 1983b), and adds further understanding to how reading develops as it becomes more proficient.

The Stages model has also had an influence on teacher training and on the development of curricula in reading and language—for those making normal progress and for those who lag behind. The Stages model has been especially useful in helping us understand the reading development of at-risk populations—economically disadvantaged students, those with learning disabilities, those with limited English proficiency, and adults with limited reading ability.

BIBLIOGRAPHY

Applebee, A. N., Langer, J. A., & Mullis, I. V. S. (1988). *Who reads best? Factors related to reading achievement in grades 3, 7, and 11.* Princeton, NJ: National Assessment of Educational Progress, Educational Testing Service.

Auerbach, I. T. (1971). Analysis of standardized reading comprehension tests. Ed.D. dissertation, Harvard University Graduate School of Education, Cambridge, MA.

Biemiller, A. (1994). Some observations on beginning reading instruction. *Educational Psychologist, 29,* 203–209.

Biemiller, A., & Siegel, L. S. (In press). A longitudinal study of the effects of the *Bridge* reading program for children at risk for reading failure.

Brody, S. (1993). Using Chall's stages in teacher education. (Personal Communication).

Carroll, J. B. (1977). Developmental parameters of reading comprehension. In J. T. Guthrie (Ed.), *Cognition, curriculum, and comprehension.* Newark, DE: International Reading Association.

Carroll, J. B. (1987). The National Assessments in Reading: Are we misreading the findings? *Phi Delta Kappan, 65,* 424–430.

Carroll, J. B. (1990). Thoughts on reading and phonics. Paper presented at the meeting of the National Conference on Research in English, Atlanta, GA, May 9, 1990.

Carroll, J. B. (1993). *Human cognitive abilities: A survey of factor-analytic studies.* New York: Cambridge University Press.

Chall, J. S. (1967). *Learning to read: The great debate.* New York: McGraw-Hill.

Chall, J. S. (1979). The great debate: Ten years later, with a modest proposal for reading stages. In L. Resnick & P. Weaver (Eds.), *Theory and practice of early reading.* Hillsdale, NJ: Lawrence Erlbaum Associates.

Chall, J. S. (1983a). *Learning to read: The great debate,* updated edition. New York: McGraw-Hill.

Chall, J. S. (1983b). *Stages of reading development.* New York: McGraw-Hill.

Chall, J. S., & Dale, E. (1995). *Readability revisited and the new Dale-Chall readability formula.* Cambridge: Brookline Books.

Chall, J. S., & Jacobs, V. (In press). The reading, writing, and language connection. In the volume dedicated to Dina Feitelson, edited by Joseph Shimron, Hampton Press.

Chall, J. S., Jacobs, V., & Baldwin, L. (1990). *The reading crisis: Why poor children fall behind.* Cambridge, MA: Harvard University Press.

Chall, J. S., & Stahl, S. A. (1985). Reading comprehension research in the last decade: Implications for educational publishing. *Book Research Quarterly, 1,* 95-102.

Chomsky, C. (1972). Stages in language development and reading exposure. *Harvard Educational Review, 42,* 1-33.

Coleman, J. S., Campbell, E., Hobson, C., McPartland, J., Mood, A., Weinfeld, F., & York, R. (1966). *Equality of educational opportunity.* Washington, DC: US Government Printing Office.

Curtis, M. E. (1980). Development of components of reading skill. *Journal of Educational Psychology, 72,* 656-669.

Davis, F. B. (1972). Psychometric research on comprehension in reading. In M. Kling, et al. (Eds.), *Final report: The literature of research in reading with emphasis on models,* (pp. 1-65). New Brunswick, NJ: Graduate School of Education, Rutgers University.

Durkin, D. (1978-79). What classroom observations reveal about reading comprehension instruction. *Reading Research Quarterly, 14,* 481-533.

Ehri, L. C. (1985, April). *Learning to Read and Spell.* Address presented at meeting of the American Educational Research Association, Chicago, IL.

Ehri, L. C., & Williams, J. P. (In press). Learning to read and learning to teach reading are both developmental processes. Murray, F. (Ed.), *Knowledge base for beginning teacher educators,* Jossey Bass.

Fink, R. (1992). *Successful dyslexics alternative pathways to reading: A developmental study.* Ed.D. thesis, Harvard Graduate School of Education, Cambridge, MA.

Freebody, P., & Byrne, B. (1988). Word-reading strategies in elementary school children: Relations to comprehension, reading time, and phonemic awareness. *Reading Research Quarterly, 23,* 441–453.

Geva, E. (1993). Discussion of J. S. Chall *The Reading Crisis: Why Poor Children Fall Behind.* Canadian Psychological Association. Toronto, October 23, 1993.

Haller, E. P., Child, D. A., & Walberg, H. J. (1988). Can comprehension be taught? A quantitative synthesis of 'metacognitive' studies. *Educational Researcher, 17* (9), 5–8.

Harris, A. J., & Sipay, E. (1990). *How to increase reading ability* (10th edition). White Plains, NY: Longman.

Iverson, S. & Tunmer, W. E. (1993). Phonological processing skills and the Reading Recovery program. *Journal of Educational Psychology, 85,* 112–126.

Juel, C. (1988). Learning to read and write: A longitudinal study of fifty-four children from first through fourth grades. *Journal of Educational Psychology, 80,* 437–447.

LaBerge, D., & Samuels, S. J. (1976). Toward a theory of automatic information processing in reading. In H. Singer & R. B. Ruddell (Eds.), *Theoretical models and processes of reading.* Newark, DE: International Reading Association.

Loban, W. (1963). *The language of elementary school children.* National Council of Teachers of English Research Report no. 1. Urbana, IL: National Council of Teachers of English.

Mullis, I. V. S., Campbell, J. R., & Farstrup, A. E. (1993). *NAEP 1992 Reading Report Card for the Nation and the States.* Washington, DC: National Center for Educational Statistics, US Department of Education.

National Assessment of Educational Progress (NAEP). (1985). *The reading report card: Progress toward excellence in our schools.* Princeton, NJ: Educational Testing Service.

Orton, S. T. (1937; reprinted 1964). *Reading, writing, and speech problems in children.* New York: W. W. Norton.

Paris, S. G., & Jacobs, J. (1984). The benefits of informed instruction for children's reading awareness and comprehension skills. *Child Development, 55,* 2083–2093.

Perfetti, C. A. (1985). *Reading ability.* New York: Oxford University Press.

Roswell, F. G., & Chall, J. S. (1992). *Diagnostic Assessments of Reading and Trial Teaching Strategies (DARTTS).* Chicago: Riverside Publishing Company.

Roswell, F. G., & Chall, J. S. (1994). *Creating successful readers: A practical guide to testing and teaching at all levels.* Chicago: Riverside Publishing Company.

Shany, M., & Biemiller, A. (In press). Assisted reading practice: Effects on performance for poor readers in grades 3 and 4.

Smith, F. (1978). *Understanding reading* (2nd ed.). New York: Rinehart and Winston.

Spear-Swerling, L., & Sternberg, R. J. (1994). The road not taken: An integrative theoretical model of reading disability. *Journal of Learning Disabilities, 37,* 91–103, 122.

Stahl, S. A. (1992). *The state of the art of reading instruction in the USA* (IIEP Research Report no. 97). Paris: International Institute for Educational Planning.

Stahl, S. A., Eubach, K., & Cramond, B. (1995). Fluency oriented reading instruction. Submitted to *Elementary School Journal.*

Stahl, S. A., & Miller, P. D. (1989). Whole language and language experience approaches for beginning reading: A quantitative research synthesis. *Review of Educational Research, 59,* 87–116.

Stanovich, K. E. (1984). The interactive compensatory model of reading: A confluence of developmental, experimental, and educational psychology. *Remedial and Special Education, 5*(3), 11–19.

Stanovich, K. E. (1986). Matthew effects in reading: Some consequences of individual differences in the acquisition of literacy. *Reading Research Quarterly, 21,* 360–407.

Stanovich, K. E., Nathan, R., & Vala-Rossi, M. (1986). Developmental changes in the cognitive correlates of reading ability and the developmental lag hypothesis. *Reading Research Quarterly, 21,* 267–283.

Sticht, T. G., Beck, L. J., Hauke, R. N., Kleiman, G. M., & James, J. H. (1974). *Auding and reading.* Alexandria, VA: Human Resources Research Organization.

Strickland, R. G. (1962). The language of elementary school children: Its relationship to the language of reading textbooks and the quality of reading of selected children. *Bulletin of the School of Education,* Indiana University, *38,* 1–131.

Thorndike, E. L. (1917). Reading as reasoning: A study of mistakes in paragraph reading. *Journal of Educational Research, 8,* 323–332.

Thorndike, R. L. (1973) *Reading comprehension education in fifteen countries.* International Studies in Evaluation III. Stockholm, Sweden: Almquist and Wiksell.

Thorndike, R. L. (1973–74). Reading as reasoning. *Reading Research Quarterly, 9,* 137–147.

Willows, D. M. (1991). A "normal variation" view of written language difficulties and disabilities: Implications for whole language programs. *Exceptionality Education Canada, 3,* 73–103.

PREFACE

MANY PEOPLE HELPED make this book possible. Among the first was the late Margaret Bullowa, psychiatrist and scholar of child language. It was she who listened to the very first ideas and it was her response which made it seem worthwhile to continue. My colleague, Helen Popp, was warmly supportive and helpful during the many years of formulation and reformulation. Several students and former students assisted with various aspects of the research; Gertrude Karger, with the section on early reading stages; Susan Harris-Sharples with the section on psychological realities; Laurie Goodman, with the content analysis of professional textbooks; and Steven Stahl with the bibliography. Emily Marston was especially helpful in all aspects of the work, and in reading and reacting to early drafts with candor and sympathy.

My thanks go also to the many students who reacted to various portions of the book in my research seminars, courses, and Institutes at the Harvard Graduate School of Education.

For typing the manuscript, I am most grateful to Mrs. Ann Cura, my secretary of many years, who saw it through its many versions with great care and warmth; to Joan Dolamore who put in long and patient hours of meticulous work; to Carol Evans and Maureen Connors who typed an earlier version, and to Vicki Jacobs for her assistance during the past two summers.

To my editor, Tom Quinn, I owe a special note of appreciation for his faith in the work, his never failing support, and for his friendship.

Although I am grateful for the assistance of many, the responsibility for the views expressed here is my own.

JEANNE S. CHALL
Cambridge, Massachusetts

CHAPTER 1

THE READING
PROBLEM

THIS BOOK IS ABOUT READING and how it develops from its primitive beginnings to its most mature and highly skilled forms. How in essence do readers change as they advance from *The Cat in the Hat* to the financial pages of *The New York Times?* I present here the theories and related research for a stage-development scheme of reading, together with suggestions and recommendations for applications in the classroom, the home, and the community. I hope that this work will add to our understanding of the reading process and to the practice of teaching reading.

My interest in reading development goes back some thirty years to my early researches in readability and vocabulary—areas of research and application concerned with successive changes in reading materials and in vocabulary knowledge with increasing age and school attainment. Many years of clinical work with children and young people who fail to learn as normally expected also spurred my interest in reading development. The progress of these students is different from the "normal," and one can experience and understand their reading as if it were in "slow motion."

A more immediate influence on the present work came from an earlier book, *Learning to Read: The Great Debate* (1967), an analysis of the research on the effectiveness of begin-

1

ning reading methods—methods that were at the time of the study, the 1960s, subjects of controversy and debate. I found from my analysis of the research that the conflicting results could be understood if I hypothesized developmental changes in reading by age and grade. Thus, although some methods seemed to produce an immediate, early advantage, other methods seemed to be more effective when comparisons were made at a later date. In essence, hypothesizing that the reading process changes, even during the beginning years, made it possible to conclude that some methods were more effective than others.

In the summer of 1972, after several years of searching for a better understanding of the transition from beginning to more mature reading (Auerbach, 1971; Chall, 1969; Simons, 1971) paralleled by intensive reading of developmental theories, I was able to outline the basic hypotheses for the proposed reading-stage development scheme. The following years I benefited from the reactions of the doctoral students in my reading research seminar, from Helen Popp's Summer Institute on Reading, Language, and Related Learning Disabilities at the Harvard Graduate School of Education, and from other institutes and my various courses in reading.

In 1976, I presented the main points of the scheme to the University of Pittsburgh Conference on Theory and Practice of Early Reading, in a paper subsequently published in 1979 in the Conference proceedings (Resnick and Weaver, 1979). Some aspects of the scheme were also presented at meetings of the Orton Society in 1974 and at the Joint Meeting of the National Conference on Research in English and the International Reading Association in 1978.

My first view was to study the course of development of what I called "literate intelligence"—the intelligence related to literacy—how reading and writing change qualitatively and how they affect and are affected by other forms of intelligence. My assumption was that the learning and uses of literacy are among the most advanced forms of intelligence, and, compared to other forms, depend more on instruction and practice. I believed then, as I do now, that the influence of the development of reading and writing—"literate intelligence"—on general cognitive development has unfortunately been underestimated. Indeed, when reading development is delayed by personal or environmental factors or both, the effects on the person, unless given special help, are too often disastrous, in spite of normal and even high general cognitive ability. Similarly, existing research evidence seems to indicate that learning to read early benefits verbal intelligence as well as reading development (Smethurst, 1975; Fowler, 1971). I decided, however, to concentrate on reading development when I realized that it might take too many years to include the relevant research and practice on writing. But some consideration is given to writing throughout the book.

Reading, like income, has both an absolute and a relative value. Just 40 years ago, an 8th-grade reading level was typical of people 25 years old or over, and that was considered above the standard of minimal literacy. Today, the average is an 11th- to 12th-grade level. Although it means a much higher reading ability, it probably has about the same relative value as an 8th-grade level had 40 years ago.

The improvement of reading among those whose progress is deficient, as well as among the highest achievers, is of great importance today. In a sense, we are newly entered on a third literacy revolution brought about by the great increase of knowledge and by the efficiency of the media to convey it. This knowledge revolution has brought with it the need for a greater level of literacy among more people than ever before. It contrasts with the two earlier revolutions—the agricultural and the industrial—each requiring much lower levels of literacy.

I hope that this book presents a broad view of what it means to progress in reading—from the beginning to the most advanced levels. Such a broad overview is needed by many —by reading researchers and by teachers, by test developers, and by reading and learning disabilities specialists. It is also needed by editors and writers of books and instructional materials, by parents, and by legislators who ultimately decide on the level and type of support given to the schools. Knowing the whole sweep makes possible a fuller appreciation of where students are, where they have been, where they are going, and what their instruction should be to bring them forward. Such a broad sweep is needed more today than in past generations. The teacher in a one-room schoolhouse had direct knowledge of how reading developed because children on all levels were usually taught in one classroom for many years. After one or two years, the teacher could anticipate what a 3rd-grade child would be doing, and if progress lagged in some way, the teacher knew enough about how reading usually developed to know whether or not to worry. Today, with the specialization of teachers by grade, and increasingly by type of child (urban, suburban, bilingual, special needs), teachers find it difficult to gain a broad sense of development and of the differences between "normal" and "other than normal."

The larger families, and particularly extended families, had similar bases for knowing when to worry. With smaller families and with greater mobility, parents now have a poorer base against which to measure the reading development of their children. Grandparents and aunts and uncles used to help provide the larger memories. Now they live in their own apartments, in different cities, states, and countries.

The uncertainty and confusion about reading that exists so widely today can be alleviated, I believe, if we realize that reading is not learned all at once, and that problems of learning vary at different stages. Reading is learned over a long period. Some people take as long as 20 years, others, more or less time. Indeed, when Goethe was very old, someone asked him when he had learned to read. He reportedly answered that although he had spent a lifetime learning, he was still learning.

The recent expansion of scientific knowledge about reading and related areas also requires a reevaluation. Reading has always been the most researched of the school subjects. But since the early 1960s the research has expanded even further, and now more is published in one year than existed from the late 1800s to the early 1960s. This great profusion of knowledge has also contributed to some of our confusion, mainly because of greater specialization among researchers who come from different disciplines and who do not seem to follow the research of other disciplines.

An understanding of how reading evolves can, I believe, help us understand some current theoretical questions as well as questions of importance to practice. With regard to theory, it can add to our knowledge of the nature of reading and of whether the process is the same for beginning reading as for mature, skilled reading. With regard to the many questions about practice, for example, one concerns many teachers. Why do the reading gains of children in the 4th and 5th grades, particularly children from homes of limited education and income, begin to decline? Why don't the significant gains in reading achievement found for primary grade children continue in the intermediate and upper grades? And in high school?

Some people say that the decline at Grade 4 may be due to the adoption, during the past decade, of stronger phonics programs (code emphasis) in the early grades. They imply that a return to a meaning emphasis in Grade 1, the method of consensus from 1920 to 1960, would bring higher reading achievement in the middle and upper grades since "reading for meaning" is the ultimate objective of these grades.

Those seeking answers to questions like these would, I believe, profit from a developmental view of reading, for the evidence is even stronger now than it was in the late 1960s for the benefits of a beginning code emphasis (Calfee and Drum, 1978; Chall, 1977, 1979a, 1982; Pflaum, Walberg, Kargianes, and Rasher, 1980). I present below a brief excerpt from *The Great Debate* (1967) on the issue of maintaining or losing gains—a reminder that this was an issue of importance in the past as well—in the studies between 1910 and 1960.

> Whether an initial code emphasis keeps its advantage in the middle and upper elementary grades, and later, depends on how reading is taught in these grades: how much the reading program stresses language and vocabulary growth and provides sufficiently challenging reading materials. If the reading programs are not challenging enough in these respects, the early advantages will probably be dissipated (p. 138).

My goal throughout this book is to present the stages of reading development in a clear, time-lapsed, "simplified" form, making it possible for the reader to gain insights into the changes that occur from stage to stage.

An understanding of how reading develops should help us

understand the highly controversial issues of what to teach, when, and by what methods—for interim and ultimate objectives.

A stage-development theory of reading is especially important in light of educational malpractice suits of the 1970s. One of these concerned a young man (Peter Doe) whose mother sued the public school system that educated him because he could not read beyond a 5th-grade level after graduating from high school. The complaint was not that her son was illiterate but that he was not literate enough to get and hold a job. An understanding of how reading develops or does not develop would help us to know how a boy of normal ability could be in school for 12 years and learn only as much as an average student who has been in school for only 5. It would further help us to know what can and cannot be read by an 18-year-old who achieves a 5th-grade level on a standardized reading test.

A developmental theory of reading can also cast some light on the minimum competency test movement. Whenever questions come up about how much reading skill is needed for what purposes and by what students, issues of development are central.

Much concern also exists over the inadequate reading and writing of many college students. Most community colleges and many 4-year colleges have extensive remedial programs in reading and writing, particularly for entering students, many of whom have developed in reading not much beyond a level typical of 8th graders. The readability levels of college textbooks have also declined—some go as low as 7th–8th or a 9th–10th grade level for college freshmen. And among those entering 4-year colleges, SAT (Scholastic Aptitude Test) scores, particularly the verbal scores (Wirtz, 1977), have declined steadily from 1967 to 1980. From 1980 to 1981 the scores have remained the same.

Equal concern focuses on the inadequate literacy of unemployed youth, up to 35 percent of high school graduates in some communities (Hunter and Harmer, 1979). And concern has grown over the low literacy level among men in the armed forces, a level considered by many to be below that required in a highly mechanized and technological enterprise (Sticht, 1975).

It would seem, then, that a better view of how reading de-

velops would contribute to a better understanding of the problems of those at all levels of achievement. And perhaps its
greatest benefit lies in what it adds to our understanding of the
large gaps in reading development among minorities, bilin-
guals, children of the poor and poorly educated, children with
reading and learning disabilities, the deaf, and others with special needs.

The chapters that follow present findings and discussions
on these questions and others. Here are some of the major
points.

My first finding reminds me of the reverse of Gertrude
Stein's observation about a rose: to read is not necessarily to
read. In other words, it is not always the same thing. The
reading of the stumbling beginner is not the reading of the fluent 3rd grader nor of the skilled college freshman. It takes
most people about twenty years to reach the highest stage of
reading development. Some do it much faster, others take
longer, and still others may not reach it.

Reading development depends upon interaction between
environmental factors (challenge and stimulation from home,
school, and community) and biological factors. The effects of
many biological handicaps can be lessened with proper stimulation and instruction.

Societies and nations have developed from limited to more
advanced stages of literacy in much the same way that literacy
develops in individuals. Currently, the more technologically
and scientifically developed nations also tend to show more advancement in literacy.

People who are significantly below average in literacy are
less successful in using other academic skills, in continuing education, and in their jobs. Present evidence does indicate,
however, that most remedial programs are effective with most
people at any age level.

Each stage of reading development has its own tasks and
crises, but the 4th grade seems to present a major hurdle. The
reasons are many and the suggested solutions are varied.
Evidence points to the need for more challenging instructional
materials. Materials in reading textbooks (basal readers) have
tended to focus on enjoyment and fun, presenting narrative fiction almost exclusively even during the middle and upper ele-

mentary grades. A developmental view of reading suggests the need for greater use of expository materials and of subject-matter textbooks and literature in the teaching of reading, particularly from Grade 4 on.

"World knowledge" and vocabulary, both developed through wide reading, are also essential for reading development. Thus education and reading are circular—the more a person has of one, the better the development of the other. The more the knowledge, the better the reading; the better the skill and uses of reading, the better the knowledge.

Not all reading is learned during reading lessons. Much is learned from reading and writing in the subject areas and from independent reading of literature, magazines, and newspapers. And from the earliest years, being read to and reading on one's own are a great help in the development of language and reading.

The book falls into three main sections: theory (Chapters 2, 3, and 4); practice (Chapters 5 and 6); and historical, cultural, and social issues (Chapters 7, 8, and 9).

Chapter 2 introduces the reading stages and Chapter 3 discusses the transitions through those stages.

Chapter 4 presents what lies behind the reading stages from psychological, linguistic, and the neuroscientific points of view, and from those of research and practice in education.

Chapter 5 concerns itself with the uses of these stages for instruction and for evaluation—in the school, the home, and the larger community.

Chapter 6 concentrates on applications of the stages to the understanding and teaching of those who have special needs.

Chapter 7 reviews old and new reading-stage schemes, as well as some of the cognitive and other stage schemes.

Chapter 8 presents historical and cross-cultural aspects of reading development.

Chapter 9 focuses on social-policy questions as they relate to the reading stages.

Chapter 10 contains conclusions and recommendations.

CHAPTER 2

A PROPOSAL
FOR READING STAGES

This chapter introduces the proposed scheme for reading stages—a scheme for studying and for understanding the course of reading development from its beginnings to its most mature forms.

Six stages are hypothesized and presented, from a kind of pseudo-reading to reading that is highly creative, through which people generally progress in characteristic ways. Individuals vary in their progression, yet most who are educated in typical schools tend to progress largely through the stages within the age limits listed.[1] Some progress at a slower pace, of course, and some at a faster pace. But in general, most people, even those with special problems and needs, follow the same sequence.

Among illiterate adults, the typical time periods for each of the stages is uncertain. Hypothetically they, too, tend to follow largely the same course of development, although like others with special needs, they have more success with some stages than with others.

How well and how fast a person progresses through the stages—whether a child or an adult learning basic literacy—depends upon the interaction of individual and environmental factors.

---

[1]The typical ages and grades vary by nations at any particular historical period and by the same nation over time (see Chapter 8).

I do not at this point present the reading stages as a theory. Instead, I prefer the less formal term "scheme," or "model," which I hope will lead to questions and hypotheses that can be either confirmed or disproven. I am hopeful, too, that the scheme can help to predict and control achievement in reading. I feel comfortable about calling it a model and even better a scheme—a scheme for arranging and interpreting facts from basic and applied research and the wisdom gained from experience in the classroom and the clinic.

The scheme focuses on what goes on in the person and in the environment to bring about reading development in each of the successive stages. The scheme is frankly macroscopic, but connections are made with microscopic research findings (Chapter 4). It does not attempt to explain what happens during a second or a minute of reading. (Such a conceptualization of reading is similar to classic germ theory in biology and medicine.) The scheme presented here more closely resembles the public health model which assumes that many diseases, even those caused by germs and viruses, can be prevented and alleviated by healthful, benevolent environments. I will not dwell on whether a "germ" or a "public health" model will be more useful for the theory and practice of reading instruction. Both are necessary. But it is important to note that environmental factors are recently gaining greater attention. More and more studies have been published on the effects of school factors on reading achievement (Bloom, 1976; Chall and Feldmann, 1966; Edmonds, 1977; Guthrie, Martusa, Seifert, 1979; Popp and Lieberman, 1977; Rosenshine, 1976; Stallings, 1975; Venezky, 1978; Weber, 1971; White, Day, Freeman, Hantman, and Messenger, 1973). At the same time, I have given greater recognition to neurological factors in reading development (Chall and Mirsky, 1978; Galaburda and Kemper, 1979; Roit, 1977; Wolf, 1979).

BACKGROUND OF THE SCHEME

I owe much to Piaget's work: his theory of stages and his stages of cognitive development (Inhelder and Piaget, 1958; Piaget, 1970). I also owe a debt to Wolff's (1960) comparison of Piaget's developmental theories with those of Freud and the psychoanalysts. With regard to advanced reading stages, the greatest influence came from Perry's (1970) study of advanced intellectual and ethical development in the college years. Although all of these theorists were influential, my major focus has been on the development of reading. My work on readability (Chall, 1958) and my work with Dale (Dale and Chall, 1948a, 1948b, 1956) influenced me greatly, as did my more than 25 years of experience as a clinician diagnosing and teaching children and young people with severe reading disabilities. The unsolved problems I uncovered while doing the research for *Learning to Read: The Great Debate* became the most recent impetus for formulating the scheme outlined here.

Generally, although the present scheme was influenced by Piaget's stages and by Wolff's analysis, my objective has not been to prove or disprove the applicability of Piaget's general cognitive theories to reading. Instead, I have sought in his work and in the work of other developmentalists ideas and methods for developing a scheme that is of value for understanding reading.

Following are some of the hypotheses used for developing the scheme:

1. Stages of reading development resemble stages of cognitive and language development. Like Piaget's cognitive stages, for example, reading stages have a definite structure and differ from one another in characteristic qualitative ways, generally following a hierarchical progression.

2. Reading is, at all stages, a form of problem solving in which readers adapt to their environment (as per Piaget) through the processes of assimilation and accommodation. In assimilation they use learned processes in reacting to new demands. In accommodation they adapt by changing or restructuring the old to accommodate the new.

3. Individuals progress through the stages by interacting with their environment—the home, school, larger community, and culture.

4. Measures of having reached a given reading stage will add a further useful dimension to standardized norm-referenced testing, as well as to criterion-referenced testing.

Such measures will add to a theoretical understanding of how reading develops and to the technology for effecting intensified improvement for those who need it more.

5. The fact of successive stages means that readers do "different" things in relation to printed matter at each successive stage, although the term "reading" is commonly used for all the stages. The different reading stages are associated with differences in such classic, basic measures of reading efficiency as eye movements, eye-voice span, and rate.

6. The successive stages are characterized by growth in the ability to read language that is more complex, less frequently encountered, more technical, and more abstract, and by changes in how reading is viewed and used.

7. The reader's response to the text also becomes more general, more inferential, more critical, and more constructive with successive stages.

8. The stages are also characterized by the extent to which prior knowledge is needed to read and understand materials. Generally, the more advanced the reading stage, the more the reader needs to know about the world and about the topic on which he or she is reading.

9. At each stage, readers may persist in characteristic techniques or habits that, if continued too long, may delay or even prevent transition to the next stage. If the accuracy, analysis, and synthesis of the decoding stage (Stage 1) are not succeeded by reading practice that requires a faster pace and a greater reliance on context (Stage 2), the reader may hold on to the successes of the earlier stage. Similarly, if the reader is not challenged with new demands for accuracy in gaining new information (Stage 3), he or she may persist longer in less accurate, more contextual reading (Stage 2).

10. Reading has affective as well as cognitive components. The reader's attitudes toward reading are related to those of his or her family, culture, and school. At all stages of development, reading depends upon full engagement with the text—its content, ideas, and values. Thus, motivation, energy, daring, and courage are aspects to be considered in the full development of reading.

THE STAGES

In this introduction to the developmental scheme elaborated in subsequent chapters, the ages and grades given for each stage are only approximations. They should be considered hypothetical, based on current educational achievements and practices. Some readers as young as age 6 may reach a level of reading categorized here as Stage 3. The average American child today reaches the beginning of Stage 3 at about age 9. Still others may not achieve it until age 12, or later, or not at all. How many now reach Stage 5 is not known, but probably fewer than the 40 percent who have some college education. That more sensitive and systematic instruction can help bring many more to this stage seems strongly possible (Bloom, 1976).

The following brief presentation of the Prereading Stage —Stage 0—is followed by a fuller treatment of the reading stages—Stages 1 to 5. In reality, some of the more advanced aspects of Stage 0 overlap with early aspects of Stage 1. One of the characteristics of Stage 1 is the child's becoming conscious of what was acquired incidentally during the Prereading Stage.

• **Stage 0. Prereading: Birth to Age 6.** The Prereading Stage covers a greater period of time and probably covers a greater series of changes than any of the other stages (Bissex, 1980). From birth until the beginning of formal education, children living in a literate culture with an alphabetic writing system accumulate a fund of knowledge about letters, words, and books. The children grow in their control over various aspects of language—syntax and words. And they gain some insights into the nature of words: that some sound the same at their ends or beginnings (rhyme and alliteration), that they can be broken into parts, and that the parts can be put together (synthesized, blended) to form whole words.[2]

The past decade has seen a growing interest in and investigation of the Prereading Stage (Bissex, 1980; Chomsky, 1979; Clay, 1966, 1975; Downing and Thackray, 1975; Durkin, 1966;

---

[2]These aspects of language development fall under the category of metalinguistic awareness (Cazden, 1974). The specific age at which they can be done varies. Some 5-year-olds can do the easy aspects, and others cannot do these at 6 or 7 or even later.

Jansky and de Hirsch, 1972; Read, 1971; Soderbergh, 1971; Wells, 1981). These investigations have identified the reading and writing activities engaged in by preschoolers, the children's problem-solving strategies, and the concepts of reading and writing held by the children during their different phases of prereading development on the way to beginning reading. It is widely reported that preschoolers today can discriminate and name most of the letters of the alphabet.[3] Many can write (print) their names and some letters dictated to them. Many children at this age have also interiorized the universal features of writing and can, when presented with various approximations to writing, select one that most resembles writing (Lavine, 1973). Some can recognize common road signs or brand names on packages and on TV commercials. Some can read some words in their favorite books. Many 3-year-olds "pretend" they can read a book, and they reveal knowledge of essential concepts of reading: holding the book right-side up, referring with a glance or pointing a finger to the words on the page while "saying" the words (i.e., telling the story as recalled), using the pictures for demonstration and elaboration, and turning the pages one at a time.

Extensive research on reading readiness and on early prediction and prevention of reading failure (Chall, 1967; de Hirsch, Jansky, and Langford, 1966; Gates and Bond, 1937; Jansky and de Hirsch, 1972) has demonstrated that the various abilities, knowledge, and skills acquired during the Prereading Stage are substantially related to success with reading at Grade 1. Although there is some disagreement among investigators as to whether individual characteristics or environment and experience is the more powerful in developing prereading skills and abilities, most agree that both are involved and that an interactional model will prove to be the most fruitful for understanding and for effecting improvement (Feldman, 1976).

There has been a great interest in the last decade or two

[3]This was not so 40 or 50 years ago. Gates (1937) found less extensive knowledge of letters and sounds.

Donald Durrell (Durrell and Catterson, 1980) has found recently in standardizing a reading-readiness measure that knowledge of names of letters may have lost its potency as a predictor of 1st grade reading since almost all children know the letters before entering Grade 1.

with finding those preschool-age children who are predicted to have difficulty in Grade 1. Various programs have been devised to stimulate and to teach these preschoolers on the assumption that good beginnings will lead to better reading development later. Parents who 30 years ago had been cautioned by educators not to teach reading to their preschoolers, watched as their own children were teaching their grandchildren to read at home (Smethurst, 1975).

Concern with prereading came also from linguists and cognitive psychologists interested in early language development. Another impetus was the growing concern about the poor reading achievement of children of low socioeconomic status. Thus, the 1960s and 1970s saw the beginnings of national efforts to study and to help the preschooler learn some of the reading tasks characteristic of Stage 0. The most widely known are the preschool and early reading shows *Sesame Street* and *The Electric Company,* which are watched by 5 million or more children. These popular TV shows, no doubt, added to the interest in early reading and writing.

The recognition that much growth in reading takes place at home during the preschool years has resulted in many how-to-do-it books for parents on teaching their young children to read (Ervin, 1979; Smethurst, 1975) as well as in books for explaining reading to parents (Larrick, 1975). The need to read to a preschooler regularly and often has been taken up by the women's magazines and by ads on TV. Much of the stimulation that parents are advised to give to their preschoolers requires more time, money (for books), and ability than may be available in some homes. Even a trip to the library is a great effort when both parents work.

It is therefore important to study how the essential prereading experiences required for optimal transition into beginning reading can best be provided by the home, school, and university.

• **Stage 1. Initial Reading, or Decoding, Stage: Grades 1–2, Ages 6–7.** The essential aspect of Stage 1 is learning the arbitrary set of letters and associating these with the corresponding parts of spoken words. In this stage, children and adults interiorize cognitive knowledge about reading, such as what the letters are for, how to know that *bun* is not *bug,* and how to know when a mistake is made. This stage has been referred to pejoratively as a "guessing and memory game," or as "grunting and groaning," "mumbling and bumbling," or "barking at print," depending on whether the prevailing methodology for beginning reading instruction is a sight or a phonic approach. The qualitative change that occurs at the end of this stage is the insight gained about the nature of the spelling system of the particular alphabetic language used.[4]

The transition from Stage 1 to Stage 2 is most vividly illustrated by Sartre's (1964) memory of how he taught himself to read. He recalls persisting and struggling with a favorite book. Determined to read it himself, he was "grunting" and sounding the syllables for hours until—with what seemed to be a flash of insight—he could read! He let out a roar and shouted the news for all to hear.

In a sense it is as if the child has recapitulated history from the early fumblings with the discovery of alphabetic writing to the equal, if not greater, intellectual feat of discovering that the spoken word is made up of a finite number of sounds. The work of Liberman and his associates (Liberman, Cooper, Shankweiler, and Studdert-Kennedy, 1967) makes this feat seem even greater. Because it is difficult to hear the same sounds when they are in different positions in a word or in different contexts (i.e., following vowels or consonants), a capacity for abstraction seems to be important, even for Stage 1.

This great discovery, usually accomplished with relief and joy but also occasionally with tears (Bissex, 1980), comes more or less dramatically to most of us who become literate. It is a phenomenon familiar to teachers of the primary grades, to remedial reading teachers, and to parents. On the surface, the child's reading does not seem to be very different, although it may be a little more fluent. On the usual tests of oral and silent reading, the scores may be the same. But the reader's understanding of reading has taken on a new structure. Therefore, new tests to capture this change are necessary.

[4]This insight is easily transferred to another alphabetic language known to the reader. The insights might well be different for ideographic languages (Maraini, 1973).

Phases exist within Stage 1, and Biemiller's (1970) study of 1st graders' reading errors seems to bear that out. Among 1st grade children who were taught by a sight-method emphasis, Biemiller found changes in oral reading errors that coincided with increasing ability in reading. Biemiller's first phase was characterized by word-substitution errors, most of which were semantically and syntactically adequate. The second phase was characterized by an increase in nonresponding and by more errors that had a graphic resemblance to the printed word, with a loss of some of the semantic acceptability. In the third phase, there was a continued concern with graphic exactness but also a return to greater semantic acceptability. All children seemed to move through these phases in the same order. The better readers progressed through them faster. The least proficient readers persisted in making the first type of error—substitution on the basis of meaning and syntax. It was only when the children appeared to let go of the "meaning" substitutions and worked instead on what the word looked and sounded like that they made substantial progress.

The Biemiller findings seem to run counter to the psycholinguistic theories of Smith (1978) and Goodman and Goodman (1977) that view true reading as reading for meaning. If one applied their theories to the Biemiller data, it would seem that children in the second phase would be rated as less skilled than those in the first since they were more "glued" to the print than to the meaning. Biemiller, in fact, concluded that the second phase, in which there is greater concern for graphic accuracy, is necessary for the transition to the seemingly easy, smooth reading in the third phase.

In essence, though, Biemiller's first-phase children were still engaging in a kind of pseudo-reading of Stage 0—the "reading" common at the prereading stage when the child retells a familiar story in a book, with the aid of a picture, mostly from recall. The nature of the "errors" during Stage 0 suggests that the print has a minimal effect on reading. Reading for these beginning 1st graders is largely an "inside out" process (F. Smith, 1979), one that depends more on the "reader" than on what is read. Similar to very mature, sophisticated readers, these beginning readers bring more to the printed page than they take from it (Dale, 1967). In one sense, beginning and very mature readers seem to behave in a similar manner toward print: they do not stick too closely to it, focusing instead on the meaning. Yet mature readers can stick to the print if they want to or need to. Going beyond it is a conscious choice for them, one based on knowledge. Young children at the pre-reading stage, and at the beginning of Stage 1, have no choice. They must supply their own words because they do not know enough about how to get the author's words from the printed page. To advance, to build up the skill for making choices, beginners have to let go of pseudo-reading. They have to engage, at least temporarily, in what appears to be less mature reading behavior—becoming glued to the print—in order to achieve real maturity later. They have to know enough about the print in order to leave the print.[5]

• **Stage 2. Confirmation, Fluency, Ungluing from Print: Grades 2–3, Ages 7–8.**[6]   Essentially, reading in Stage 2 consolidates what was learned in Stage 1. Reading stories previously heard increases fluency. Stage 2 reading is not for gaining new information, but for confirming what is already known to the reader. Because the content of what is read is basically familiar, the reader can concentrate attention on the printed words, usually the most common, high-frequency words. And with the basic decoding skills and insights interiorized in Stage 1, the reader can take advantage of what is said in the story and book, matching it to his or her knowledge and language. Although some additional, more complex phonic elements and generalizations are learned during Stage 2 and even later, it appears that what most children learn in Stage 2 is

[5]This may be similar to the seeming maturity of young children's art work. Their finger paintings resemble those of Jackson Pollack, and their drawings may smack of Miro. Yet can children's works be considered works of art? Should they be discouraged from their later struggles with seemingly awkward horses and stereotyped houses? Perhaps reading, too, must go from what seems like a finished, rounded act at the beginning to what seems more halting and dull in order to reach the maturity of choice and the finished, rounded act. See in this connection, Gardner (1980).

[6]It is possible that Stage 2 continues throughout one's life and is characterized among adults by reading popular fiction, magazines, mysteries, and some parts of the daily newspaper—reading from which one does not learn much that is new or exciting but that is confirming and satisfying.

to use their decoding knowledge, the redundancies of the language, and the redundancies of the stories read. They gain courage and skill in using context and thus gain fluency and speed.[7]

Relevant data regarding the reality of Stage 2 comes from the strong predictiveness of the reading achievement test scores at the end of Grade 3, as compared with those at the end of Grades 1 and 2 (Kraus, 1973). Kraus, who also referred to Bloom's (1964) data, found that by Grade 3, if a pupil scores significantly below the norms on achievement tests and does not receive special help, he or she will continue to experience failure throughout the school years.

The reality of Stage 2 may also be seen in the effects of campaigns to increase adult literacy. Stage 2 seems to be the main point at which most such campaigns fail. These efforts here and in Third World countries indicate that although most adults can get through Stage 1, they begin to falter at Stage 2. Reading a newspaper or a pamphlet containing new agricultural information, which requires at least Stage 3 reading, is difficult or impossible for most. The following explanation may prove useful. After the literacy classes complete their Stage 1 programs, there are not enough readable materials available—material that is familiar in its use of language and content—for the new literates to gain the fluency of Stage 2. Nor is there usually a compelling need to keep on reading.

What kind of environment fosters the development of Stage 2? Essentially, it requires an opportunity for reading many familiar books—familiar because the stories are familiar, the subjects are familiar, or the structure is familiar, as in fairy tales or folktales. (At one time, the Bible and religious tracts were familiar.) Familiarity with the language patterns of these

---

[7]The difference between reading a story at Stage 0 and at Stage 2 was illustrated to me by a brother and sister, aged 7 and 4. Each wanted to read to me the little Nutshell Library book, *Pierre*, by Maurice Sendak. The 7-year-old, the Stage 2 reader, grabbed it first. He was older and stronger. He then read it through fluently, with an obvious sense of the meaning. The 4-year-old sister grabbed it in turn, over his strong protest. "She can't read," he insisted. "I can too," she said. He went along with my tolerance of her immaturity, and the Stage 0 child read the story through with such fluency and expression that I might have accepted her performance as reading if it were not for her Stage 2 brother's protestations that she wasn't really reading the words.

books also helps. Generally, the greater the amount of practice and the greater the immersion, the greater the chance of developing the fluency with print that is necessary for the difficulty to come—the acquisition of new ideas in Stage 3.

For children of low socioeconomic status, although a discrepancy is reported from the Prereading Stage on, the gap seems to widen at Stage 2.[8] The child whose parents cannot afford to buy books or whose own patterns of recreation and work do not include borrowing books and magazines from a public library loses the time needed for practice. If the parents do not read regularly to the child, development of language may be slower (Chomsky, 1972). Even more important, the child loses out on the emotionally confirming responses that books and reading matter bring.

• **Stage 3. Reading for Learning the New: A First Step.** When readers enter Stage 3, they start on the long course of reading to "learn the new"—new knowledge, information, thoughts and experiences. Because their background (world) knowledge, vocabulary, and cognitive abilities are still limited at this stage, the first steps of Stage 3 reading are usually best developed with materials and purposes that are clear, within one viewpoint, and limited in technical complexities. This is in contrast to Stage 4 where multiplicity of views, complexity of language and ideas, as well as subtleties of interpretation are the expected.

In a sense, entering Stage 3 fits the traditional conception of the difference between primary and later schooling: in the primary grades, children learn to read; in the higher grades, they read to learn. During Stages 1 and 2 what is learned concerns more the relating of print to speech while Stage 3 involves more the relating of print to ideas. Very little new information about the world is learned from reading before Stage 3; more is learned from listening and watching. It is with the beginning of Stage 3 that reading begins to compete with these

---

[8]SES is used here and throughout the chapter to refer to the usual kinds of experiences children are exposed to in homes classified by the different socioeconomic levels. I do not mean the income of the family but the overall experiences, particularly the experiences of reading and literacy (Bloom, 1976).

other means of knowing. However, at the beginning of Stage 3, learning from print is still less efficient than learning from listening and watching. Hypothetically, by the end of Stage 3 the efficiency of reading may equal and begin to surpass that of the other means of gaining new information, particularly listening (see Chapter 3).

Stage 3 reading is also characterized by the growing importance of word meanings and of prior knowledge. The need to know some new things, if more is to be learned from reading, becomes greater. Readers need to bring knowledge and experience to their reading if they are to learn from it (Chall, 1947, 1950; Kintsch, 1974). They also need to learn a process—how to find information in a paragraph, chapter, or book, and how to go about finding what one is looking for efficiently.

It is significant that in traditional schools, the 4th grade, age 9, was the time for starting the study of the so-called subject areas—history, geography, and natural science. The curriculum in the first three grades included the language arts and math. The content subjects were not included until children had mastered enough of the literacy skills to deal with the books used to teach them about times and places and ideas removed from their direct experience.

The findings from the readability research of the past fifty years seem to fit this stage as proposed (Chall, 1958; Klare, 1974–1975). Stage 3 fits the data on and the experiences with the distinctions between primary level reading materials and materials at the 4th-grade readability level and above. The materials at 4th-grade level and higher begin to go beyond the elemental, common experiences of the unschooled or barely schooled. To write out even the simplest informative materials—materials that present ideas that the reader does not already have—a readability level of at least Grade 4 is usually required. Materials at Grade 4 readability level begin to contain more unfamiliar, "bookish," abstract words (ones that are usually learned in school or from books) and a higher proportion of long and complex sentences. (Such words may be learned from TV but probably only from the public service programs.) While the learner is in the decoding (Stage 1) and confirming (Stage 2) stages, the task is to master the print; with Stage 3 the task becomes the mastering of ideas. Because this is a task quite different from, and probably more difficult than, those of Stages 1 and 2, it can be mastered only in a limited way. I propose that for most children, Stage 3 reading means learning how to learn from reading, but essentially from only one point of view.

The reading in this stage is essentially for facts, for concepts, for how to do things. If there is any reading for nuance and variety of viewpoint, it is probably in the reading of fiction. One may hypothesize that the time taken to progress from Stage 3 to Stage 4 relates to the time it takes to acquire knowledge in the many areas needed to read and understand the multiple viewpoints encountered in Stage 4.

One might further divide Stage 3 into two phases: Phase A, covering the first half, from about grades 4–6 (ages 9–11), and Phase B, covering grades 7–8 and/or 9 (ages 12–14).

The first phase, Stage 3A, includes development of the ability to read beyond egocentric purposes, to reading about conventional knowledge of the world.[9] At the end of Stage 3A (Grade 6), individuals are able to read serious material of adult length but falling somewhat short of the reading difficulty of most adult popular literature.

Stage 3A does not usually require special knowledge for reading informational materials or fiction. Indeed, "first books," that is, introductions to subjects, are commonly read by 4th–6th graders.

Stage 3B, junior-high level, brings readers closer to the ability to read on a general adult level. *The Reader's Digest* and other popular magazines, popular adult fiction, and local newspapers are within the reader's ability by the end of this phase. *Newsweek, Time,* and other news magazines are still somewhat beyond this stage.

As readers move from the first to the second phase of Stage 3, they also grow in their ability to analyze what they read and to react critically to the different viewpoints they meet. Much can be done here in reading critically, but it is better and more consistently done in Stage 4 when more of what

[9]According to the Werner and Kaplan study (1952) of language development, it is about this time when word meanings and language become more conventional in a worldly sense (see Chapter 3).

is read is known and the reader's critical abilities are more developed.

Stage 4. Multiple Viewpoints: High School, Ages 14–18. The essential characteristic of reading in Stage 4 is that it involves dealing with more than one point of view. For example, in contrast to an elementary school textbook on American history, which presupposes Stage 3 reading, the textbook at the high-school level requires dealing with a variety of viewpoints. Compared to the textbooks in the lower grades, the increased weight and length of high-school texts no doubt can be accounted for by greater depth of treatment and greater variety in points of view. Stage 4 reading may essentially involve an ability to deal with layers of facts and concepts added on to those acquired earlier. These other viewpoints can be acquired, however, because the necessary knowledge was learned earlier. Without the basic knowledge acquired in Stage 3, reading materials with multiple viewpoints would be difficult.

How is Stage 4 acquired? Mostly, through formal education—the assignments in the various school textbooks, original and other sources, and reference works in the physical, biological, and social sciences; through reading of more mature fiction; and through the free reading of books, newspapers, and magazines. Dealing with more than one set of facts, various theories, and multiple viewpoints, as one must in Stage 4, gives one practice in acquiring ever-more-difficult concepts and in learning how to acquire new concepts and new points of view through reading.

• Stage 5. Construction and Reconstruction—A World View: College, Age 18 and Above. Stage 5, the most mature stage, I take from Perry's (1970) study of intellectual development during the college years. He contrasted a quantitative approach to knowledge (Stage 4) with a more qualitative approach:

> In our reports, the most difficult instructional moment for the students—and perhaps therefore for the teachers as well—seems to occur at the transition from the conception of knowledge as a quantitative accretion of discrete rightness (including the dis-

crete rightnesses of multiplicity in which everyone has a right to
his own opinion) to the conception of knowledge as the qualitative assessment of contextual observations and relationships
(Perry, 1970, p. 210).

When Stage 5 is reached, one has learned to read certain
books and articles in the degree of detail and completeness that
one needs for one's purpose, starting at the end, the middle, or
the beginning. A reader at Stage 5 knows what not to read, as
well as what to read. To reach this stage is to be able to use se-
lectively the printed material in those areas of knowledge central to one's concern. Whether all people can reach Stage 5
reading, even at the end of four years of college, is open to
study. Some evidence, however, suggests that more college
students reach this qualitative stage earlier than they did in previous generations (Perry, 1970).

Stage 5 can be seen as reading that is essentially constructive. From reading what others say, the reader constructs
knowledge for himself or herself. The processes depend upon
analysis, synthesis, and judgment. The reader makes judgments as to what to read, how much of it to read, at what pace,
and in how much detail. And when many sources are used,
even if only two, he or she decides what synthesis is to be
made. What does this mean? It means a struggle to balance
one's comprehension of the ideas read, one's analysis of them,
and one's own ideas on them.

Past knowledge about the subject and broad general
knowledge are needed for selecting what to read, for comprehending it, and for making a useful synthesis. Previous knowledge and familiarity with the ideas make a rapid reading rate
possible. If the texts are unfamiliar, a slower, study-type pace
is needed.

Generally, Stage 5 means that one has the ability to construct knowledge on a high level of abstraction and generality
and to create one's own "truth" from the "truths" of others.
While difficult philosophical and historical works may require
Stage 5 reading to be understood, much fiction can also be understood at more than one level. *Moby Dick,* for example, can
be understood as an adventure story or as a profound tragedy
of retribution.

Relationships among the Reading Stages. I have hypothesized that each stage presupposes skills acquired in the previous stage, that these are generally subsumed as new skills are acquired, and that each stage is subsumed by the next stage. Stage 1, the decoding stage, is assumed to build on the skills, attitudes, and knowledge developed in the Prereading Stage. This does not mean that a child cannot learn to read without the full range of prereading skills and abilities. Beginning reading programs where children did not have these skills have succeeded through modifications of the program (Gates, 1937). However, the existing literature on readiness does indicate that achievement on prereading factors is a good predictor of early reading achievement, at least through the end of Grade 2 (Stage 1) (Bond and Dykstra, 1967; de Hirsch, Jansky, and Langford, 1966; Durkin, 1966; Jansky and de Hirsch, 1972).

Stage 1, in turn, appears to be a necessary condition for Stage 2 because scores on decoding tests have a positive and significant correlation with scores on oral and silent reading tests (Chall, 1967, 1978a; Walmsley, 1976). Since these standardized reading tests cannot be restricted to the use of only those words and phonic elements taught specifically in each child's reading program, it is a tenable hypothesis that mastery of Stage 1, particularly the ability to identify words not directly taught, is necessary for proficiency in Stage 2.

Although Stage 2 subsumes Stage 1, decoding does not stop altogether.[10] The learning and use of correspondences between spoken and written words continues in Stage 2 and other stages. Correspondences are used for new proper names and for new words not immediately recognized, and, in fact, it continues during Stages 3, 4, and 5. In Stage 5, particularly, decoding is used for reading foreign names, new technical words, and new alphabetic foreign languages. Indeed, it would seem that a Stage 1 type of reading was needed to break the code of the Rosetta Stone—although probably all who tried did most of their other reading on a Stage 5 level. One tenable

[10]The degree of direct teaching at Stage 2 is relatively less than at Stage 1, but wide reading must be encouraged. The classroom should contain many books that are easy, familiar, and interesting enough to invite reading, and it should provide the time and the atmosphere to read them.

hypothesis is that typical literacy behavior does not stay at one stage only. Those who read at Stage 5 for study and work may relax with a mystery at Stage 2. Although the general character of reading changes with each succeeding stage, the abilities of previous stages remain for use in situations that require them.

Stage 3, the first stage of reading to learn, presupposes abilities to use context and fluency in reading that are acquired in Stage 2. Without these characteristics, the reading of materials with new concepts, names, and facts would be difficult. Only when the fundamental decoding skills are mastered (Stage 1) and fluency has become habitual (Stage 2) can reading become useful as a tool for learning, even when the new information is relatively straightforward and unencumbered by a variety of viewpoints and subtleties. Because Stage 3 reading requires accurate attention to facts and details, decoding skills acquired at Stage 1 are still used. And because it requires confidence to move ahead even if a word or idea is not gotten immediately, Stage 3 makes use of Stage 2 fluency.

In a similar manner, Stage 4 subsumes Stage 3, and Stage 5 subsumes Stage 4. Understanding of one viewpoint on a subject or topic must be developed so that multiple viewpoints can be understood. From multiple viewpoints, a world viewpoint that depends on the ability to reconstruct and construct anew from what one reads may be achieved.

VALUES OF A READING STAGE THEORY

For Instruction.   Reading stages can contribute to a better understanding of how reading is acquired and how the total environment, as well as the school environment and instruction, may be optimized for pupils at the different stages. It would appear that children who enter 1st grade and are at the beginning of Stage 1 should have more specific and systematic instruction than those who have made some inroads into decoding.[11] This is because the relations between sounds and let-

---

[11]Many children entering Grade 1 are past Stage 1 and well into Stage 2 because of *Sesame Street* and *The Electric Company* and the general acceptance by parents of the efficacy of early reading.

ters, elementary decoding skills, are usually not discovered by the learner but require direct instruction.[12] Toward the end of the decoding stage, the knowledge and skills acquired are usually sufficient to become self-generative. That is, some growth can be achieved with practice on one's own.[13]

If I have characterized Stage 3 properly, then the focus of reading instruction in the middle grades should be on literature and reading in the various subject areas—textbooks, reference works, and other sources.

A qualitative, developmental way of looking at reading may provide a useful set of questions to ask, particularly about the failure points. For example, we may ask why there has been a consistent failure point reported for Grade 4 or 5, the point of transition between Stages 2 and 3. The appropriateness of the optimal challenge, the proper materials and instructional strategies for effecting a transition from Stage 2 to Stage 3, needs to be questioned. Thus, the concept of proper match or challenge, a concept used often in the 1930s, might gain from a fresh look. How and where to teach reading in the intermediate and upper elementary grades (Stage 3) could also profit from a fresh look. Is it better done by the teacher from a reader, a collection of stories? Or is it better done by the teaching—of literature, science, social studies—from content materials? Or are both needed?

• **For Evaluation.** A reading stages model can help to provide the broad general principles of reading development needed to construct meaningful tests—norm-referenced, criterion-referenced, or diagnostic. These stages have been used recently, in fact, by Gagné (1978) in a set of guidelines for the development of diagnostic-prescriptive reading tests. When some test publishers claim to measure the "379" reading comprehension skills needed by 4th graders, one wonders

[12]This is currently being debated. Much of the research in reading as well as in math for the primary grades seems to indicate that direct instruction is more effective (Rosenshine, 1976). There seem to be opposing views on this matter (Almy, 1975).

[13]Of course, some children do invent their own spelling systems and teach themselves to write and read (Chomsky, 1976, 1979; Durkin, 1966; Read, 1971). These children are exposed to much "literate" stimulation and receive a great deal of reinforcement for these activities. These conditions, however, are probably not met in most homes in the United States.

whether some of the current technology designed to help teachers is going to lead to a general state of paralysis. However, tests are needed, and schools at least, if not teachers, seem to be ready for criterion-referenced tests and other tests of mastery. An understanding of what distinguishes reading at the various stages of development would be one of the essentials for selecting and constructing the crucial subtests and items. Norm-referenced tests could also benefit from a better knowledge of the qualitative changes in reading (Auerbach, 1971).

• **For Studying "Literate" Environments.** The stages scheme can lead to systematic study of the environments in school and at home that foster reading development. Availability of books is essential for growth in reading. Are books more essential for some stages than for others? A tenable hypothesis is that availability of books is particularly essential for growth at Stage 2 and beyond.

• **For Studying the Effects of Classroom Environments.** Stages may also be useful in studying the effects of different kinds of classroom structure and organization. One might hypothesize that for Stage 1, in which the children have not already learned letters and sounds and do not have insight into the fact that the two are related, much has to be taught directly and practiced systematically. For children who are learning such things, a more structured learning environment might lead to more definite gains than one in which the children work more on their own and are expected to discover their own generalizations (Stallings, 1975; White, Day, Freeman, Hantman, and Messenger, 1973).

It would seem that some direct instruction is again needed for Stage 3 when the emphasis is on reading to acquire new, exact knowledge. With the acquisition of knowledge comes a need for more words of lower frequency and the ability to learn them from context and from dictionaries, encyclopedias, and other references. It is at this stage, too, that the old, yet new, question arises: Who should do the teaching of reading— and what should be taught? Should emphasis be on reading literature? On content? On exercises designed to teach the various reading comprehension skills? A recent research study on how reading comprehension is taught in the middle grades found that most time was spent on distributing and checking reading exercises (Durkin, 1979).

• **For Those Who Have Difficulty with Reading.**   The stage scheme may help us to gain a better understanding of the reading and other educational problems of those who experience persistent difficulties—those who have reading or learning disabilities and those whose retarded reading is attributed to deficiencies in their linguistic development.

With regard to the poor reading performance of children with reading or learning disabilities, it is notable that the basic characteristic of such children is the significant discrepancy between their reading achievement and their mental ability. They do not generally have problems in understanding or producing language. At the risk of oversimplifying the complexity of their problems, one may say that generally their ability to derive meaning from print lags significantly behind their ability to understand by other means. Their difficulty is usually not with understanding ideas and language. If they have difficulty with language, it is with its phonological aspects—sound discrimination, segmentation, blending, and sequencing.

Experience from clinics and classrooms indicates that children with reading or learning disabilities have great difficulty with Stage 1 (decoding) and Stage 2 (fluency). Indeed, the more severe the reading or learning disability, the more there seems to be a problem with decoding and fluency (Chall, 1967). Furthermore, compared to children of their chronological and mental age, the transition from Stage 1 to Stage 2 is more difficult and takes longer for the disabled children. It takes a long time before they are comfortable with even the simplest book. They almost seem glued to the print, or they still guess wildly at the words they see.

The difficult transition from the decoding (Stage 1) to the confirmation stage (Stage 2) was noted by many of the early investigators of reading disability—Gray, Gates, Orton, and Fernald (see Chall, 1967). This problem continues to be of concern. Samuels and his associates (Samuels, Begy, and Chaur, 1975–1976) have been developing techniques for effecting this transition and moving toward "automaticity."

An overlong stay in Stage 1 is also serious for a child when the rest of the class moves into Stage 3 and he or she cannot cope with Stage 3 reading. Some provision needs to be made for the pupil's continued conceptual and informational development, which in most schools comes primarily from written materials. If this is not provided while the pupil is learning to read on a lower level, deficiencies in cognitive development may ensue, although the original problem was with decoding rather than with the meaning components of reading.

With respect to the poor reading performance among bilingual, minority, and low SES children, the reading stages scheme suggests that Stage 1 should present the least relative difficulty to them. Although these children may have had fewer literacy experiences by age 6, with good instruction little difference should persist during Stage 1 because what needs to be learned at this stage is specific, finite, and when learned, self-generative. With good teaching and a good program that provides direct teaching and an opportunity for much practice, little difference should exist among students of different backgrounds in learning at Stage 1. Indeed, such claims were made by Weber (1970) in the first of the school effectiveness studies, and they are being made by the authors and publishers of some of the highly structured reading systems. See, for example, SWRL's Beginning Reading Program (Southwest Regional Laboratory for Educational Research and Development, 1972), Distar Reading (Englemann and Bruner, 1969), and the Stanford Computer Assisted Instruction Program in Initial Reading (Atkinson, Fletcher, Chetin, and Stauffer, 1970).

The gap for low SES children, I would hypothesize, begins to widen at about Stage 2, the stage requiring much reading and daring and ease about one's performance. It is probably difficult to achieve a Stage 2 level from school readers and workbooks alone. Children's books should be made available in school and out (Weber, 1971).

Stage 3 also needs great care. The literary and "bookish" language of textbooks, encyclopedias, and other informational books creates another hurdle. It would seem, therefore, that concepts, vocabulary, and strategies necessary for reading such books need to be taught. Although it may be possible for children with rich and varied literary experiences to move more smoothly from Stage 2 to Stage 3—from the fluent reading of simple children's books to the reading of textbooks in order to acquire new information—it is less likely that children with more limited literary experiences can do the same without help.

For the less advantaged children to compete favorably with their more privileged peers, they must be helped to proceed through these reading stages. For success with Stages 3, 4, and 5, they must be helped to improve systematically their knowledge of words, facts, and ideas, knowledge that children of higher SES backgrounds may acquire around their dinner tables, from books on the family shelves, from their own collections of books, and from the magazines cluttering the coffee table. Because the opportunities for such learning may not be provided by most lower SES homes, it is essential that the school provide them during the reading stages when they are most needed.

• **For Research.** A stage theory might help to prevent some of the persistent controversies that occur in the field of reading research and practice. The research in reading seems to be particularly subject to misunderstandings. It is not uncommon for investigators to disagree over the meaning of *reading,* when each is concerned with a different stage of its development. The proposed stages should help to clarify what is or is not being studied or discussed.

The reading stages may also help to provide a framework for analyzing and synthesizing various models of reading. It appears that the psycholinguistic theories of reading by F. Smith (1971 and 1979) and the Goodmans (Goodman and Goodman, 1979) make little provision for a decoding stage (Stage 1) and seem to show little concern for the kind of accuracy required in technical and scientific reading (Stage 3 and beyond). Indeed, it is often suggested in their theories that decoding retards reading for meaning and that relying on context for recognition of words and meanings is the ideal reading strategy at all times, including the initial stage. To a great extent, the theories of Smith and the Goodmans, when applied to beginning reading, resemble the sight and sentence methods of the recent past and the language experience methods of the present. According to those models, there is one reading process—reading for meaning—which is essentially the same at the beginning level and at the highly skilled level.[14]

Stage theory may add to our knowledge of what happens as the individual learns to read at an ever-increasing level of maturity. Although we use only one word—*reading*—for what happens at the various stages, important quantitative and qualitative changes take place. Quantitative measures of change already exist—the standardized reading tests for measuring the abilities of readers and the readability formulas for measuring the difficulty of the reading materials. The standardized reading tests are similar to existing measures of mental ability in that they measure growth in maturity in terms of ages or grades. Such quantitative estimates have their value in that they can help to effect a match between reading materials and readers. They also help to determine whether progress has been made from year to year.

What such tests do not provide, however, is information for the researcher, teacher, or clinician about the specific aspects and components of reading that have been mastered and those yet to be acquired. As is the case with most intelligence tests, no provision is made in standardized reading tests for translating the scores into qualitative descriptions of the read-

---

[14]In an early paper, Goodman (1968) outlines a three-level model of the development of reading proficiency. In the first level, the child learns to assign phonetic values to either letters, letter patterns, or whole word shapes to create an aural input. This aural input is recoded into oral˙language (through the use of the child's knowledge of the language) which, in turn, is decoded into meaning. This seems to correspond to Stage 1 proposed here. In Goodman's second level, the process is "telescoped" so that the child is dealing with larger graphic units at greater fluency (similar to Stage 2 proposed here). At his third level, the child goes directly from print to meaning without an intermediate phonemic recoding stage.

More recently, the Goodmans (Goodman and Goodman, 1979) have argued that children can achieve the third level of reading proficiency, going from print to meaning, from the very beginning, without instruction in the phonic aspects of written language.

ing process that suggest the necessary next steps for instruction and practice. This is particularly important in providing for the millions who have serious reading problems. It would help to know, for example, what an 8th grade reading level on a standardized reading test means when it is achieved by a 4th grader, an 8th grader, a 12th grader, or an adult seeking a high-school equivalency certificate. Does such a score indicate mastery of decoding, fluency, and reading for facts and concepts? At what level? Tests of these different qualities would help us in research and in practice.

• **For theories of the reading process, and of instructional theories of reading.** The proposed reading-stage scheme may help explain some of the similarities and differences among the reading process theories that are of interest today. Most can be distinguished by their relative emphasis on certain aspects of the reading process. For example, some theories tend to view reading as mainly a "top-down" process, while others view it as a "bottom-up" process, or a combination of both. Generally a "top-down" theory emphasizes prediction and guessing from context—for both word recognition and comprehension—based on overall understanding of the text. A "bottom-up" theory emphasizes the hierarchical aspects of reading—from letters to words for word recognition, from literal to interpretive skills in reading comprehension.

According to the proposed reading-stage scheme, style of processing would tend to vary according to the reader's stage of development. This can be seen in Table 2-1, Column 1, where we have classified Stage 0 as top-down, for there are few, and only rudimentary, word perception skills available for reading. The "pseudo-reading" of the preschooler is based primarily on prediction and memory. The style changes at Stage 1, when it becomes primarily a bottom-up process, focusing on word perception and decoding. The processing style changes somewhat at Stage 2. It continues in the bottom-up approach of Stage 1, with an increasing backup of a top-down process. From Stages 3 to 5, the emphasis shifts to top-down, with secondary emphasis on bottom-up for materials that become very difficult or unclear.

Table 2-1
PROCESS CHANGES BY READING STAGES

	READING PROCESS "STYLE"	MEDIUM OR MESSAGE?	DECODING OR MEANING EMPHASIS	PREVIOUS KNOWLEDGE NEEDED FOR COMPREHENSION	PREFERENCE FOR ORAL OR SILENT READING
	(1)	(2)	(3)	(4)	(5)
Stage 0 To Age 6	Top-down	Message to medium	Meaning	Needs to know the stories that child pretends to read	Oral
Stage 1 Grade 1–2.5	Bottom-up	Medium to message	Decoding (meaning)	++Words and syntax	Oral
Stage 2 Grades 2–3	Bottom-up to top-down	Medium and message	Decoding (meaning)	+++Familiarity of selections, words, and syntax	Oral/silent
Stage 3 Grades 4–8	Top-down and bottom-up	Message and medium	Meaning (decoding)	++++Knowledge of word meanings, concepts, information	Silent
Stage 4 Grades 9–12	Top-down and bottom-up	Message	Meaning	+++++Much background knowledge, abstract and technical words, concepts	Silent
Stage 5 Grade 13	Top-down and bottom-up	Message	Meaning	++++++Much general and specific knowledge	Silent

Some evidence suggests that the method by which a reader first learns may be a factor in the process, for example, the way context and prediction are used (Barr, 1974). But other evidence from eye-movement, eye-voice span, and error (miscue)* studies shows that the changes in processing are related generally to reading development.

Another issue on which most reading theories take a position is whether reading is primarily getting "the message" or acquiring skill in "the print medium." Another way to view this theoretical issue is in terms of what the learning task is or what creates the difficulty. Is it the printed text? Or is it the meaning of the message?

Table 2-1, Column 2, refers to whether the focus is on the meaning or on the print medium for each of the reading stages. This category is similar to the top-down/bottom-up, with the message emphasis on the side of the top-down style. Here, too, the prereader of Stage 0 seems to resemble more the mature reader than the beginning reader. The emphasis before the beginning is on the message. Then for Stage 1, the reader's major attention is on the medium, although the message also gets part of the attention. Somewhere during Stage 2, more attention begins to be focused on the message, and by Stage 3, most of the focus shifts to the message. During Stages 4 and 5, readers' facility with the medium is usually highly efficient. Because the content and language of what is read becomes harder, the focus of attention is on the message.

Another theoretical issue on which the various reading theories differ is whether they view reading as primarily a process of decoding or meaning (see Table 2-1, Column 3).

The meaning/decoding emphasis category tends to overlap somewhat with the top-down/bottom-up and medium/message categories. If we project it onto the reading stages, we see that at Stage 0, the meaning emphasis seems appropriate. The person cannot use decoding skills that do not yet exist. The "pretend" reading is based mainly on memory and predic-

---

*A study of miscues by Moore (1980) found correlations among the cuing systems and traditional performance measures suggesting "a focus on syntactic and graphic details at earlier grade levels and a movement toward semantic processing at grades five and six" (p. 75). Moore concludes, ". . . the findings of the study of the development of reading strategies of children in grades one to six have been reasonably consistent with other miscue studies. Developmentally it would seem that as a child became a more proficient reader in terms of traditional performance measures there is a movement away from the syntactic, and the combined syntactic/graphic dimensions to more concern for semantic meaning" (p. 89).

tion. During Stage 1, the emphasis is on decoding, with concern also for meaning. Beginning with Stage 3, and continuing to Stages 4 and 5, the focus shifts to meaning, with decoding as needed to recognize unfamiliar words.

Column 4 concerns the amount of background knowledge needed in order to comprehend the materials that are typically read at each stage. As we see from Column 4, the amount of background information needed increases by stage level.

The last theoretical issue concerns the preference for oral or silent reading. For the past 60 years, most reading theories have stressed the importance of silent reading for comprehension, with cautions against oral reading (E.L. Thorndike, 1917). Some have even proposed starting with silent, non-oral methods right from the start in Grade 1 (McDade, 1937). Column 5 presents a theoretical view of preferences by successive stages. The preference for oral reading in Stages 0 and 1 comes from many sources—the need to associate print with speech (found from studies on phonemic significance in early reading) and the need to practice the decoding process overtly. Further support for oral reading comes from the eye-movement studies. At Grade 1, readers need many fixations per word before they recognize it.

At Stage 2, silent reading begins, along with oral reading. It is in a real sense a transition stage between oral and silent reading. Automatic recognition of words and the increasing fluency in Stage 2 are a preparation for the silent reading needed in Stages 3 and beyond (Perfetti, 1977). Beginning about Stage 3 and continuing during Stages 4 and 5, silent reading becomes more efficient. Indeed, at the two highest levels, silent reading becomes faster than oral.

It should be emphasized, however, that even at Stages 3 and beyond, both a slower reading rate and oral reading can contribute to getting the meaning of what is read and to esthetic appreciation. Poetry, Shakespeare, the Bible, Dickens, and other texts read primarily for esthetic and affective purposes become more graspable and more personal with oral reading.

Table 2-2 is concerned with several theoretical issues of importance in instruction. Here, too, we attempt to show how preference for a position tends to be associated with the particular stage of reading development. The first issue is that of an open-indirect versus a structured-direct teaching environment (see Column 1). This issue has been the subject of much discussion and research.

Table 2-2
INSTRUCTIONAL ISSUES BY READING STAGES

LEARNING ENVIRONMENT	TIME FOR LEARNING AND USING READING	MATERIALS OF INSTRUCTION, MATERIALS READ*
(1)	(2)	(3)
Stage 0 Open-indirect	+	+Picture books, alphabet books, writing materials
Stage 1 Structured-direct	++	++Basal readers and workbooks, trade books for beginners
Stage 2 Open-indirect/ structured-direct	+++	+++Basal readers and workbooks, trade books of fiction and nonfiction
Stage 3 Structured-direct/ open-indirect	++++	++++Basal readers, workbooks, subject matter textbooks, reference works, children's books
Stage 4 Structured-direct/ open-indirect	+++++	+++++Reading in content areas and literature, newspapers and magazines
Stage 5 Structured-direct/ open-indirect	++++++	++++++Wide reading of books and periodicals for study, work, and recreation

*One can also use games, TV, and computers.

We classified as "open-indirect" those learning environments in which the rules and processes are presented indirectly in a less structured manner, to be inferred or discovered by the students. For reading, it may include self-selection of instructional materials and much "individualized" reading. A "structured-direct" reading instructional environment is more teacher-directed and usually more hierarchically organized.

Column 1, Table 2-2, presents as most optimal for Stage 0 an open or unstructured environment for most children. For those with special needs, a structured environment may be more effective. Stage 1, we propose, will be more effective, generally, under a more structured, direct-teaching program because there is much to be learned that cannot be discovered on one's own. At Stage 2 fluency is developed with much reading on one's own. But because much is yet to be learned in decoding and word recognition, there is need also for direct teaching and structure.

For Stages 3 through 5, both structure-direct and open-indirect environments are needed. Direct teaching appears first because students have much to learn in order to read ever more difficult texts, with ever more abstract and sophisticated responses. They need to learn more vocabulary and background information, and these are seldom achieved by self-discovery alone.

The second issue concerns time for learning and uses of reading. In Column 2 we indicate the amount of time for learning and reading use that is needed for development at each successive stage. We propose that at each successive stage, more time is required because reading becomes more difficult and covers a broader range of information and style.

Column 3 lists the instructional materials typically used today. It should be noted that the materials become more varied, branching out from basal readers at about Stage 3 to include content textbooks, literature, the print media, and so forth.

Table 2-3 contains excerpts from typical materials that can be read by readers at successive stage levels. We should note that the selection for each succeeding stage contains more unfamiliar or low-frequency words, longer sentences, and more difficult concepts. The topic and the language become more abstract and more removed from common events and experience at succeeding levels. Thus, if one views these passages as a very simple and rough measure of mastery of a stage, one can hypothesize what has to be learned to advance to the next stage.

When a person can read and understand such selections at a given level, it usually means that he or she can also read at the lower levels with understanding.

Table 2-3

Stage 1	"May I go?" said Fay. "May I please go with you?"[a]
Stage 2	Spring was coming to Tait Primary School. On the new highway big trucks went by the school all day.[b]
Stage 3A	She smoothed her hair behind her ear as she lowered her hand. I could see she was eyeing *beauty* and trying to figure out a way to write about being beautiful without sounding even more conceited than she already was.[c]
Stage 3B	Early in the history of the world, men found that they could not communicate well by using only sign language. In some way that cannot be traced with any certainty, they devised spoken language.[d]
Stage 4	No matter what phenomena he is interested in, the scientist employs two main tools—theory and empirical research. Theory employs reason, language, and logic to suggest possible, or predict probable, relationships among various data gathered from the concrete world of experience.[e]
Stage 5	One of the objections to the hypothesis that a satisfying after-effect of a mental connection works back upon it to strengthen it is that nobody has shown how this action does or could occur. It is the purpose of this article to show how a mechanism which is as possible psychologically as any of the mechanisms proposed to recount for facilitation, inhibition, fatigue, strengthening by repetition, or other forms of modification could enable such an after-effect to cause such a strengthening.[f]

[a] *American Book Primer,* p. 19.
[b] Ginn 720, Grade 2², p. 48.
[c] Ginn 720, Grade 5, p. 66.
[d] Book F: *New Practice Reader,* Graves et al., Webster, New York, 1962.
[e] Kathryn, A. B., *College Reading Skills.* From Mason and J. Bresig, *Modern Society,* 3d ed., Prentice-Hall, Englewood Cliffs, N.J.,
[f] E. L. Thorndike, "Connectionism." *Psychological Review,* 1933, *40,* pp. 434–490.

CHAPTER 3

TRANSITIONS THROUGH THE READING STAGES

How DOES ONE MOVE from one reading stage to the next? Piaget's concepts of assimilation and accommodation—two ways of adapting to the environment—are useful for understanding reading development as well.

Essentially, reading tasks may be viewed as problems to be solved. The solution may lie in assimilation, that is, in adapting to the new task in a manner used previously to adapt to the old. That is, new reading tasks may be treated as essentially similar to the older, known tasks, with similar solutions. In the second kind of problem solving, accommodation, the reader uses new forms of thinking to solve new problems, by changing, by restructuring his or her knowledge and abilities. That is, one accommodates oneself.

These two forms of adaptation are separate only in theory. In actual practice they are closely related. Every act of assimilation contains some aspects of accommodation and accommodation assumes some assimilation. For reading, those tasks that require skills and abilities already mastered by the reader should be accomplished by assimilation, while those tasks beyond the reader's present masteries should be acquired by accommodation. Thus, "easy" reading can be done by using skills already mastered, that is, assimilated. Harder reading tasks can be acquired only by restructuring the reader's skills and abilities, that is, through accommodation.

Let us use these two concepts in discussing how the reader moves from stage to stage, solving problems of increasing complexity and subtlety.

TRANSITIONS FROM STAGE 0 TO 1

During the transition from prereading (Stage 0) to decoding (Stage 1), reading tasks change in many ways. The pretended pseudo-reading of Stage 0 depends on memory and picture understanding. No real recognition of separate words occurs, nor does a person have the knowledge that the printed words "match" the spoken words. There is only a kind of global matching of story parts with pictures and other reminders of the remembered story.

To make the transition from Stage 0 to Stage 1, words and letters must now be recognized and "matched" with spoken words and sounds. If the transition from Stage 0 to Stage 1 is made by assimilation, dependence on picture clues and memory of the story content will continue. This is, in fact, Phase 1 reading in Grade 1 as described by Biemiller (see Chapter 2, p. 17). The child's errors involve mainly substitutions that "make sense" linguistically, i.e., the semantic meanings and syntax are sensible, although the words that are read aloud do not match the text as written. Ilg and Ames (1950) also found "having to be told the words" and word substitutions to be the commonest errors in early reading.

If the transition is by accommodation, the reader focuses his or her attention on the words as written and on the letters in the words. So to move from Stage 0 to Stage 1 by means of accommodation, the reader restructures his or her knowledge and skills. The concept of reading also changes—from a global, "inside-out" notion that reading is memorizing stories, or creating stories from pictures, to reading the words that tell the story. The child's concept of reading if he accommodates to Stage 1, therefore, is closer to Hamlet's reply when asked what he was reading—"Words, words, words."

The style of Stage 1 differs from that of Stage 0. Stage 0 is more global, impulsive, "inside-out," that is, it comes more from inside the reader and less from visual matching to the outside text. Stage 1 is by contrast more "outside-in," more reflective, more dependent on what is on the page.

How is the transition effected? How can children be helped to make this accommodation? Probably the most effective way for most children is to receive instruction in the letter names and sounds, in recognizing words, and in reading connected texts (to help in recognizing common words and in practicing decoding). Writing also helps, as does the reading of simple books and being read to from books of interest that the child cannot yet read alone.

Some children do make the transition largely on their own, through being read to and encouraged to read and write on their own under the loving eyes of parents who are always there to confirm the child's efforts (Bissex, 1980). Children's early writing and "invented spelling" gives them practice in associating the written letters to the sounds (Chomsky, 1979; Read, 1971). To be effective, this requires high motivation of parents and children, high task orientation, and many books and writing materials. Although reports of such self-learning stress the independent aspects of the child's learning behavior, one might hypothesize that it is the long hours of joyful teaching and time invested gladly by the parents in their child's reading and writing that probably account in considerable measure for the excellence of the results reported. The "time on task" by parents and children who learn informally at home has not been recorded, as far as I know. But one might guess that in all probability it outweighs the limited amount of teaching and practice that each child receives in a 1st grade classroom. The time, then, that can be spent on reading at home is considerable. Such time and loving individual attention is not possible in a 1st grade class of even 20 or 25 children. Overall, both teaching and practice, whether the teaching is direct or indirect, facilitate the child's accommodating to Stage 1.

Does the reading method matter? Considerable research evidence indicates that a "code emphasis," that is, an emphasis on learning the printed words and letters that stand for spoken words and sounds, makes a difference in how a child accommodates to reading. Generally it has been found to be more effective for most children than methods that put first emphasis on the meaning of what is read. "Code emphasis" makes possible the earlier development of insights into the relation of print and speech—the key cognitive restructuring needed for Stage 1. Generally, children taught by a meaning emphasis (or sight method) in Stage 1 make slower progress (Chall, 1967).

The early errors made by children taught by code or meaning emphasis also tend to vary, with the sight-trained tending to make more substitution errors and the decoding group making more errors of phonics (Barr, 1974; Calfee and Drum, 1978).

It would seem as if meaning-emphasis methods tend to extend the reader's adaptations of Stage 0 to Stage 1. They tend, as in Stage 0, to rely heavily on pictures and on substituting words that make sense semantically, although they have little graphic resemblance to the printed word. In essence, they seem to rely on assimilation, using older structures longer.

Code-emphasis children tend to accommodate earlier in Stage 1, responding differently from the ways they responded in Stage 0. In Stage 1, they focus more on the printed words and letters, rather than on pictures and memory as they did in Stage 0. When children learn something about letters and sounds and how they work in words, they seem to accommodate more in reading new texts. Instead of assimilating by using their pseudo-reading of Stage 0, relying on memory of the story and on pictures for making "story sense," they accommodate, searching not only for the word that makes sense, but for the word that "is written" by the use of letter-sounds. Their errors in connected as well as in single-word reading tend to be phonemic as well as semantic and syntactic (Barr, 1974; Biemiller, 1970; Calfee and Drum, 1978; Weber, 1970).

But the desire to use the new structures must be great for the child to give up the older, more comfortable habit of relying on memory and making up the rest when memory fails. Indeed, the first accommodation to the "real" reading of Stage 1 is knowing that one doesn't know a word—an increase of no responses in oral reading of connected text (Biemiller, 1970). Those who cannot or will not give up the certainty of Stage 0 seem to make slower progress through the early phases.

The unknowns in Stage 1 are "new" words—words not recognized immediately, although known in speech and when heard—and new letter-sounds and how they are used in recognizing words. Typical Stage 1 learnings are sound/letter correspondences—spelling and sounding principles, generalizations, and patterns; sight recognition of common words and of words first learned through sounding; and reading of short selections. Most of the words and letter-sounds have to be learned from those who know them—teachers, parents, siblings, classmates. There is much asking and telling, practicing "orally" and being confirmed.

During the 1800s these learnings were taught from spelling books, such as *Webster's Blue Back Speller,* and *Town's Spelling and Defining Book.* Earlier and later, they were called primers. Now they are taught through pre-primers, primers, readers, and workbooks (Chapter 5).

Some published reading programs, as well as some teaching methods, may put a greater emphasis on meaning and sight recognition from the start, encouraging adaptation through assimilation of Stage 0 strategies. This was the prevailing method used from 1920 until about the late 1960s. Since then, more published programs have a heavier code emphasis at the beginning, putting an earlier stress on accommodating to Stage 1 (Chall, 1977).

The essential transition from Stage 0 to Stage 1 involves gaining insight into the alphabetic principle in "solving" words not immediately recognized. Indeed, it is this major learning in Stage 1 that hastens a favorable transition to Stage 2, which requires an even greater facility and ease with decoding and word recognition.

THE TRANSITION FROM STAGE 1 TO 2

Transition from Stage 1 to 2 requires adaptation to texts that contain language and content that begins to approach the natural language and thought of the reader (see p. 18). Essentially,

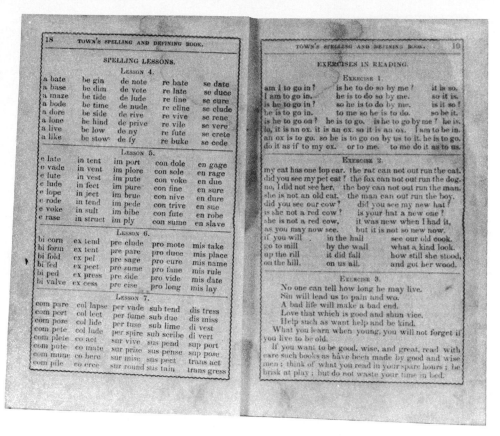

Pages 18 and 19 from Town's Spelling and Defining Book *(1846) show a concern for spelling and sounding, and for connected, meaningful reading.*

Note particularly page 19, Reading Exercise 3, which can be used as a vignette of the work ethic and its emphasis on learning and achievement.

the change in reading matter is from the highly controlled vocabulary and limited content of Stage 1 to a more extensive vocabulary, language, and content.[1] Stage 2 reading strategy requires some of the sweep and confidence of the "message making" of the prereader of Stage 0. To persist in the cautious, word-by-word reading characteristic of much of Stage 1 would be dysfunctional for Stage 2. As in Stage 1, the natural mode is still mainly "oral." But in Stage 2, particularly toward

[1]Traditional, religious societies tend to use religious texts, in their regular unadapted, unsimplified forms, beginning with Stage 2. See Chapter 8.

The following have the second sound of th, *as,*
in thou.

Thine	teeth*	blithe	then	soothe
thy	those	wreath	thus	they
bathe	tithe	writhe	the	there
lathe	these	sythe	them	their
swathe	though	seethe	thence	ou
clothe	thee	breathe	than	thou
loathe	lithe	this	booth	mouth
meethe	lithe	that	smooth	

* The noun *teeth*, has the first sound of *th*, and the verb to *teeth* its second sound. The same is observable of *mouth* and to *mouth*. This is the reason why these words are found under both heads.
The words *mouth*, *moth*, *cloth*, *oath*, *swath*, *bath*, *lath*, have the first sound of *th* in the singular number, and the second in the plural.

Examples of the formation of plurals, and other derivatives.

Bay,	bays	stain,	stains	saint,	saints
day,	days	brain,	brains	heap,	heaps
lay,	lays	chain,	chains	tear,	tears
pay,	pays	pain,	pains	hear,	hears
pray,	prays	paint,	paints	spear,	spears
sway,	sways	claim,	claims	creed,	creeds
way,	ways	strait,	straits	trait,	traits
mail,	mails	plague,	plagues	chief,	chiefs
nail,	nails	key,	keys	leak,	leaks
sail,	sails	knave,	knaves	speak,	speaks
weep,	weeps	green,	greens	sheaf,	sheaves
seam,	seems	yield,	yields	leaf,	leaves
fly,	flies	stride,	strides	poll,	polls
cry,	cries	guide,	guides	soul,	souls
dry,	dries	smile,	smiles	coal,	coals

sky,	skies	toe,	toes	bowl,	bowls
buy,	buys	foe,	foes	rogue,	rogues
sigh,	sighs	bow,	bows	post,	posts
flight,	flights	glow,	glows	host,	hosts
light,	lights	flow,	flows	toast,	toasts
sight,	sights	blow,	blows	coast,	coasts
life,	lives	snow,	snows	door,	doors
wife,	wives	hoe,	hoes	floor,	floors
knife,	knives	foal,	foals	oar,	oars

TABLE XIII.
Lessons of easy words, to teach children to read,
and to know their duty.

LESSON I.
NO man may put off the law of God:
My joy is in the law all the day.
O may i not go in the way of sin!
Let ne not go in the way of ill men.
II.
A bad man is a foe to the law.
It is his joy to do ill.
All men go out of the way.
Who can say he has no sin?
III.
The way of man is ill.
My son do as you are bid;
But if you are bid, do no ill.
See not my sin, and let me not go to the pit.
IV.
Rest in the Lord, and mind his word.
My son, hold fast the law that is good.
You must not tell a lie, nor do hurt.
We must let no man hurt us.

Several pages from Noah Webster's, The American Spelling Book (1824), *illustrating early concern for both decoding (phonics and spelling) and for reading with understanding.*

the end of the stage, reading begins to be "silent," to oneself. For most children at Stage 2, however, reading will still be a kind of subvocal oral reading, with whispering or lip movements until the end of Stage 2, in Grade 3. Ilg and Ames (1950) found that by age 9 (Grade 4) children "may do better in silent reading and may prefer silent reading, but when reading for facts and information may retain better when they read orally" (p. 296).

If the cautiousness of Stage 1 continues too long, and too great an emphasis is put on perfect accuracy and "sounding" of the text beyond a point of need, Stage 2 may be held back. That is, if children are too "glued to the print," without help in freeing themselves from it, they may not develop as rapidly in the fluency and reading for meaning needed in Stage 2. This could become dysfunctional for the development of Stage 2, which is characterized by a more fluent, freer approach to reading that relies more heavily on the meaning of the text and the use of context. Too analytic an approach at Stage 2 may hold up silent reading comprehension.

Accommodation to Stage 2 would take a more courageous, even daring attitude, combining the "inside-out" (top-down) approach that makes use of context and story knowledge and the "outside-in" (bottom-up) approach used for decoding. For Stage 2 reading, the individual needs confidence and ease in using Stage 1 learnings, and confidence in trying the new strategies that are needed in Stage 2. The reader also needs to rely more on knowledge of language, of ideas, and of facts to anticipate meanings as well as new words. The reading style of Stage 2, therefore, seems to be closer in style to that for Stage 0 than for Stage 1.

Accommodation to Stage 2 requires daring and reflecting on one's daring. The child learns implicitly that the correct word or answer is based not only on sounding, or only on memory, or only on context—it is based on all of these. The integration is more difficult than knowing each separately. So the reader in Stage 2 makes many mistakes, and he or she should be given this freedom, along with "tips" on how to make corrections.

The changes in oral reading errors of primary grade children noted by Ilg and Ames (1950) are relevant here. The most common errors to age 8 were substitutions of visual forms (either substitutions of a single letter, short words that looked alike, or in long words, using some of the letters given and guessing the rest). At age 8, substitutions of meaning nearly equaled those of visual substitutions. By age 9, substitutions of meaning predominated over visual substitutions.[2]

The reading materials for Stage 2 differ from culture to culture and by historical periods. I believe they have one characteristic in common—they are within the oral tradition of a culture and of the children, linguistically, cognitively, and stylistically. In traditional religious societies of the past and

[2]See in this connection the results of miscues analysis studies (Moore, 1980).

present, prayers, homilies, the Bible, the Koran, all are used in their unadapted and unsimplified forms. In modern Western countries, the trend has turned from religious to national content, to more literary folk and fairy tales, to more modern stories. Much criticism recently has been leveled at the content of today's beginning reading texts—from concerns about inadequate ethnic representation to concerns for emotional and cultural significance, and for more appropriate difficulty.

TRANSITIONS FROM STAGE 2 TO STAGE 3

The transition from Stage 2 to Stage 3 also requires changes in attitudes and strategies, as well as in growth in general knowledge, in language, and in cognitive abilities. The materials typically read during Stage 3 are considerably different from those at Stage 2—the vocabulary goes beyond the reader's everyday word knowledge, the number and difficulty of concepts increases, the sentences are more complex, and more sophisticated background knowledge is assumed (see Chapters 2 and 5). Accommodation to Stage 3 requires a higher level of reading skill, greater world knowledge, and a higher level of language and cognitive development.

It matters little for modern Stage 2 readers whether the hero was called James or Joseph. It matters a great deal in the reading of historical and scientific materials at Stage 3. Correctness and accuracy in reading what the author wrote is one of the characteristics of Stage 3 reading.

The personal characteristics associated with Stage 3 reading are reflectiveness and the ability to accumulate facts and other details. According to Freudian theory, children are in their latency period during the time that most are reading at Stage 3. It is a time of keen interest in the world, a time for collecting objects, things, facts, and knowledge.

Stage 3 style shifts back to the more reflective and analytic style of Stage 1, away from the flowing and "guessing" of Stage 2 but using the fluency of Stage 2. The reader has to know again, as in Stage 1, when he does not know. If the reader uses the strategies of Stage 2 for Stage 3 tasks, that is, if he or she simply assimilates, the reading might be too quick and superficial, leading to poor recall of names, places, and sequences of events. The attitude toward the easy familiar stories of Stage 2, when carried over to Stage 3, may produce a rate that is too fast for the more demanding Stage 3 reading.

Accommodation to Stage 3 is achieved through the learning of subject matter—science, social studies, and literature. It is acquired during the reading and study of subject matter textbooks, reference works, biography, historical and science fiction, specialized and general magazines, and popular and "classic" children's books. Oral and written reports on what is read help make meaningful what is read to oneself and to others.

Stage 3 may be viewed as the average minimal level needed for the great majority of people in an industrial society—a level at which one can acquire new information and vicarious experiences from newspapers and magazines, and from books that are written on not too complex a level (Chapters 7 and 8).

THE TRANSITION FROM STAGE 3 TO 4

Stage 4 may be viewed as the minimal reading competence required in a knowledge society, one in which communication of information is the most valued pursuit. It assumes the ability to read efficiently complex materials on a wide variety of topics, from a variety of viewpoints. A greater quantity of reading is typical for Stage 4 as compared to Stage 3, as is a greater openness to the reading materials and to the different views they present. Now the accumulation of facts of Stage 3 gives way to the search for relationships and viewpoints. In Stage 4 it is as if the reader's full range of knowledge, viewpoints, and generalizations opens up from the more limited range of Stage 3.[3]

The reading strategies of Stage 4 are more like "pattern recognition" of different ideas and points of view than recognition of individual ideas. An efficient reading rate is almost es-

---

[3]But some readers at Stage 3 do begin to branch out into wide reading of books and magazines. A few, perhaps, like Francine Nolan of *A Tree Grows in Brooklyn*, want to read all the books in the public library, from A to Z.

sential at Stage 4 if the reader is to "cover" school assignments and is to "keep up" with a daily newspaper, a weekly newsmagazine, and an occasional bestseller.

With Stage 4, the volume of materials to be read increases, as does their complexity and the complexity of the responses expected as compared to Stage 3. Now the precise detail characteristic of Stage 3 must be let go. At Stage 4 the full mass of knowledge in print begins to be available to the reader, because it can now be read. Stage 3 reading is not sufficient for that.

The reading at Stage 4 is in some ways more global than at Stage 3, with much groping and sampling. Much more material needs to be read on a variety of topics, more than in Stage 3. Much of it remains for some time as "patterns in parallel," with the reader having little idea of how it can be pulled together. If the Stage 4 reader assimilates and uses Stage 3 strategies when Stage 4 is called for, reading is too slow and careful, making it difficult to absorb and integrate the different viewpoints.

I recall vividly the difference between Stage 3 reading and that of Stages 4 and 5. When I was in the 6th grade, we studied World War I. I came home from school one day full of enthusiasm over what I had just learned. I now know, I confided to my father, a veteran of the First World War, the cause of the war. He listened patiently, with some pride, but with amusement at my recitation of *the* cause. His four years with the cavalry gave him another view. In high school, our history textbook was more extensive, listing many causes of World War I. I lost the *one* cause of my very sure Stage 3 days when I did a report on the "many" causes and discovered that I was not sure of any. I had lost the assurance of the single Stage 3 point of view and had entered into the multiplicity of views and skepticism of Stage 4.

Reading at Stage 4 may in some ways seem impulsive, with seemingly little integration. For integration to take place, the reader needs to know more and value more of what is being read. This usually comes later at Stage 5. With the more extensive reading of Stage 5, with deepening knowledge through discussion and writing, and with growing conviction and point of view, more can be pulled together.

Accommodation to Stage 4 takes place when the reading

tasks, particularly those in school, cover a multiplicity of knowledge—facts, ideas, opinions, views—with discussions and written assignments designed to force the student to grapple with that multiplicity. Most content areas in the secondary school lend themselves well to providing the needed challenge and practice—English (literature and composition), history, the social sciences, science, and the like.

THE TRANSITION FROM STAGE 4 TO 5

Passage from Stage 4 to 5 is the most difficult, for more than the other transitions, it seems to depend on the reader's cognitive abilities, accumulated knowledge, and motivation (Perry, 1970). Making a transition from Stage 4 to 5 means that the reader engages in tasks that require the synthesis, reorganization, and critical reaction to what is read in often difficult and contradictory texts.

On an assignment in a graduate seminar which asks students to synthesize a limited number of research reports, some students seem to rely on a Stage 4 strategy, placing greater emphasis on an analysis of the individual research studies and less on synthesizing the ideas from the different studies. Those who use a Stage 5 strategy focus on an overall view gleaned from a reading of all of the individual research studies.

For Stage 5 accommodation, a great deal of knowledge is needed, as well as confidence and humility. Above all, the reader needs a feeling of entitlement. One needs to believe that one is entitled to the knowledge that exists, to think about it, use it, and to "make knowledge" as did those whose works they read.

To make the transition to Stage 5, it is helpful, Perry (1970) says, to watch the stumblings of one's teachers. In reading, most of one's stumbling is hidden. It can be discovered, however, in oral discussion and in written reports. These may be shared with students who are often relieved to know that their mentors are still grappling with the same process.

Accommodation to Stage 5 is accomplished better when one has a viewpoint, or dares to have a view, not for all time but for now. One needs courage also to expose to others the view gained from reading in speaking and writing. And to expose it means to open oneself not only to acceptance and praise but to rejection and ridicule.

Some of the conditions of a successful transition to Stage 5 are: broad knowledge of the content that one will be reading at Stage 5; high efficiency in reading, personal courage, daring, confidence, and humility; and an environment that encourages Stage 5 reading—the college or professional school that expects and teaches for it, and a community that rewards it.

It is in college and graduate school that most students learn to give up their Stage 4 reading, with its concern for reporting the different views without really being able to integrate them. One seems at Stage 5 to read and write less, but to think and agonize more. In this process, many different ideas and views are fused into one's own.

It is probably not the case that Stage 5 is achieved simultaneously by the same person in different areas of knowledge. Indeed, transition to Stage 5 (and also to Stage 4) may not be reached at the same time for all kinds of reading tasks and materials. There may be faster stage development in areas of special personal interest or of particular emphasis in the school curriculum. Even while most of their reading is at Stage 2, for example, some children may read of rocks, fossils, dinosaurs on a Stage 3 or even a 4 level. The variations in stage development for the same person become more obvious at the high school and college levels when greater specialization and concentration take place. Some can do Stage 5 reading in the behavioral sciences, Stage 4 in biology, and Stage 3 in physics and chemistry. Some adults reach Stage 5 for one specialized area of knowledge but may still function at Stage 4 or even at Stage 3 in other areas of knowledge.

TRANSITION THROUGH THE STAGES: CONCLUDING REMARKS

In sum, the basic characteristics of the stages seem to follow an ebb and flow. Stage 5 mirrors the "reading" of the preschooler in Stage 0 in some ways: both require great daring leaps, and the use of one's own ideas of what is in the text for "reading" what *is* there. The child in Stage 0 who retells stories while looking at the pages of a book does not rely on recognition of the individual words and letters but on recall of the stories. The Stage 5 reader also pays less attention to the print (less than in previous stages), not because he or she doesn't know the words, but because the content is so well known that the reader can concentrate on the ideas. Both care more about the message than the medium. They attend more to meaning than to mechanics.

The ebb and flow from stage to stage also moves from openness to greater structure, then back again to openness. Stage 0 is open, and the child is helped by invention and daring. In Stage 1, when the reader learns the basic elements and rules of recognizing words, a "structured" approach usually works better. There are rules to be learned and followed. At Stage 2 the reader returns to the daring of Stage 0 and applies more gracefully the elements and decoding rules learned in Stage 1 with an emphasis also on the message. In Stage 3 he or she returns to the concentration of Stage 1, this time for new ideas and meanings. At Stage 4, a new openness to ideas is needed. Stage 5 continues this openness requiring courage and commitment to using the knowledge gained (see Table 2-1, Chapter 2).

If the prereader already seems to do what the most mature readers do after 13 or more years of instruction and practice, why do we have to instruct him or her? Indeed, this has been asked and is being asked by serious reading theorists and researchers. Some answer that we do not have to instruct. They appear to propose that reading develops best when the reader is left in his or her natural state, as in Stage 0, and subsequently acquires skill by much reading for meaning. Direct teaching of decoding and other so-called reading skills is to be discouraged, they say, because it holds up reading progress. They stress that reading must be natural, like language acquisition, with no differentiation of skills and no differentiation by developmental levels (Goodman and Goodman, 1977; Smith, 1978). Others favor a developmental, hierarchical view (Gough and Hillinger, 1980; Samuels, 1976; Weaver, 1978).

Perry (1970) finds that these two views exist with regard to learning and teaching at the college level. The natural, global view would teach college students the "truth" from the start—that knowledge is uncertain. Those who prefer the hierarchical view of learning would teach that knowledge and acquiring it are different at different points, helping students see that up to a certain point they are doing fine but that at a later point, they must move on, using a different strategy and approach.

Those who take a natural view of reading, envisioning the ideal as Stage 5 (or Stage 0), would teach reading as if it were essentially Stage 5 (or Stage 0), emphasizing meaning, integration, content, interpretation, and creative reactions from beginning to end.

The developmental view tells the reader in essence that reading is one thing at one time, and another thing at another. After students get the idea of using letters and sounds in Stage 1, for example, in order to get them to Stage 2, we say, look here at these stories. When you read them, you have to concentrate on what they mean. What you did until now (in Stage 1) you will need, but you need something more here. You have to move along easy now, making good guesses, in addition to sounding. Don't fuss too long on each word or you'll lose the thought of what you read. Read ahead if you are not sure of a word.

Then, when things are going just fine with Stage 2, we change the reading matter and we say: This is not for fun alone (as in Stage 2). This is for learning, for remembering, and for understanding the world. You really have to try to remember what it says about *who, what, when,* and *how,* because these things are important to learn. You can't do that by moving along as fast as you did for your stories (in Stage 2), skipping words you didn't know and making guesses. That was good then, and still is good for such stories. But with these you have to make sure that you read what the writer wrote.

When the student gets the idea of the more substantive reading needed for Stage 3, being asked to know what the author really means to convey and what the words mean, he or she begins to be confronted by even more reading in a variety of subjects. It is then (Stage 4) that the reader is encouraged to speed up, giving up some accuracy temporarily. In Stage 4, more ideas are gained for the same effort (time in reading) as compared to Stage 3 reading, so that more facts, ideas, and feelings are gleaned from the reading.

Then in college, the Stage 4 reader is told that this level isn't good enough. A good reader synthesizes and has a more realistic and worldly view of knowledge. Knowledge must be treated as relative—true for given situations at given times. The reader is asked to produce "pieces of sculpture"— creations and re-creations of what is read, combined with what is known and imagined—instead of the strings of beads of knowledge that worked well in high school (Perry, 1970).

I take the position here that the second view of reading—the developmental view—is the more valid in light of present theory and research findings. It fits better the available evidence from research in the classroom, the laboratory, and the clinic (Chapter 4).

Although I prefer the developmental theory for a scientific explanation and for instruction, I do not take the position that the "naturalistic" view does not work at all. It works, but, I believe, mainly where the learners have high motivation, high cognitive and language development, much stimulation and help in their homes, and highly individualized teaching in school with a plentiful supply of books. But even these children appear to achieve better when reading is taught in a more developmental manner (Chall, 1967; Guthrie et al., 1979; Rosenshine, 1976, 1979; Stallings, 1975).

HOW DEPENDENT IS EACH STAGE ON MASTERY OF EARLIER STAGES?

Stage 1, it would appear, is needed for mastering Stage 2. In order to read the simplest connected texts with any fluency, it is necessary to recognize common words and to be able to decode those not recognized. If too few of the unknown words can be decoded, the reader may, in fact, resort to a lower level of reading, Stage 0, relying mainly on guessing the words from memory. Stage 2 functions mainly because of the use made of what is learned in Stage 1—knowledge of the relations between

letters and sounds and the skills that are based on that knowledge. With weak Stage 1 skills, energy remains concentrated
on decoding instead of on meaning where it should now focus.

Stage 3 reading relies on the fluency acquired in Stage 2, a
skill needed to cope with the more complex and varied reading
matter typical of Stage 3. In order to deal with the more difficult vocabulary and syntax of Stage 3, the rhythm and flow of
Stage 2 are needed. If they are not available, the slow rate and
the hesitations hinder concentration on the meaning.

It is, of course, possible to reach Stage 3 by other means.
Those who broke the code of the Rosetta stone could read the
message (Stage 3) after solving the mystery of the alphabetic
code (Stage 1). But the alphabetic code had to be broken before the message was revealed. It is doubtful whether the cryp-
tographers achieved, or needed to achieve, the fluency of Stage
2. If the alphabetic principle is understood, it seems possible
to go directly into Stage 3, at a slow pace. Fluency may come
later, with practice. Indeed, the Koranic Schools of the Middle
East (Wagner and Lofti, 1980) and the Heders of the Orthodox
Jewish Schools tend to do just that—go from teaching of the alphabet to the reading of adult texts. Stage 2 fluency probably
comes later in Stage 3 (see Chapter 8). It may be achieved,
also, because their religious tradition has already made these
texts familiar to the children.

Stage 4 is highly dependent on mastery of Stage 3. It
seems that the greater complexity of Stage 4 reading, which
contends with much data and many interpretations, requires a
prior experience of reading for a more limited purpose.

For Stage 5 reading, much depends upon what has been
acquired earlier in Stages 3 and 4. To reconstruct knowledge
from reading requires great efficiency, skill, and depth.

The characteristics of a given stage, after they are brought
to a point of efficiency, continue in some form in the next
stage. The characteristics of the earlier stages are not completely abandoned. Instead, they form the underlying structure of the new stage, and they serve as a safety mechanism
when the skills of the new stages are not immediately applica-
ble.

Decoding, the main development of Stage 1, therefore, remains with readers throughout each of the successive stages. It

is most useful in coping with reading matter that is appreciably above the reader's normal level, requiring "sounding" of unrecognized words and names. Even at Stages 4 and 5, decoding is needed, particularly for reading foreign names, places, names, and rare and technical words.

Each successive stage has a characteristic structure, and it absorbs the characteristics of the previous stages. Each succeeding stage is more varied and complex—and demands of the reader more complex reactions—from word recognition to literal comprehension, to highly analytic and critical reading. The reading materials become more difficult—more abstract, less common in vocabulary and syntax—and assume more previous knowledge (see p. 39, Table 2-3).

In a sense, none of the stages is ever fully mastered. One continues to grow and become more proficient in the skills of a stage even as a new stage is entered. It may be useful to view the transition to the next higher stage as resting on competency in the earlier one. Thus Stage 1 (decoding) can move into Stage 2 (fluency) before all of the relations between letters and sounds are learned. The greater proficiency in decoding that is needed later can be picked up with Stage 2 reading.

Is it possible to start to read late in life and become a Stage 5 reader? It is written of many religious leaders in antiquity that they first learned to read as mature adults, at the age of 40 or more. One could hypothesize that they could reach the highest stages of reading, although they began to read at such late ages, because they were steeped in the oral traditions of their cultures which formed the basis for the written scriptures. When they learned the alphabetic principle of the written language, they could read the scriptures at a high level of individual interpretation because they had for many years been interpreting the oral versions. This would suggest that reading at a high level is enhanced where the background knowledge, the complex language of the texts, and the mode of critical inquiry and synthesis required are already available.[4]

---

[4]This principle appears to be the basis of the literacy programs of Paolo Freire among impoverished farmers of South America. His first steps are to make them conscious of the need for literacy and their entitlement to it. Where this knowledge and attitude toward literacy already exists, it is possible to proceed to Stage 1 reading.

Why, then, are 12 to 16 years needed by most people to-day to reach Stage 5? Probably because of the knowledge and judgment aspects of reading. These really take a lifetime for almost everyone, and then such achievement may occur only in one or two areas of specialization. Indeed, in a real sense, liberal arts training is designed to prepare the student for Stage 5 reading in several areas of knowledge in the arts, sciences, and humanities, preparing the student to read, understand, use, and contribute to the knowledge held to be important for educated people.

The difference in the nature of reading, as experienced at the three advanced stages, can be seen in the following answers to the question: Is what you just read true?

Stage 3: Yes, I read it in a book. The author said it was true.

Stage 4: I don't know. One of the authors I read said it was true, the other said it was not. I think there may be no true answers on the subject.

Stage 5: There are different views on the matter. But one of the views seems to have the best evidence supporting it, and I would tend to go along with that view.

CHAPTER 4

REALITY OF
THE READING STAGES:
EVIDENCE FROM
PSYCHOLOGY,
LINGUISTICS,
NEUROSCIENCES,
AND EDUCATION

THIS CHAPTER BRIEFLY SUMMARIZES the evidence relating to the proposed developmental reading stages. This evidence comes from several areas of scholarship: basic research and theory in the psychology and teaching of reading, linguistics and psycholinguistics, and the neurosciences. Another line of evidence comes from educational research, both theory and practice.

We do not attempt a complete coverage of the published literature. The literature on reading alone is vast, with several thousand books and articles published every few years. We searched, instead, for those theories, research findings, and practices that relate to reading development and to our proposed reading stages. First we searched the literature on the basic psychological processes related to reading development. To assure inclusion of the most important studies, we relied especially on such widely accepted works as those of Buswell (1922) on eye movements; Gibson and her associates (Gibson, Barron, and Garber, 1972; Gibson, Pick, Osser, and Hammond, 1962; Gibson and Olum, 1972) and M. D. Vernon (1971) on perception; Gibson and Levin (1975) on the psychology of reading; and Levin (1980) on eye-voice span.

I am mindful that evidence of validity for a scheme such as the one proposed here will ultimately require many observations and experiments and the cooperation of many scholars. But they can do this only after the scheme is made available to them. I present, therefore, the published evidence from research and from educational practice that I consider relevant to the stage scheme, not as sufficient, but as a necessary first step.

The full findings from psychology, linguistics, and the neurosciences appear in Appendix A. Only the highlights appear here. The evidence from education comes in the second part of this chapter.

EVIDENCE FROM PSYCHOLOGY

• **Psychological Processes**   At what age do children perceive that given words and letters are the same or different? At what age can they use visual information not in direct focus? A review of the available research on visual perception indicates a steady growth with age and school grade. Thus, most children can see similarities and differences in letter-like forms before age 5 (Stage 0). The speed at which letters are matched increases in Stage 2 (Grades 2 and 3) and continues to increase through Stage 3 (Grade 4). Some investigators tend to see this increase with age as a result of maturation, while others view it as influenced mainly by stimulation.

Children begin to use visual information not directly in focus at Stage 2 (Grades 2.5–3) when reading becomes more fluent. Attentional processes also increase considerably during

Stages 1 and 2 (Grades 1–3). The ability to use knowledge of spelling patterns and phonological or sounding rules seems to begin in Stage 1 (Grade 1) and works fully for most children by the end of Stage 2 (Grades 2 and 3). It becomes more efficient during the first part of Stage 3 (Grade 4). So, although most children can use phonological rules at Stage 1, it seems that only when the phonological and spelling systems are fully functioning and efficient can the more mature reading of Stage 3 occur.

From studies of oral reading errors, we learn also that by the time children reach the beginning of Stage 2 (the middle of Grade 2) they can integrate decoding (phonics) with their use of context, that is, the sense of what is read and the meaning of surrounding words along with the grammatical structure of sentences (Gibson and Levin, 1975; Vernon, 1970).

Appendix A contains greater detail on these studies, the specific processes measured, their findings, and how they parallel the proposed stages.

• **Eye Movements**   The movement of the eyes across print has served as a means of studying the basic reading process since the 1800s. The findings from the classic as well as from the newer eye-movement studies are quite consistent. All show fast growth in efficiency of eye movements during the primary grades and a slowing of the rate of growth from about Grade 4 or 5 until the college years. The proposed stages tend to parallel the growth curve of these eye-movement studies. The greatest growth in efficiency comes at Stages 1 and 2, when basic word recognition, phonics, and fluency are acquired—when the major reading task is "mastering the medium." At Stage 3, when the main task shifts to "mastering the message," growth slows down. Since eye movements have been viewed by researchers as a "window" on the reading process, they give indirect evidence of the changes that take place in our proposed reading stages (Buswell, 1922; Gellat, 1978).

• **Eye-Voice Span**   The eye-voice span (EVS), the distance that the eye is ahead of the voice during oral reading, has also been used by psychologists to study the reading process, its development, and factors that are related to it. Early in the history of reading research, it was found that the eye-voice span for mature readers was longer than that for less mature readers. The research findings from EVS have also been quite consistent. Similar to eye movements, the EVS undergoes fastest development in the early years of schooling with a peak at Grade 4, and a slowing rate from Grade 5 on (Levin, 1980).

These studies were concerned primarily with what used to be called the "mechanics" of reading. They now are called the visual-auditory perceptual aspects of reading, or decoding. They also fall into what I call the "medium" aspect of reading, and all seem to have their greatest growth during the first three or four years of reading development (Stages 1 and 2). The growth continues, but at a slower pace in the later elementary, high school, and college years (Stages 3, 4, and 5).

These laboratory findings tend to be confirmed by correlational studies attempting to study the association of various background factors to reading achievement at different stages of development (Chall, 1967; Hammil and Larsen, 1974). The correlational studies have found that visual and auditory perceptual factors are more highly correlated with general reading achievement than are language and cognitive factors during the first years of reading development. Beginning with Grade 4, language and cognitive development are more highly related to reading than are the visual-auditory perceptual factors. Similar findings have been reported for individuals with learning disability (See Appendix A, p. 204).

EVIDENCE FROM LINGUISTICS

Research on language development indicates that most children have sufficient knowledge of syntax for reading at Grade 1 (Strickland, 1962). Most also have a sufficiently large listening and speaking vocabulary. A review of the research on vocabulary size (Lorge and Chall, 1963) estimated that most children entering Grade 1 probably know about 4000 words.*

*Estimates of the number of words that first graders and other students know vary considerably. For first grade, estimates have ranged from 2000 to 25,000 words. See Lorge and Chall (1963) for a review of these studies and some of the methodological issues involved in the discrepancies—e.g., different ways of defining knowledge of a word, different forms of testing, and different sizes of dictionaries from which words are sampled. See also Anderson and Freebody (1981).

The task for them is therefore to learn to recognize them and to "sound out the words." By present day standards, it takes about six years, to Grade 6, for most students to learn to *read* about 6000 words. The typical 6th grade basal reader contains about 6000 different words. Comparisons of the ability to comprehend material that is heard with similar material that is read also suggest that it takes about eight years (Grade 8) for the average person's reading comprehension to "catch up" with his listening comprehension. (See Appendix A.)

At least for the primary and part of the upper elementary grades (Stages 1, 2, and 3), the language of most children seems to be sufficient for their reading. With Stage 3 and beyond, a more advanced level of syntax and a greater range and complexity of word knowledge are needed.

Beginning about age 10 or 11, the child's word knowledge seems to go through a qualitative change, not only in the number known, but in the difficulty (frequency) of the words they know (the words become less common and more abstract). Perhaps the greatest change is in the way words are defined. The definitions change from the concrete to the more abstract and general. Younger children more often define words by use and demonstration. Older children give more synonymous explanations. To a child of 8 or younger, an "orange" is "what you eat." To the older child, it's a "fruit" or "a citrus fruit" (Feifel and Lorge, 1950; Werner and Kaplan, 1952). That this great change comes at about Grade 4, or Stage 3 by our scheme, is extremely interesting. That is also the time when schools traditionally began to teach "reading for the new" through systematic teaching of the content subjects, such as history, geography, and natural science. This was the time when the curriculum began to include "knowledge of the world" as one of its objectives.

The linguistic research on phonemic development—the development of an awareness of a language's sound system —also shows a break between the first three grades and the later grades, i.e., between Stage 2 and below, and Stage 3 and above. We see this in the ability to separate sounds in words and to synthesize them. The research in phonemic development, as well as that of the development of vocabulary and the relationship between listening and reading comprehension, parallels that of reading development (Chall, Roswell, and Blumenthal, 1963; Liberman and Shankweiler, 1979).

The materials typically read in the various grades also change—the language increases in difficulty, the ideas become more abstract, and the comprehension expected at each succeeding stage becomes less literal and more inferential. The material requires more thought, although it is possible, by varying the complexity of the questions, to obtain a lower or a higher level of comprehension on the same materials.[2] (See Table 2-3, p. 39.)

EVIDENCE FROM THE NEUROSCIENCES

The research findings from the neurosciences on students with reading and learning disabilities are similar in many respects to those found for the general population of students. The research on those with learning disability also indicates changes with age, and particularly the critical nature of age 9 (Grade 4, Stage 3). Satz and his associates (Satz, Friel, and Rudegair, 1976) found that younger children with severe reading disability, ages 6–8, had special difficulties in the perceptual areas while older children had greater difficulties in the language and cognitive areas.

Similar findings were reported by Birch and Belmont (1964) from studies of auditory-visual integration among normal and retarded readers aged 5–11 years. The correlation of perceptual factors with reading for both normal and retarded readers was greatest at Grade 1. After Grade 2, no significant relationship of perceptual factors with reading was noted. Correlations of IQ with reading increased with age.

Other research suggests that language difficulties are the central problem for most children with learning disabilities, the young as well as the older (see Roit, 1977; Vogel, 1974; and especially Vellutino, 1979, in Appendix A, who proposes that perceptual difficulties can be interpreted in terms of language difficulties).

[2]Perry, in a Bureau of Study Council Annual Report, reported that Harvard College final examinations in the 1970s contained more higher level questions than those in the 1800s.

A somewhat different concept comes from the work of Mattis, French, and Rapin (1975), who found three patterns of reading disability among 53 dyslexics examined: a language disorder group, an articulatory and graphic dyscoordination group, and a visuo-perceptual disorders group.

EVIDENCE FROM EDUCATIONAL RESEARCH
AND PRACTICE

• **Organizational Breaks in Schools**   Many practices in the schools seem to parallel the reading stages proposed here. One of the clearest parallels is that of school organization. For about two centuries, the schools have distinguished between the primary school (first three years of school), the intermediate school (the next three years, Grades 4–6), the upper elementary (Grades 7–8), and high school (Grades 9–12). A later break was the junior high school (Grades 7, 8, and 9) from a three-year secondary school (Grades 10–12). The most recent break is the middle school (Grades 5–8). Beyond the elementary school, the oldest break has been at the secondary level (Grades 9–12). The break at college remains the same, although increasingly it means a two-year as well as a four-year college.

Even with the recent changes in organization, these breaks have tended to remain quite stable. Where the range has changed, the differences do not exceed one year or, at the most, two. The organizational breaks have pretty much stayed within the basic structure of the primary grades, the intermediate and upper elementary grades, high school, and college.

The reading stages proposed here tend to parallel these traditional and contemporary school breaks. The primary grades—once called the language school—parallel Reading Stages 1 and 2. The intermediate and upper elementary grades (the middle grades and beginning of junior high) parallel Stage 3, reading to learn a variety of subjects and values. Academic work in traditional and contemporary high schools requires the broader reading that is characteristic of our proposed Stage 4.

College-level work, when up to traditional academic standards, requires and gives practice in Stage 5 reading.

The curriculum objectives of some modern alternative "open" elementary schools seem to imply that reading and writing are used to acquire "new" learnings right from the start of Grade 1. Observations in these schools, however, reveal that the "new" learnings in the primary grades, if they are stressed, are generally acquired through listening and through the audio-visual media. Even in these schools, printed materials are used as we describe here in Stages 1 and 2, unless, of course, the students can already do Stage 3 reading. Reading to learn new information and ideas usually takes place about the same time as in traditional schools—at about Grade 4. Thus, although some contemporary schools have modified their curriculum goals, the reading demands on the students seem to remain about the same unless they are advanced in their reading development.

A new model of school organization for the 1980s has recently been proposed by Ernest L. Boyer, former U.S. Commissioner of Education.[3] Boyer's sequence calls first for a Basic School, "a four- or five-year block of time when each child becomes well grounded in fundamental skills . . . each student must learn to read, write and speak with clarity and to compute accurately. . . . In the Basic School, the mastery of language must come first."

The Middle School (to replace junior high) is to be a five-year sequence that will focus on a central core curriculum in order to introduce all students to "people, ideas, literature, and events that have fundamentally shaped the course of history." The Middle School would continue a rigorous exposure to the basics of language and mathematics. Students would also study their contemporary world, examining the organizational, economic, and social structures, and begin to think about the future.

Transition School (two to three years) is to be a "capstone to formal schooling," a time for specialization and develop-

[3]In *The New York Times Educational Supplement* (January 7, 1979), Ernest L. Boyer, "Commissioner's Model for the 1980's," United States Commissioner of Education.

ment of unique talents in and beyond the classroom, with schools specializing in business, health, social service, and the like.

Boyer's new school organization plan and its goals overlap appreciably with our proposed reading stages. His four- or five-year Basic School covers reading Stages 1 and 2, putting major stress on acquiring the basic skill of reading. Stage 3 seems to cover the five years of his Middle School. The core of knowledge about "people, ideas, and literature" acquired by students during this period requires a good command of Stage 3 reading—and, in turn, enhances the development of Stage 3 reading through the reading tasks required.

Boyer's Transition School (the last two to three years of high school) would be a time of specialization, when the student tries on different ways of looking at the world and of working in it. This curriculum goal requires sophisticated reading skill on at least a Stage 4 level. The specialization and in-depth treatment of issues and knowledge required give students practice in Stage 4 reading, good preparation also for the Stage 5 reading required in college.

Boyer's emphasis on growth in language throughout the school sequences is significant. "Language and general education would be stressed throughout all of formal education. But if the basic skills were well mastered in the early grade years and the core curriculum were well taught, students in the upper grades could begin to specialize and spend time productively off campus."

• **The 4th Grade "Slump"** A common point of weakness in reading development reported in the research and also in practice comes at about Grade 4. Many changes have been observed at this grade—in the children, in the curriculum, and in instructional materials. The 4th grade is critical in the development of eye movements, eye-voice span, word recognition, phonics, and so on. For each of these, the rate of growth is steepest during Stages 1 and 2, with a kind of plateau reached during Grade 4, when development continues but at a slower pace. The acquisition of 4th grade reading is thus a major milestone in a child's education, and an inability to reach 4th grade reading when the student begins to study subject matter (e.g., science, social studies) can cause serious problems for the student, the student's teacher, and the parents.

Difficulties with 4th grade reading are found particularly among children who lagged behind in Stages 1 and 2.[4] The difficulties may not have been evident in the early grades, for the uses of reading are not as demanding. Difficulties show up when the reading requirements shift and reading is used increasingly as a tool for new learning. Until quite recently, in fact, some school systems considered children for remedial reading only at the 4th grade and higher.

The Grade 4 slump can be viewed as a failure to make a smooth transition from Stage 2 to Stage 3, when the linguistic, cognitive, and conceptual aspects of the text are more demanding. Teachers of children who experience the 4th grade slump report that some are able to read the stories in their "readers," but not their content textbooks which contain a more extensive vocabulary and concept load and require more background knowledge.

The 4th grade slump may also come from poor development of skills largely acquired in Stages 1 and 2, decoding and fluency. But Stages 1 and 2, while necessary for Stage 3, are not sufficient for its development. In order to move easily to reading the more difficult content materials of Stage 3, students need to know more words and concepts, they need more information and background knowledge, and they need to reason on a more mature level. Thus, growth in language, knowledge, and in cognition are needed along with growth in decoding and fluency.

We may also view Grade 4, the beginning of Stage 3, as the beginning of the literary tradition, as compared to the oral tradition that is more characteristic of Stages 1 and 2.[5] In schools of a generation or two ago, the transition into Stage 3 reading

[4]This is common among children with severe reading disabilities and with children whose reading skills have still not caught up, particularly in word recognition and fluency. It also appears among children who find it difficult to concentrate because of lack of interest or because of emotional problems.

[5]In an oral tradition, reading is on a lower level of proficiency and serves primarily to confirm the knowledge which has been obtained "orally" or by means other than reading. In a literary tradition, higher levels of literacy are reached which take the reader beyond the knowledge acquired orally.

was eased by systematic instruction and practice in the reading of subject-matter textbooks. It was usually in Grade 4 that textbooks in history, geography, and the natural sciences were formally introduced.[6] These were often read as a class, students taking turns reading portions orally and answering questions put to them by the teacher or writing answers after silent reading assignments. The textbooks also served as homework that required reading parts of the text and writing essay responses. Discussions based on these readings, as well as the drawing of maps and charts, and the writing of précis made these books more than just vehicles for learning history, geography, and the like. They also served as a means for practicing reading and writing, for "learning the new." Even earlier in American schools, reading textbooks, beginning with about Book 4 or 5, contained selections from major areas of knowledge.

This practice has changed. There is less systematic teaching and learning of content subjects in the middle grades, and less systematic practice of reading and writing in these areas. Indeed, a recent book on reading in the intermediate grades states that the main purpose of teaching content in the middle grades is not to learn the content, but to develop the pupils' interest in different subjects.[7]

The critical nature of 4th grade reading can be seen also in the significant change in the content of standardized reading tests. Here, too, there is a difference in the reading passages for the primary grades as compared to Grade 4 and above. In the primary grades (Stages 1 and 2), the selections are about familiar, everyday happenings, and mostly narrative. Beginning with Grade 4 (Stage 3), the test selections become informational, and the ideas and language of the passages become less familiar, more abstract, and more literary (Auerbach, 1971; Popp and Lieberman, 1977).

The difference between Stage 2 and 3 appears to be similar to the changes in word meanings found by Werner and Kaplan (1952) and Feifel and Lorge (1950) among 10–11-year olds—the

---

[6]Some schools have subject matter textbooks beginning with Grade 1, but these usually serve as supplementary "readers," not for learning new content.

[7]There may be a reversal of this view soon since the increase in research and in practice on reading in the content areas.

difference lying in the greater abstraction beginning with Stage 3. If the transition is made in the student's language and if it is transferred to reading, the beginning of a great leap occurs in the 4th–5th grade. Those who have not mastered early reading, and who for some reason do not make the linguistic and cognitive transitions, usually have difficulties also at Grade 4 (Stage 3).

A reading difficulty at Grade 4 and above is very real to those who experience it, for it means not only a struggle with reading lessons but even more with "the school subjects" since the textbooks are usually at or near grade level. Grade 4 has, traditionally and in modern schools, meant the beginning of systematic study of the curriculum, particularly social studies and science. In essence, the ability to read at a 4th or 5th grade level means the taking of beginning steps into the "world of knowledge" in printed form—knowledge that can be acquired only if one knows how to read the texts that contain it. Once readers learn to do Stage 3 reading, it is possible for those with high ability, motivation, and much practice to advance to Stages 4 and 5, perhaps, with little additional formal reading instruction. Indeed, many of our founding fathers were probably among such "self-educated" readers. In an early study of adult readers, W. S. Gray found that adults who left school after Grade 5 and continued to use their reading tended to retain and increase their reading ability. Those who stopped formal schooling before they reached Grade 4 (Stage 3) usually lost the skill they had attained (Gray, 1956).

• The 4th Grade Milestone and Readability Measurement   A 4th grade level also has great meaning in readability measurement. Readability is concerned with the comprehension difficulty of connected texts and has developed numerous measuring instruments—readability formulas—that are used on samples of books and other texts to predict the level of reading needed to read and understand it.

Materials of a readability level of 4th grade and higher are very different from materials with readability levels at the 3rd grade and below. Materials at grade levels 1 to 3 are quite simple in vocabulary and syntax and are usually about elementary,

FOURTH READER.

I.—THE WHISTLE.

1. When I was a child, seven years old, my friends, on a holiday, filled my pockets with coppers. I went directly to a shop where they sold toys for children; and, being charmed with the sound of a whistle that I met by the way in the hands of another boy, I voluntarily offered him all my money for one.

2. I then came home, and went whistling all over the house, much pleased with my whistle, but disturbing all the family. My brothers, and sisters, and cousins, understanding the bargain I had made, told me I had given four times as much for it as it was worth.

3. This put me in mind what good things I might have bought with the rest of the money; and they laughed at me so much for my folly that I cried with vexation.

4. This, however, was afterward of use to me, the impression continuing on my mind; so that often, when I was tempted to buy some unnecessary thing, I said to myself, "Don't give too much for the whistle"; and so I saved my money.

The next few pages are reproduced from The Fourth Reader of Appleton's School Readers *(1883). These also illustrate the more serious nature of the content as compared with modern readers. Note also the depth of questions asked on the text.*

71

5. As I grew up, came into the world, and observed the actions of men, I thought I met with many, very many, who gave too much for the whistle.

6. When I saw any one too ambitious of the favor of the great, wasting his time in attendance on public dinners, sacrificing his repose, his liberty, his virtue, and perhaps his friends, to attain it, I have said to myself, "This man gives too much for his whistle."

7. When I saw another fond of popularity, constantly employing himself in politics, neglecting his own affairs, and ruining them by that neglect, "He pays, indeed," said I, "too much for this whistle."

8. If I knew a miser, who gave up every kind of comfortable living, all the pleasure of doing good to others, all the esteem of his fellow-citizens, and the joys of benevolent friendship, for the sake of accumulating wealth, "Poor man," said I, "you do indeed pay too much for your whistle."

9. When I met a man of pleasure, sacrificing the improvement of his mind, or of his fortune, to mere bodily comfort, "Mistaken man," said I, "you are providing pain for yourself, instead of pleasure: you give too much for your whistle."

10. If I saw one fond of fine clothes, fine furniture, fine horses, all above his fortune, for which he contracted debts, and ended his career in prison, "Alas!" said I, "he has paid dear, very dear, for his whistle."

11. In short, I believed that a great part of the miseries of mankind were brought upon them by the false estimates they had made of the value of things, and by their giving too much for their whistles.

Adapted from Benjamin Franklin.

For Preparation.—I. Allusions, historical, geographical, and literary.
II. Spelling and pronunciation ; words to be copied, and marked with diacritical marks, hyphens, and accents. III. Language-lesson. IV. Words
and phrases to be explained in the pupil's own words, giving the meaning
as used in the lesson (*not* the general definition). V. Style and thought.
Numbers I. and V. to suggest topics of conversation on the reading-lesson;
Numbers II., III., and IV. to be prepared by the pupil. There may be
some points in Numbers I. and V. that are too difficult for many of the
pupils for whom this Reader is intended. The teacher will use his discre-
tion in selecting topics from these numbers for explanation to his class.

I. Benjamin Franklin, an eminent American philosopher and states-
man, born at Boston, Mass., January 17, 1706. His father was a soap and
candle maker. Benjamin learned the printer's trade, and removed to Philadelphia. He discovered the identity of lightning and electricity. His
efforts secured the alliance of the French with America in the Revolution.
He also assisted in making important treaties, and in forming the Consti-
tution of the United States. (See Lesson LXV.)

II. Write out and mark the pronunciation of frĭends, filled,
whĭs'-tle, lăughed, un-nĕç'-es-sa-ry, neg-lĕct'-ing. (See Webster's
diacritical marks on page 98, and in the introduction to the spelling lessons of the Appendix.)

III. "Children"—what change is necessary to make this word refer to
only one? What meaning does *ing* give to the word *whistling?* Find
other words in which it makes the word refer to continued action. Dr.
Franklin wrote "says I" (7, 8, 9, 10) for "said I"—why incorrect?

IV. "Coppers"—what coin does this mean? What does "charmed"
mean (1)? "Voluntarily"? (willingly, of his own accord.) "Disturbing"
means what? Who is a *cousin?* What is a *bargain?* What is *folly?*
—*vexation?* "Impression continuing on my mind"? (i. e., I remembered
it.) "Ambitious of the favor of the great"? "Fond of popularity"? (in
this case, desiring the people's votes.) Who is a *miser?* What is the
meaning of *esteem?—benevolent?—*"accumulating wealth"?—comfortable?
—"contracted debts"? (ran in debt.) "Ended his career" means what?
"False estimates they had made of the value of things"? (i. e., made mistakes about the worth of things.)

V. Do you think of any other examples to add to these of Dr. Franklin,
in which people have "given too much for the whistle"? Write out such
a case in your own words. What is meant by "the great"? How can
they bestow "favor"?

familiar ideas and things (Chall, Bissex, Conard, and Harris-Sharples, in press). Materials at 4th grade readability begin to resemble adult, natural writing. The higher vocabulary range and the more complex syntax enable the construction of a text that contains new ideas. Levels below 4th grade use too restricted a vocabulary and syntax to permit writing that informs beyond the existing knowledge and language of the reader.

A list of 3000 words compiled by Edgar Dale is the measure of vocabulary difficulty in the Dale-Chall readability formula (1948b). This list is highly predictive of the readability level (comprehension difficulty) of texts ranging in difficulty from the 4th grade to the college graduate level. The 3000-word list contains the essential, fundamental, most frequent words (in meaning and recognition) in the language—words that can be read and understood by 80 percent of children in fourth grade. Knowledge of these familiar words usually means that the student can read at about a 4th grade level (beginning Stage 3). To advance beyond this level, readers would need to know words beyond the 3000—words less familiar, more abstract, specialized, more technical or literary.

Indeed, it is only at about a 4th grade readability level and higher that it is possible to write "information-type" reading materials and narrative of a substantial nature. The easiest information books, often called "the first book" of space, or music, or stamps, are usually written on a 4th or 5th grade readability level. The widely used children's encyclopedias usually average a 5th–6th grade readability level.

Knowledge of the 3000 commonest words in a foreign language has also been considered a breakthrough in mastering the language. Various studies have found that the commonest 3000 words in a language usually comprise about 90 percent of the words in its popular adult literature. Thus, the commonest 3000 have been used to construct basic teaching materials (Bongers, 1947). When these are mastered, most students can begin to cope with more difficult content materials, beginning at a Stage 3 level.

The "magic 3000" is also relevant for learning to read Chinese. It appears that literacy is judged in present-day China as knowing the 3000 commonest characters. Adult Chinese newspapers, it is reported, contain about 3500 characters (Taylor, 1981).

A 4th grade reading level (beginning Stage 3) is a kind of watershed for children and adults with reading and related learning disabilities. A recent autopsy of the brain of a young man with a history of severe dyslexia is significant in this connection. Upon examination, his brain was found to be different in regions considered important for language and reading development (Galaburda and Kemper, 1979). According to his past clinical records, after many years of special remedial instruction in reading, he had been able to reach only a 4th grade reading level (beginning Stage 3). Although it is risky to draw conclusions as to why he could not seem to get much beyond Reading Stages 1 and 2, it is appropriate, I believe, to propose a hypothesis that the transition from Stage 2 to Stage 3 and higher is qualitatively different from the transitions in the earlier stages. While going from Stage 0, to 1, to 2 may be difficult, moving to Stage 3 is probably more difficult still. The phenomenon was observed by Orton (1937/1964) who reported excellent success (at Stages 1 and 2) with the special remedial procedures developed for children with specific reading disabilities. But, he noted, many had difficulty making transitions to the use of reading for study and recreation, and he urged more and earlier practice in the reading of books designed to bring this about.

The most recent evidence for difficulty in making the transition to Stage 3 comes from the test results of the National Assessment of Educational Progress (NAEP, 1981). The national tests given during 1970, 1975, and 1980 at ages 9, 13, and 17 permit some hypotheses with regard to reading development. However, it must be noted that the population was cross-sectional—the children studied over time were different children although of the same ages. Essentially, what interests us most is that in the two re-test periods, 1975 and 1980, the 9-year-olds (age 9, Grade 4) showed significant gains. The other two age groups, the 12-year-olds (Grade 8, end of Stage 3) and the 17-year-olds (Grade 12, end of Stage 4), made few significant gains. Some evidence, in fact, showed a decline in inferential comprehension. This may be another kind of evidence of changes in reading development between the primary levels and the intermediate and higher levels, i.e., from mastering the print medium to mastering the meanings of ever more complex messages.[8]

 • **Functional Literacy**   A 4th–5th grade reading level (or a 4th or 5th grade educational attainment) has, for about 50 years, been the criterion of functional literacy. A reading level below Grades 4–5 was used during World War II by the army to classify those who were in need of basic literacy training. Such training programs were designed to bring the armed forces to a 4th–5th grade level of reading—a level that would permit the use of reading for learning. This basic cutoff at Grades 4–5 remains essentially the same today.

Since World War II, however, the minimal goal of many literacy programs has increased to 8th grade and higher. Many states offer assistance to achieve high-school equivalency (Stage 4). Some programs in the U.S. Navy are designed to bring men to a reading level of about 11th–12th grade (Stage 4), a level needed to read very difficult technical manuals.

Thus, while the need to read more difficult, technical manuals (Sticht, 1975) and other instructional materials is becoming increasingly common, it is significant that even today, the lowest level of literacy that is required for entry into the information system of the army is a 4th–5th grade reading level (beginning Stage 3).

[8]There may be still another essential factor that explains the NAEP score breaks. One can hypothesize that the current low scores for the 12- and 17-year-olds stem from the fact that they had insufficient time to benefit from the improvements in the methods, materials, and emphasis that began in the late 1960s and continued through the middle 1970s.

CHAPTER 5

APPLICATIONS OF READING STAGES TO TEACHING AND TESTING

THIS CHAPTER TAKES UP teaching and testing. The first part concentrates on teaching—both the formal and the informal teaching by schools, the home, and the community. Second, we focus on evaluation, on the testing of individuals, and on evaluating programs for teaching reading. Testing is treated separately from teaching only for purposes of clarity. In reality, testing and teaching are highly interrelated and are best viewed as parts of instruction.

I use the reading-stages scheme presented in the previous chapters as a model for understanding what happens to people as they learn to read at higher and higher reading levels. I am concerned not so much with the great variety of reading skills that may need to be taught as I am with the broad changes as progress is made through the reading stages. And I am equally concerned with what the school, the parents, and the community contribute to bringing it about. In learning what the nature of reading is at the different stages of development, teachers, principals, parents, librarians, and policy makers may be helped to promote effective instruction and stimulation.

I have included charts and tables to convey the changes that occur in readers as they progress through the stages. Illustrations and excerpts from textbooks and other reading materials give further insight into what is read and can be read at the different stages.

This chapter serves, as did Chapter 2, as a vehicle for conveying the overall picture of development in reading—from its fumbling and stumbling beginnings to the "ease" and "grace" of skilled reading. This chapter, therefore, focuses more on practice than on theory.

Growth in power and skill in reading, or in any other complex skill, is so minute from day to day, with ups and downs, movings forward and fallings back, that it is often difficult to experience directly an overall picture of growth and change. In failing to see the growth, we fail also to see the contribution made by the teacher, parents, and others to the child's reading development. We also fail, too often, to note the effects of the student's own efforts.

I hope that the child's teachers—including principals, librarians, school-board members, educational publishers, and parents—will gain here a view of reading development similar to that of a lapsed-time film of an unfolding flower. It is more difficult to do this for reading, for we must capture the sixteen years, more or less, of schooling and living that it takes most people to achieve the high level of reading at Stage 5.

INFLUENCES OF THE PERSON
AND THE ENVIRONMENT

Basically, reading is taught and learned. Without the proper educational stimulation from the school, the home, and the community, most of us would be illiterate. Indeed, nearly half of the people in the world, mainly in the developing countries, are still illiterate because they do not have enough schools and teachers.

Literacy across nations, and within nations, is highly related to economic development. The IEA study of *Reading Comprehension in 15 Countries* (R. L. Thorndike, 1973) found that the more developed the nation, the higher its average reading achievement, with students in the developing nations at all age levels reading significantly below those in the developed, industrialized nations. Within countries, the children of the more affluent families scored significantly higher in reading than the children of the less affluent.

More recent studies find that schools with given characteristics (strong leadership and high expectations, for example) contribute significantly to the reading achievement of their pupils, particularly of those whose parents have not had advanced schooling (Edmonds, 1977; Popp and Lieberman, 1977; Rutter et al., 1979; Venezky, 1978; Weber, 1971).

This does not mean that biological, cognitive, and other individual characteristics are unrelated to reading development. They are significantly related at all levels (Carroll, 1977). But there is growing evidence that much of what was considered genetic about intellectual development, for example, is learned in environments that stimulate it (Fowler, 1971; J. McV. Hunt, 1961).

Even children diagnosed as neurologically impaired, or who have neurological development that is associated with difficulties in learning to read and write, can be taught with special procedures (Chall and Mirsky, 1978; Denckla, 1977; Roswell and Natchez, 1977). Thus, although biological and genetic factors are not to be ignored in understanding the course of reading development, I take the position that the environmental stimulation that fosters reading and language and cognitive development has a strong influence on reading development and has only recently begun to be appreciated.

One biological difference seems quite real—the difference in reading achievement between boys and girls. It has been reported for many years by different researchers and teachers. Most surveys report that on Reading Readiness Tests (Stage 0) and in beginning reading (Stage 1) girls are ahead of boys. How long the girls remain ahead is not clear, but it appears that by Stage 3 many boys seem to catch up; however Project Talent, which tested at 10th grade, found girls significantly ahead in reading (Flanagan, 1976). And children with reading and related language disabilities, those who remain for a long time on

Stages 1 and 2, are predominantly boys.

The reasons for the differences are many, and they can be divided into the social-cultural and the biological. Gates (1961) held that the difference was mainly cultural in that girls had the advantage because there were more women teachers than men and also that the stories in the readers had a feminine orientation. The biological explanation used most often is that girls, as a group, develop faster than boys of the same age, particularly in the left cerebral hemisphere that is responsible for language.

Little doubt exists that the biological and the cultural interact. Several studies have found that under certain kinds of instruction, boys as a group achieve as well as the girls (Atkinson, 1974). Some cross-cultural comparisons of reading have found that the male/female differences either do not exist in some countries or that boys are superior to girls in reading (Dwyer, 1973; Preston, 1962).

Research in the 1970s and early 1980s continued to report beneficial effects of optimal school environments for the development of reading, particularly among children with a high risk of failure, whether of a biological or a cultural nature. The research evidence is accumulating that school administrators (Edmonds, 1977; Venezky, 1978; Weber, 1971), teachers (Chall and Feldman, 1966), textbooks (Chall, Conard, and Harris, 1977), and the additional help given pupils when they need it (Kraus, 1973; Smith, 1972) are crucial in children's reading development.

How well a child or an adult reads at any point depends upon the interaction between personal and environmental conditions. The relationship is dynamic in that changes in personal characteristics require adjustments in the reading environment for optimal stimulation and further growth. A limitation in the personal development of the learner does not mean that learning cannot take place. Instead, the research indicates the need for proper adjustments in the environment for continued reading development.

The central importance of education in reading achievement is further indicated by the fact that remedial reading works. A recent analysis of studies comparing children who receive remedial reading with comparable children in need of help who did not receive it found that the gains from remedial reading—short and long-term gains—were significant and substantial (L. Smith, 1972). The long-term gains, even after five or ten years, were also significant. When those receiving remedial reading were compared to control groups (equal in mental ability, neurophysiological factors, extent of reading retardation, social class, and so on), those pupils who received remedial instruction read significantly better than those who did not.

Environmental factors in the home have also been found to be significantly related to reading achievement. During the late 1960s, the factor found to be most related to achievement was socioeconomic status of parents (Coleman, 1966; Jencks, 1972). Children from homes of lower social status scored lower on verbal and reading tests than those of upper middle status. This difference continues to be found in the National Assessment of Educational Progress (NAEP, 1981).

A more recent analysis of these SES differences indicates that the status is of less importance than what the parents do with and to their children with regard to their education and reading (Dave, 1961; Bloom, 1981). Called the "thrust toward education," it has included things such as taking the children to the library, or the museum, or the zoo. It is these educational experiences rather than the income of the parents that related highest to educational achievement of children.

While the large-scale studies of the effects of the environment were carried out nationally and internationally, other studies of biological-neurological factors in learning to read were undertaken. These studies point to the fact that severe difficulties in learning to read are found in large numbers of children. Some estimate the percentage at 2%, others at 7%, and still others at 10–15% of the population (Chall, 1977). Federal law 94-142 has given recognition to the fact that while perhaps most reading problems stem from factors in the environment, the cause of others is medical. Yet for these children, too, environmental stimulation from the home, school, and community must be optimal. For children who are diagnosed to have a medically based learning disability, the major remedial treatment is usually individually designed remedial instruction, an environmental modification.

A POINT OF VIEW REGARDING
THE READING STAGES

1. Individual people progress through the reading stages at different rates. Even with an equal number of years of formal schooling, different people reach different stages of development. The rate of advancement depends upon an interaction between individual (biological, motivational, cognitive, and so on) and environmental (home, school, community) factors.

2. The age and grade specifications for the different stages vary also from culture to culture and group to group. The grades and ages used here are based on the school standards and achievements of average children in the United States during the 1970s and early 1980s. As individuals change (e.g., new medical treatments for neurologically different children) and as school conditions change (more appropriate methods and materials, availability of better reading materials, more instruction), so age and grade expectations will change.

3. The characteristics and descriptions given for the different stages serve primarily as models, not as prescriptions and not as standards. They are presented to convey how reading develops and changes. I hope that this understanding will lead to improved environmental stimulation—in school, at home, and in the wider community—that matches better the development of the person.

4. There are many ways to bring about the same results in reading. Our best lessons are from history. The early primers in England and in the United States in the 1600s and 1700s consisted mainly of selections from the Bible. Students had spent time earlier learning their letters.

In the 1800s many reading primers started the child on learning letters, then words. During the years between 1910 and 1960, most children learned to read little simple stories from the start, with little and later teaching of letters and sounds.

In the 1960s some children were taught the letters by their parents and "invented" their own spelling systems. In the late 1960s millions of young children were learning the letters and sounds from TV on *Sesame Street* and *The Electric Company*. From the late 1960s through the 1970s and early 1980s the beginning readers and workbooks also contained an earlier emphasis on letters and sounds.

These procedures for teaching the beginning reader seem quite different, yet all are designed to accomplish the major beginning reading task—decoding. They all were designed to teach how to relate the spoken to the printed word and some "rules" about relating letters to sounds.

Today acquisition of Stage 1 and Stage 2 is also facilitated by the beginner books (Dr. Seuss's *Cat in the Hat* and others; Random House) that were first published about twenty-five years ago. These little books make possible early application and use of decoding skills in Stage 1 and Stage 2. This was achieved in earlier years through reading and rereading of selections in the primers and reading textbooks and, in the child's own writing, copying and spelling.

5. A person's progress through the stages is not a straight upward path. At any reading stage, the level of the individual's performance also depends on the relative novelty and difficulty of the task and the extent of instruction received. If the task is new, and no additional instruction is received, the reader may drop temporarily to a lower level of functioning already abandoned. For example, a child or an adult beginner who has learned to apply decoding skills on a fairly familiar text (Stage 2) will start "guessing" when material is too difficult (requires Stage 3 reading), i.e., it contains too many words that need to be decoded, too many that are not recognized immediately, and too many whose meaning is not known. With time and with instruction, reading will be smooth again.

6. The reading stages should not be seen as static and fixed. A person may be in transition toward a higher stage from an earlier one at any point. The transition may not be complete for all aspects. Indeed, at the higher levels, when reading becomes more varied in terms of content, one may be at Stage 4 in one area of knowledge and at Stage 3 in another.

A person may function at differing levels at any one time. One measure of maturity is the reader's ability to function on a sufficiently high level when presented with a reading task that requires it.

7. The stages do not mean that all children of a given grade or age are to be at the same reading level, nor do they mean that they are to be instructed at the same level.

The stages are proposed as a means for teaching each person at his or her level of development. The stages assume that most people progress through the same developmental stages and therefore can be helped by those who understand the course of that development.

8. To reach the most mature stages of reading is of value to both the individual and to society. No evidence suggests that too many highly literate and highly educated people are a burden to society.

STAGES OF READING DEVELOPMENT: AN OUTLINE FOR PRACTICE

Table 5-1 presents a general outline of the reading stages for teachers, parents, educational publishers, librarians, and others who make decisions about children's reading. I hope that this outline enlarges an understanding of the stages first presented in Chapter 2. It is designed to be of particular interest to those who make the practical decisions that control the ways children are taught to read. Let me call attention first to column 5 which presents the relationship between listening and reading. I believe that considerable insight can be gained by all who teach if students' levels of reading development are understood in relation to their levels of listening comprehension. Column 5 reveals the general slow development of reading in comparison to listening. Although the 1st grader's achievement in reading is considerable, it pales in the light of the fact that 1st graders can understand and use about 6000 different words. If he or she finishes the first-grade reader successfully, that child will be able to read only about 300 to 500 words—less than 1 out of the 10 words he or she can understand when heard.

Table 5-1

STAGES OF READING DEVELOPMENT: AN OUTLINE OF THE
MAJOR QUALITATIVE CHARACTERISTICS AND HOW THEY ARE ACQUIRED

1 STAGE DESIGNATION	2 GRADE RANGE (AGE)	3 MAJOR QUALITATIVE CHARACTERISTICS AND MASTERIES BY END OF STAGE	4 HOW ACQUIRED	5 RELATIONSHIP OF READING TO LISTENING
Stage 0: Prereading, "pseudo-reading"	Preschool, Ages 6 months–6 years	Child "pretends" to read, retells story when looking at pages of book previously read to him/her; names letters of alphabet; recognizes some signs; prints own name; plays with books, pencils, and paper.	Being read to by an adult (or older child) who responds to and warmly appreciates the child's interest in books and reading; being provided with books, paper, pencils, blocks, and letters.	Most can understand the children's picture books and stories read to them. They understand thousands of words they hear by age 6 but can read few if any of them.
Stage 1: Initial reading and decoding	Grade 1 & beginning Grade 2 (ages 6 & 7)	Child learns relation between letters and sounds and between printed and spoken words; child is able to read simple text containing high frequency words and phonically regular words; uses skill and insight to "sound out" new one-syllable words.	Direct instruction in letter-sound relations (phonics) and practice in their use. Reading of simple stories using words with phonic elements taught and words of high frequency. Being read to on a level above what child can read independently to develop more advanced language patterns, knowledge of new words, and ideas.	The level of difficulty of language read by the child is much below the language understood when heard. At the end of Stage 1, most children can understand up to 4000 or more words when heard but can read only about 600.

Table 5-1 (cont.)

STAGES OF READING DEVELOPMENT: AN OUTLINE OF THE
MAJOR QUALITATIVE CHARACTERISTICS AND HOW THEY ARE ACQUIRED

1 STAGE DESIGNATION	2 GRADE RANGE (AGE)	3 MAJOR QUALITATIVE CHARACTERISTICS AND MASTERIES BY END OF STAGE	4 HOW ACQUIRED	5 RELATIONSHIP OF READING TO LISTENING
Stage 2: Confirmation and fluency	Grades 2 & 3 (ages 7 & 8)	Child reads simple, familiar stories and selections with increasing fluency. This is done by consolidating the basic decoding elements, sight vocabulary, and meaning context in the reading of familiar stories and selections.	Direct instruction in advanced decoding skills; wide reading (with instruction and independently) of familiar, interesting materials which help promote fluent reading. Being read to at levels above their own independent reading level to develop language, vocabulary, and concepts.	At the end of Stage 2, about 3000 words can be read and understood and about 9000 are known when heard. Listening is still more effective than reading.
Stage 3: Reading for learning the new	Grades 4-8 (ages 9-13)	Reading is used to learn new ideas, to gain new knowledge, to experience new feelings, to learn new attitudes; generally from one viewpoint.	Reading and study of textbooks, reference works, trade books, newspapers, and magazines that contain new ideas and values, unfamiliar vocabulary and syntax; systematic study of words and reacting to the text through discussion, answering questions, writing, etc. Reading of increasingly more complex fiction, biography, nonfiction, and the like.	At beginning of Stage 3, listening comprehension of the same material is still more effective than reading comprehension. By the end of Stage 3, reading and listening are about equal; for those who read very well, reading may be more efficient.
Phase A	Inter-mediate, 4-6			
Phase B	Junior high school, 7-9			

86

Table 5-1 (cont.)

STAGES OF READING DEVELOPMENT: AN OUTLINE OF THE

MAJOR QUALITATIVE CHARACTERISTICS AND HOW THEY ARE ACQUIRED

1 STAGE DESIGNATION	2 GRADE RANGE (AGE)	3 MAJOR QUALITATIVE CHARACTERISTICS AND MASTERIES BY END OF STAGE	4 HOW ACQUIRED	5 RELATIONSHIP OF READING TO LISTENING
Stage 4: Multiple viewpoints	High school, grades 10–12 (ages 15-17)	Reading widely from a broad range of complex materials, both expository and narrative, with a variety of viewpoints.	Wide reading and study of the physical, biological, and social sciences and the humanities; high quality and popular literature; newspapers and magazines; systematic study of words and word parts.	Reading comprehension is better than listening comprehension of material of difficult content and readability. For poorer readers, listening comprehension may be equal to reading comprehension.
Stage 5: Construction and reconstruction	College and beyond (age 18+)	Reading is used for one's own needs and purposes (professional and personal); reading serves to integrate one's knowledge with that of others, to synthesize it and to create new knowledge. It is rapid and efficient.	Wide reading of ever more difficult materials, reading beyond one's immediate needs; writing of papers, tests, essays, and other forms that call for integration of varied knowledge and points of view.	Reading is more efficient than listening.

By the end of Stage 2 (Grade 3), reading "moves up" toward the level of listening, but still, only about one-third of the words known from listening can be read. At the end of Grade 3 (end of Stage 2), when the fundamentals of phonics have been generally mastered and most students can read about 3000 words (sufficient for beginning Stage 3), reading is still "behind" listening. Only some time toward the end of Stage 3 does reading catch up to listening, making it as or more efficient than listening as a means of learning.

Different methods of teaching reading have produced different rates of development, some effecting significantly higher reading gains than others. But the discrepancy between listening and reading remains substantial for most methods, with reading behind listening for most children through the end of Stage 3.

In Stages 4 and 5, reading is generally more efficient than listening. For good readers at these stages, reading is also faster than listening, especially when the materials are very complex. This is not surprising. Scientific papers read at professional meetings, for example, are usually understandable when read but very difficult to understand when heard.

Column 3 gives an overview of the major qualitative characteristics as the individual moves from stage to stage. A useful way to conceptualize these changes is in terms of the relative emphasis of the two major aspects of reading: the medium (alphabetic writing that corresponds to the sounds of words) and the message (the story, the poem, the recipe, the legal document) that is read. In column 3 we note the major change from a focus on the printed medium in Stages 1 and 2 to a greater emphasis on the message in Stages 3, 4, and 5.

Column 4 presents an overview of how reading is acquired. It makes clear the importance of a teacher—an adult or older sibling or classmate—and of reading materials and tasks. It shows that reading development depends on a variety of activities for optimal growth. Although the basic instruction in Stages 1, 2, and 3 is usually provided by the school, full development in these stages depends also on the home and the community.

The progression through the stages is also characterized by a growing facility with recognizing and decoding words; learning the meaning of ever more difficult, uncommon, abstract words, concepts, and ideas; and acquiring more and more knowledge of the world necessary for understanding what is read.

READING MATTER: CONTENT AND DIFFICULTY

The complexity of the reading matter also increases with each stage of development. Table 5-2 contains samples of materials that can be read by students at successive stages. They become more difficult, more technical, more abstract, and more varied. The higher readability levels of materials at successive stages reflect harder and more abstract words, more difficult syntax, and greater conceptual load, for example. (See Table 2-3.)

Reading tasks also change with the successive stages. In Stages 1 and 2, we expect that the reader can render what is written into speech—to say the words and to recall the content. The cognitive task grows more complex with Stage 3 when readers are expected to comprehend, recall, and make inferences. At Stages 4 and 5, readers are expected to be more analytical, critical, and creative in reacting to what they read.

It is important to remember that most people do not always function at the same stage level for all of their reading. Particularly at Stage 3 and beyond, the materials and tasks vary so widely that it is possible for readers who have relatively rich backgrounds and vocabularies in some subjects to have limited backgrounds and vocabularies in others. Further, the same selection may be easier when literal comprehension is called for and harder when a more analytic response is called for.

Table 5-2 Stage 1
MICE ARE NICE

I have something nice to show you. Look! Do you know what they are? They are my pet mice.

Take my word for it. Mice are fun. They are not hard to get. I got mine when Mother drove me to the pet shop.

Moving On, Teacher's edition, 1980. New York: American Book Company. Page 59. (Book 1)

Table 5-2 (cont.) Stage 2
VOYAGER TO OUTER SPACE

"All aboard for outer space!" Dad said. "This afternoon you're going to the Planetarium, and you'll take a pretend rocket trip to the moon!"

"Wow, that sounds great!" John said. He and Jean had been talking about space and planets.

"What's the name of the place we're going to?" Jean asked.

"The Planetarium," said Dad. "A planetarium is a place where you can see planets and millions of stars on a big dome-shaped ceiling."

Building Dreams, Teacher's Edition, page 236. New York: American Book Company. (Book 3-1)

Table 5-2 (cont.) Stage 3A
THE MOON

The moon is the earth's only natural satellite. It is believed to be a solid object, ball-shaped, and much smaller than the earth. It travels around the earth in a path that is almost a circle.

We see the moon because it reflects sunlight to our eyes. However, only the side of the moon toward the sun is brightly lighted. The shadowed side is usually too dark to be seen.

The photographs at the left were taken about three days apart. Notice the changes in the amount of surface that can be seen.

Thurber, Walter A., and Durkee, Mary C. *Exploring Science, Fire.* Boston, MA: Allyn and Bacon, Inc., 1966, p. 158.

Table 5-2 (cont.) Stage 3B

For many years the Great Nebula in Andromeda was a puzzle to astronomers. It differed from the other objects they were able to observe with their telescopes. But when telescopes were built larger and larger, the form of the Nebula became clearer. It turned out to be a great spiral whirlpool of tens of thousands of millions of suns. It was another galaxy like the Milky Way.

Within recent years many other faraway galaxies have been brought into view by the giant telescopes. In the whole universe there are probably millions of them. But our own Milky Way galaxy so far seems to be among the largest.

The vast spaces beyond the earth are rapidly being explored by more and more astronomers, using bigger and better telescopes. The largest telescopes can now pick up light from stars hundreds of millions of light years away, and reveal strange facts about these faraway points of light.

Knox, Warren; Meister, Morris; Stone, George; Wheatley, Dorothy. *The Wonderworld of Science, Revised,* Book 6. New York: Charles Scribner's & Sons, 1957, pp. 188–189.

Table 5-2 (cont.) Stage 4
THE ANCIENT MAYAN EMPIRE

Archaeologists are trying to reconstruct the great Maya Empire. It had already begun to fall apart when the first Spaniards arrived in Central America hundreds of years ago. All that is left of the empire today are remains of buildings, such as the glistening white pyramids that rise out of the tangled jungles, the rich palaces of the kings, the great stone courts where the Mayan people played ball, and the temples of fire and human sacrifice. Some of the walls are covered with reliefs of strange human figures, repulsive serpents, and the beautiful Quetzal bird. Although these have been dug up by archaeologists, they still guard the secrets of that amazing people.

Over 800 sites of Mayan cities have been discovered, but no more than a dozen have been carefully excavated. Even in the four that have received the most attention, only some of the monuments have been cleared of jungle growth. Sequences of picture carvings, something like the hieroglyphics of ancient Egypt, have never been deciphered. A great deal about the Maya Empire is yet to be learned.

The Oxford History of the American People.

WHAT IS LEARNED IN READING, AND WHEN, AND WHERE?

Table 5-3 presents the main contributions to reading typically made by the school, the home, and the community. As with other characterizations of the reading stages, this one is not to be considered prescriptive. It represents what is generally done in most schools, homes, and communities at this time in our history to foster growth in reading at the various stages of reading development.

The table attempts to capsulize the learnings typical of each reading stage. To keep it short enough to be practical and memorable, much had to be omitted. Still, I believe that it gives a useful overview.

Not all schools do as this abstract version of reality indicates. Nor do homes and communities all participate in reading development just in this "way." We have noted, however, that similar stages of development can be reached by different means, and it may not be at all detrimental to do things differently, providing that development is achieved. Even though the real world may vary, I believe it worthwhile to know the typical and expected.

Table 5-3
HOW AND WHERE LEARNING TAKES PLACE

STAGE	WHAT IS LEARNED	SCHOOL	HOME	COMMUNITY
Stage 0	"Pretends" to read; recognizes some letters and few words; prints name; reads a few signs.	Books are read to children; children are encouraged to look through books, to "read" them, to scribble; letters are displayed.	Adults read to child, talk to child; provide books, paper, and pencils; show interest in child's efforts to read and write: arrange trips to zoo, museums, etc.	Public library furnishes books for infants and preschoolers; inexpensive children's books available for purchase in supermarkets and bookstores; educational TV screening and treatment for "high risk" children who may experience difficulty in learning to read.
Stage 1	Decoding recognizes high-frequency words; reads very simple stories. Does simple writing.	Readers and workbooks used in class; library books used for independent reading in classroom and school library; stories read to children, writing and spelling taught; diagnostic and remedial services available.	Adults read to child; adults listen to child read and provide feedback; provide books for child to read and paper and pencils for writing; take trips to points of interest.	Public library has adequate facilities; books for children available in supermarket or bookstore; diagnostic and remedial treatment services available for children with difficulty in learning to read.

Table 5-3 (cont.)
HOW AND WHERE LEARNING TAKES PLACE

STAGE	WHAT IS LEARNED	SCHOOL	HOME	COMMUNITY
Stage 2	More fluent reading (less word-by-word) from simple books; uses decoding and intelligent guessing to figure out new words; pays more attention to meaning of what is read. More writing.	Readers and workbooks used as well as trade books; writing and spelling taught, more silent reading for meaning than for Stage 1; school and classroom libraries used; diagnostic and remedial services provided.	Books provided for child's independent reading; adults or siblings continue to read to the child; visit library regularly with child; limit TV viewing to provide time for reading; arrange educational trips.	Public library facilities and availability of inexpensive books for purchase in supermarkets, shopping malls, department stores, bookshops, and through book clubs; good children's TV on literature, science, etc.; diagnostic and remedial services provided.
Stage 3	Reading to learn the new from readers, subject textbooks, reference works, and trade books; comprehension of materials increasingly more complex in language and thought.	Readers and workbooks at increasing levels of difficulty; reading, study, and written assignments using subject-matter textbooks and encyclopedias; use of dictionary; special work in vocabulary building; school and classroom libraries available, as well as diagnostic and remedial services.	Quiet time for reading, homework, and projects; books from public libraries, educational trips to museums, etc.; a children's encyclopedia or easy access to it as well as a dictionary; newspapers and magazines; limits TV viewing to give child time to read and study.	Public library and inexpensive books for purchase available; educational TV, newspapers, and magazines also available; diagnostic and remedial services for those in need.

Table 5-3 (cont.)

HOW AND WHERE LEARNING TAKES PLACE

STAGE	WHAT IS LEARNED	SCHOOL	HOME	COMMUNITY
Stage 4	Reading greater quantities and varieties of increasingly difficult materials representing a multiplicity of viewpoints.	Textbooks, reference works, and other materials of increasing complexity in the student's curriculum (literature, social studies, science, humanities, and technical subjects) combined with writing; reading instruction focuses on efficiency (rate), vocabulary building, study skills, and critical reading; school library and diagnostic and remedial services provided.	Newspapers, magazines, dictionaries, and reference works; discussions; limits on TV viewing to provide sufficient time for reading.	Public library and inexpensive books for purchase available; diagnostic and remedial services for those who make below-average progress.
Stage 5	Creating and re-creating from reading and other sources of information; reading of great variety of difficult materials, analytically, critically, and creatively.	Reading of everything necessary for courses and individual interests and recreation; diagnostic and remedial services available.	Books, magazines, newspapers; discussion of ideas; writing.	Public library and inexpensive books and other printed media available; diagnostic and remedial services available for students who lag behind in reading and other linguistic skills and for students who need help with efficient reading, i.e., rate and study skills.

CURRENT PRACTICES:
PROGRESS AND CONCERNS

As a whole, the greatest progress during the past decade has been made at the early stages—particularly at Stages 0 and 1. Recent research confirms the importance of the development of language, familiarity with books, writing, and learning of letters during the preschool years for Grade 1 reading (Bissex, 1980; Durkin, 1979; Jansky and de Hirsch, 1972; Popp, 1978). With the Children's Television Workshop's *Sesame Street* and *The Electric Company*, more children are entering 1st grade knowing the letters and able to do "a little reading." Therefore, more children are entering school better prepared for the reading they will be doing at the start. Efforts are also being made to provide library services for infants (at the New York Public Library, for example) and to provide free books for disadvantaged children (Reading is Fundamental).

Research is needed on realistic ways to develop children's reading in homes of limited and modest means, where both adults work, where no money is available for buying books and magazines, and where the adults do not feel comfortable enough about their own reading to read to their children.

The effect of neurological difficulties on an early start also needs investigation. Although most children seem to gain from an early start at home, could an early start in school bring greater frustration, particularly to neurologically "high-risk children"? If regular classroom instruction starts later, fewer are at risk since the extra time means that, in general, more children will be neurologically ready for beginning reading. If so, would it be better to wait for maturation or to provide early assessment and special instruction (de Hirsch and Jansky, 1972; Popp, 1978; Peter Wolff, personal communication)?

Still another question is whether the learnings of Stage 0, most usually gained at home, are essential for progress in Stage 1, or whether they can be learned during Grade 1. Because schools, homes, and communities vary in how much they can provide for children, we need to know optimal procedures for early success.

Methods of teaching beginning reading have changed in the past decade. In the late 1960s reading textbooks began to devote a greater amount of space to the teaching of decoding and introduced decoding earlier. This trend, together with the earlier teaching of the preschooler in the home by parents and through *Sesame Street* and *The Electric Company,* has probably contributed to the increase in reading achievement nationally noted among 9-year-olds by the National Assessment of Educational Progress in 1981 (Chall, 1977, 1979). The fact that most of these gains do not seem to continue after Grade 4 indicates a possible lack in Stage 3 and/or Stage 2 instruction.

Stage 2 school practices seem to depend heavily on the reading textbooks with short selections and exercises in workbooks and worksheets. Unless the school has a good supply of trade books in its library and classrooms, and unless children have books of their own to read, too little reading is done to develop the fluency needed at this stage. The exclusive reading of basal textbooks and workbook exercises may be an effective strategy for Stage 1 but insufficient for developing fluency at Stage 2.

Stage 3 procedures are probably the weakest, and perhaps the most difficult to improve. The greatest gap between reality and need lies, I believe, in the kinds of materials read during Stage 3 in Grades 4–8. More emphasis needs to be placed on reading of expository materials in the content areas—history, science, civics, health, careers, and so on. It would seem that more of the learning-to-read time in Grades 4 to 8 should be spent on reading content materials in various disciplines rather than on short, narrative selections.

There is also need at Stage 3 for systematic vocabulary development and for a greater focus on knowledge acquired from reading.

The long-time concern with the lack of gains in reading beginning with Grade 4 indicates difficulties with reading at about Stage 3 or perhaps even earlier. What aspects of reading are more deficient at Stage 3 is not clear, although several hypotheses seem tenable. Fluency may have been inadequately developed in Stage 2. Decoding may still be weak. Limited meaning vocabularies and insufficient background knowledge in the subject areas under study may also be involved.

Stage 4 requires a great deal of reading of a great variety of materials and viewpoints. One of the greatest problems here is time—particularly since TV viewing takes as much if not more time than the student spends in school, let alone the time spent reading.

Stage 5 is not easily achieved and requires much knowledge, reading skill, and efficiency, and ability in analysis and synthesis. Most of all, it requires teachers and mentors who themselves are doing Stage 5 reading—facing the realities of re-creating and creating knowledge for themselves.

Essentially, then, the most effective way to bring about the full development of a person's ability to read and the uses to which he or she puts that reading is to attend carefully to changing needs at each successive stage. Schools and teachers cannot do this alone. Parents, siblings, and the community must provide the needed incentives, materials, practice, and services. Reading is not learned once and for all but throughout a lifetime in which the individual is challenged to react to ever more difficult materials in ever more sophisticated ways. Early successes help the later ones, but they do not assure them.

EVALUATION

This section discusses evaluation and assessment. The first part focuses on assessing readers—children, young people, and adults—over the course of their reading development from stage to stage. The second part concentrates on ways to assess the "reading" environment—the school program, the home, and the community—for instructing and stimulating readers through the stages.

• Assessing a Person's Reading Development A reading evaluation should cover at least two aspects: the development of essential reading abilities and the development of the uses of reading.

Most widely used published reading tests measure only reading abilities. There are no widely used tests of the uses of reading, particularly in relation to the development of skills and abilities. Thus, while many kinds of tests make judgments about a person's reading skills and abilities, none are available to judge how reading is being used.

Table 5-4

SUGGESTIONS FOR EVALUATING READING AT THE SIX STAGES

	SKILLS AND ABILITIES ACQUIRED	KNOWLEDGE AND USES OF READING
End of Stage 0: Kindergarten	Prints[a] or writes name.	Identifies pictures in books;
	Names letters of the alphabet and prints[a] some.	Knows that books are for reading and usually enjoys being read to.
	Recognizes some common signs and labels.	Pretends to read by retelling story while looking at pages of book previously read to him/her.
	Hears rhymes in words.	
	Begins to understand that certain words begin with certain sounds.	Plays with and knows uses of books, pencils and paper; may engage in early writing (invented spelling).
Published tests available for end of stage 0	Reading Readiness Tests and standardized tests for beginning Grade 1	See Evanechko (1973) and Clay (1972)
End of Stage 1: middle Grade 2	Quick recognition of about 600 high frequency words in child's 1st grade basal reading text.	Understands the alphabetic principle; knows the relation between commonest sounds and letters.
	Can "sound out" one syllable phonically regular words.	Reads independently books of a limited number of high frequency words, e.g., *Green Eggs and Ham, The Cat in the Hat, Little Bear.*
	Reads orally, simple connected text containing high frequency words such as in 1st grade basal reader.	
	Silent reading less proficient than oral reading for most.	
Published tests available for Stage 1	Standardized Reading Tests (for groups) Grades 1 and beginning 2; Standardized Oral Reading Tests (individually administered); Tests of Word Analysis Skills (phonics, individually administered)	Observations based on above.

[a]These are usually done in capital letters at the beginning.

Table 5-4 (cont.)

SUGGESTIONS FOR EVALUATING READING AT THE SIX STAGES

	SKILLS AND ABILITIES ACQUIRED	KNOWLEDGE AND USES OF READING
End of Stage 2: End of Grade 3	Reads orally with fluency up to beginning 4th grade level and can "sound out" and use context to read most words not immediately recognized. Reads materials of same difficulty silently with good comprehension. Knows most of the basic phonic elements and can use them. Uses a "beginner's" dictionary	Much reading in school and at home of books that have more print and fewer pictures than in Stage 1; the preference in stories begins to differ for boys and girls.
Published tests available for Stage 2	Standardized Reading Tests (silent); Standardized Oral Reading Tests; Word Analysis Skills (individually administered)	See Huck Inventory (1966).
End of Stage 3A, first phase: End of Grade 6	Can read orally and silently (with comprehension) a variety of materials and styles up to a beginning 7th grade readability level: literature and popular writing, textbooks in social studies, science, etc. Reads easier parts of adult newspapers and magazines; uses dictionary. Strong meaning vocabulary.	Reads widely children's fiction and nonfiction, children's newspapers, magazines, and easier parts of adult newspapers and magazines. Uses library efficiently; uses children's dictionaries and encyclopedias. Begins to develop efficient study habits.
End of Stage 3B, second phase: End of Grade 8	Can comprehend what is read and learn new information and ideas from a variety of material up to a beginning 9th grade readability level: adult literature; popular fiction; science and social studies texts; adult encyclopedias and other reference works.	Reads adolescent and adult fiction and nonfiction. Uses print materials efficiently—textbooks, adult dictionaries, encyclopedias, trade books, print media—for study, written reports, and own interests. Uses library efficiently.

Table 5-4 (cont.)

SUGGESTIONS FOR EVALUATING READING AT THE SIX STAGES

	SKILLS AND ABILITIES ACQUIRED	KNOWLEDGE AND USES OF READING
End of Stage 3B, second phase: End of Grade 8	Has a good meaning vocabulary, general and technical; uses an adult dictionary. Can read adult newspapers and magazines.	
Published tests available for Stage 3	Standardized reading tests; Standardized oral reading tests; (tests of advanced word analysis skills, mainly for those having difficulty).	See Huck Inventory (1966) for books read.
End of Stage 4: End of Grade 12	Can read analytically and critically from a broad range of fiction and nonfiction of different styles and content: (readability levels up to beginning college) books, textbooks, newspapers (*New York Times*), and magazines (*Time, Newsweek,* etc.). Extensive meaning vocabulary, general and technical.	Reads widely for own needs and for academic requirements; has efficient study strategies; locates materials needed and uses efficiently for written reports and study. Reads newspapers, magazines, novels, etc.
Published tests available for Stage 4	Standardized reading tests for high school seniors and for college freshmen.	Harvard Reading Test (Perry) Observations based on above.
End of Stage 5: College	Can read all kinds of materials—up to highly difficult, specialized, technical, and abstract—for own needs. Can analyze and synthesize knowledge from reading, general and specialized.	Reading is used with great efficiency and speed for learning and for personal needs.
Published Tests available for Stage 5	Several standardized reading tests at the college level.	

[b]Because Stage 3 covers so many years, we list the characteristics for evaluation separately for Grades 4-6 as Stage 3A and for Grades 7-8 as 3B.

We suggest, in Table 5-4, such an evaluation scheme. It includes concern for growth in skills and abilities and in the uses of reading. The scheme covers all six stages. Where published tests are available, we indicate that. Generally, our purpose here is to give the reader an overview of what to look for in judging whether individual readers are or are not "making it," and if not, what absence of skills and abilities may be holding them back. Also, what uses are they making of reading? This assessment does not go into reasons why; that analysis is considered in the next chapter.

Admittedly, these suggestions are not complete. Their main purpose is to help focus on how to judge the main characteristics of the stages presented in previous chapters. For most purposes, we suggest a simple yes/no judgment on both the "skills" and on the "uses." For each stage, I have also listed the published tests whose results might be useful additions to such judgments.

The most widely used published reading tests are the "norm-referenced," standardized tests of achievement. Standardized on large representative populations, they permit comparison of a student's scores with those of others who are the same age or grade.[1] Most students take standardized tests about four or more times during their 12 years in elementary and high schools. Some take such tests every year. A good norm-referenced standardized test that is administered and interpreted properly (together with a test of capacity) can give useful information for evaluating the individual's reading ability and for judging whether the student is progressing appropriately.

Criterion-referenced tests designed to assess the student's mastery of specifically defined reading skills are also helpful in assessing progress. But while norm-referenced tests cover the complete range of K–college, criterion-referenced tests cover limited characteristics of reading.

Some subtests of norm-referenced tests and some criterion

[1]Common score conversions are: grade score equivalents (a 4.5, for example, means that the individual scored as well as the average child in the fifth month of Grade 4); percentile (a 75th percentile means the individual did better than 75% of those in his or her grade); and Stanine (6th Stanine means a high average score falling in the upper 40%).

tests can be used to make estimates of some of the components of the stage development characteristics. The word-analysis or word-study subtests of norm-referenced tests for the early elementary grades, for example, can give evidence of decoding proficiency at Stage 1 or 2.

Probably the most useful tests for specific skills are the individually administered diagnostic tests. They offer useful data for evaluating aspects of the stage-development characteristics—such information as oral reading accuracy and rate (and kinds of errors), decoding skills, and silent reading comprehension. But these tests, like the others, do not assess the changes in the uses of reading and in its conceptualization.

Most tests—whether norm-referenced, criterion, or diagnostic—tell only where the person is. A judgment as to whether the score or its translations are good enough requires other information. To make that judgment, one compares the person's scores to the "normative" grade or age expectations or to scores obtained by others of the same cognitive development. The latter is, in fact, the criterion used in diagnoses of individuals with severe difficulties in learning to read. Because most people are expected to perform as others of their age or grade do, I suggest that the first judgment of progress be made against grade and age norms. Also, because cognitive or language development is a better measure of someone's "potential" reading ability, that criterion is used as well. (See Chapter 9, Reading and Social Policy, for additional discussion of this question.)

Table 5-4 has included only a limited set of items for each stage in order to give focus to the changes in abilities and uses of reading as the person develops. It may be fleshed out for the preschooler by consulting Ilg and Ames (1970; see Appendix B) and Bissex (1980).² Bissex is also of interest for assessment of writing. Rozin and Gleitman (see Appendix B) give a more theoretical view of early reading changes and accomplishments.

The table may also be used to suggest individual instructional needs. Each of the characteristics close to the age of the person assessed may be simply checked off. Together with the

²See also Clark (1976), Clay (1966), and Soderbergh (1971).

grade equivalent scores, and scores on knowledge of skills from diagnostic and criterion tests, an estimate can be made of where the reader stands with regard to stage development. This can be compared to the chronological age or grade placement of the student to judge whether development is average, below average, or above it. The same can be done for the uses of reading.

I also suggested that even if the development of skills is found to be normal for the person's chronological age, it should be compared with his or her cognitive development. Finally, these estimates should be turned into guidelines for further instruction. And if this instruction does not work, especially for those who are developing at a slower pace than expected, referral for further evaluation and possibly other kinds of instruction should be made.

• Evaluating Programs and Reading Environments

No standard measures are available for evaluating schools, homes, and communities with regard to their optimal influence on reading development. The findings from recent research studies, however, point to the significance of certain factors in schools that contribute to the positive reading development of students.

School Personnel   Research during the past 10 years on what makes schools effective points first to the importance of people—the principals, teachers, and reading specialists—in how well students do. Generally, the principal sets the spirit, the tone, and the expectations for achievement which are essential in the overall reading program. As early as 1971, George Weber found that 3rd grade children in four inner-city schools who achieved as well as children in more affluent suburban schools were those whose principals and teachers had a high regard for reading and expected the children to achieve well. The reading programs were strong, including systematic phonics, regular and frequent evaluation by reading specialists, availability of many books which the children were encouraged to read in school and at home. The Weber study has been replicated by other researchers including Edmonds (1977);

Guthrie et al. (1979); Kean et al. (1979); Popp and Lieberman (1977); and Venezky (1978). Conducted in many cities, all of these studies concluded that schools make a significant difference in the reading achievement of children.

It may sound strange that what seems so obvious a truth could become a new research finding. Most laymen assume that schools matter in students' achievement in general, and most definitely in reading. And yet many thought otherwise based on two widely read studies of the 1960s and 1970s —Coleman's *Equality of Educational Opportunity* (1966) and Jenck's *Inequality* (1972). Both found that the strongest factor in achievement was the SES background of the child. The school factors, in their studies, had very little influence. The current trend to measure each school as a unit, in contrast to the earlier studies that measured across great numbers, is one explanation for the difference in results.

Other school personnel are important in the child's reading development, particularly reading specialists and teachers. Many studies have found that when reading specialists are working actively with teachers and children in evaluation and remediation, overall reading achievement is improved (Weber, 1971; Popp and Lieberman, 1978). Long recognized by parents as central in the achievement of their children, teachers have also been found to make a significant difference in the reading development of children (Chall and Feldmann, 1966; Jansky and de Hirsch, 1972).

Monitoring children's test results has been found to be important. It may be done by a principal, a reading specialist, or a test specialist. But it must be done with diligence and sensitivity to avoid having too many children in junior and senior high school unable to read their assignments and, in fact, barely literate.

Many studies have found that the classrooms in which pupils make more progress spend more direct time in learning and practicing reading (Stallings, 1975). Also effective are direct versus indirect teaching methods, that is, more explaining and discussing by the teacher as compared with dependence on the children's self-discovery. Direct teaching is more effective particularly among children who have not been the better learners (Rosenshine, 1979). Related to these findings are the reports in recent studies about the greater effectiveness of structured organization versus open classrooms (Bennet, 1976; Rosenshine, 1976, 1979; Rutter et al., 1979).

Published Reading Programs   Most elementary schools (K–6) use a published reading program, a basal reading series,[3] as the major vehicle for teaching reading. An analysis of beginning reading basal programs widely used in the 1970s was done by Popp (1975) based on an earlier analysis by Chall (1967). Popp used a comprehensive scheme for analyzing readers, including aspects of content and motivation. With regard to method, she found an earlier and heavier emphasis on phonics in the beginning basal readers of the 1970s when compared to those analyzed by Chall (1967) which were published in the late 1950s and early 1960s. Basal readers have been evaluated more recently by EPIE (1970) to assist school systems in selecting published reading programs.

Some recent changes have involved an increase in ethnic representation, the earlier introduction of comprehension skills, and earlier and heavier phonics programs in basal readers. Although these changes generally have been in the direction suggested by research, considerable criticism with regard to each of these remains. Recently Durkin (1979) found inadequate attention given to teaching reading comprehension in the most widely used basal readers for the intermediate grades. Beck and MaCaslin (1977) and more recently Flesch (1981) claim that the phonics programs in the most widely used basal readers are not as effective as the phonics programs in other published reading series.[4] The various phonics programs may be distinguished by a traditional classification—analytic (indirect) versus synthetic (direct) phonics. The programs in the most widely used basal series tend to teach word parts and individual letters and sounds by starting with the word and "analyzing out" the parts. They do not usually teach separate letter-sound associations or phonic blending. Instead they rely

[3]These include textbooks with reading selections, teacher's manuals containing instructions on how to teach the selections, and workbooks for the students. Some also contain tests and various other supplementary materials (see Chall, 1967).

[4]For example, Distar, Open Court, Economy, etc. These programs may be classified as synthetic (direct).

on the child's inferring the connection between letters and sounds.

In a synthetic (direct) approach, the letters and corresponding sounds, and the phonic "rules" are taught more directly—more like, "this is the letter *m* and it has the sound *m*."

In my analysis of beginning reading programs (Chall, 1967) I found evidence for the superiority of an earlier and heavier teaching of phonics, whether the program was analytic or synthetic. There was insufficient evidence with regard to the superiority of synthetic versus analytic phonics. An update of the research to 1982 suggests, however, that decoding programs with a direct (synthetic) approach tend to be more effective than those with an indirect (analytic) approach (Chall, 1983).

Another characteristic of basal reading programs is that they are graded for difficulty. Some programs are easier: they cover less and are slower paced, grade for grade. Some are harder. Little research exists on optimal difficulty (Chall, Conard, and Harris-Sharples, in progress). Much current practice seems to suggest that publishers and teachers tend to think the easier the material, the better the results (Conard, 1981). But recent research suggests that the easier the textbooks (readers and subject-matter textbooks), the lower the reading achievement in the long run (Chall, Conard, and Harris, 1977). The most widely used basals seem to have gotten more difficult over the past decade, although a steady decline in difficulty has been reported for reading textbooks from the 1800s to the middle 1960s (Chall, 1967). Still other characteristics to look for in basal reading series are quality of writing and variety of content.

With regard to textbook materials in the content subjects, our developmental scheme suggests that they be used to develop reading abilities, beginning with the 4th grade, together with children's encyclopedias and other reference works and trade books related to the topics studied.

What should the difficulty of content-area textbooks be in relation to the reading ability of students? The study by Chall, Conard, and Harris (1977) comparing the difficulty of textbooks used in elementary and high schools over a 30-year period with SAT scores found that those students who had used the more challenging textbooks scored higher than those who used easier textbooks. Although an optimal level of readability cannot be established definitely from the available research, it would seem that books that are either too hard or too easy may not be optimal.

What about the great profusion one finds in many schools of boxes, kits, workbooks, worksheets, and so on? Several recent studies at the intermediate levels suggest that such procedures might take too much management time at the expense of time needed for teaching (Durkin, 1979; MacDonald, 1976).

The Availability of Books   Probably the most important factor in reading development is the wide reading that depends upon the easy accessibility of books. From the earliest studies of the reading of adults and children (Marston, 1982), accessibility was found to be the most important factor, with readability and interest following. This means that books (and magazines and newspapers) are read when they are near at hand, are readable, and are interesting. A classroom library collection, a school library collection, or books at home bought or borrowed from a public library are, therefore, very important. Textbooks are important, but they are not enough. Each stage requires much more reading than that which textbooks provide. Table 5-3 and also Table 5-4 contain ideas for the kinds of materials that are appropriate for the different reading stages. It is the responsibility of the home and community, as well as the school, to provide them.

This is only a very brief guide to the variety of materials which are suitable for the different stages and whose use further enhances the transition and movement to higher stages. For specific books which are especially useful in the home, Larrick's *A Parents' Guide to Children's Reading* (1975) gives helpful suggestions to parents on the books to read to young children and on the books to help children select for their own reading. Her more recent work gives additional suggestions on how parents can help their children's reading.

I hope that Table 5-3 makes vivid the fact that reading development does not come from reading textbooks alone, nor from workbooks, nor from worksheets, nor from an intensive 6-week set of practice exercises with a microcomputer. They teach the skills and some of the *how-to-do-its*. But they are not alone sufficient because they do not provide the needed applications to the real world. Further, broader based practice and application are necessary before reading can serve as a means of acquiring knowledge and opinions.

The table is divided into the materials used in schools, both text and nontext materials, and those used in homes and communities. A great amount of reading is needed at all stages for optimal development, with increasing amounts needed at successively higher stages. This means that the school, the home, and the community must cooperate in assuring that children have the materials to read, the time to do so, and that they actually do read.

The availability of books is, as expected, more of a problem for children whose parents are of limited financial means. The RIF program (Reading is Fundamental) has for years carried on a program of providing books free to children whose parents cannot afford to buy them. Paperback book clubs also provide all kinds of inexpensive books that can be bought through the school.

A plentiful classroom collection in the early grades and a school library collection for the intermediate and upper elementary grades—with privileges to borrow books for home use—would help make book reading habitual for children in poor urban centers as well as in affluent suburbs. High schools are known by their libraries, as are colleges.

The Home and Community   It should be evident from all of this how much the home and community contribute to a child's reading development. The home is the first teacher of reading, and it remains important throughout the student's development although the school takes on greater importance with time.

The community, too, is essential. It decides how much money schools spend on textbooks, on a school library, on classroom libraries, and on special testing and remedial services. It also decides on the nature of the public library and the services it should provide.

The amount and kind of independent reading done by children may also be influenced by the media—particularly by

TV. Currently, there is growing concern about the great amounts of time spent watching TV by children of all ages. Will it prove harmful to their cognitive and reading development? An analysis by Wilbur Schramm (1977) suggests that TV might indeed affect reading as a "thief of time." Some recent evidence indicates that reading may be negatively affected by too heavy TV watching at Grade 4 and above (Hornik, 1978). It would appear, then, that strong incentives are needed to encourage reading. Certainly, for today's children who spend so much time on TV, books must be readable, interesting, and, above all, available.

CHAPTER 6

READING DEVELOPMENT ABOVE AND BELOW THE EXPECTED

IN THIS CHAPTER I deal with those whose reading achievement is either significantly above or below that expected on standardized tests and other accepted measures. First I treat those who are able to read significantly above their age or grade placement. Then I consider those children and adults who test below the expected norms, many of whom have severe difficulty learning to read and write for one or more reasons.

Theoretically, about 16 percent achieve significantly above the norm and the same percent significantly below it, i.e., the average for the grade or age group. This represents a difference at either end of one standard deviation.* In terms of reading achievement, it means about one and one-half to two reading grade equivalents (and one stage) above or below the norm. It is significant also for the uses of reading in learning content, e.g., math problems, social studies, science, and literature.

My discussion of precocious readers as well as of those readers with difficulties concentrates mainly on the kinds of

---

*Some people consider two standard deviations from the mean to be a more appropriate measure. With this criterion, about 3 percent of the population would be considered significantly below and 3 percent significantly above.

strengths and weaknesses they present at various reading stages. I will not attempt to present the more complex causes of severe reading disability. Although such questions are of great importance, what is, I believe, of equal importance is the developmental differences—both strengths and weaknesses—that may be found among those whose reading development differs from the normal. My purpose throughout the chapter is, therefore, not to present the underlying neurological, psychological, linguistic, educational, or social/cultural causes of reading difficulty. Rather, my purpose is to learn what aspects of reading and related language are strong and weak at the different stages and, further, to suggest how knowledge of these might help teachers, parents, and reading specialists plan more effective programs for continued reading development.

A recent conceptualization of reading by John B. Carroll (1977) is particularly helpful in this respect. He hypothesized that reading may be viewed as the interaction of three main factors—language, cognition, and reading skills. The first two we have classified earlier (Chapters 2 and 5) as "the message" and the third as "the medium." Problems with reading may appear in light of difficulties with one, two, or all three of the factors at any one time. Further, according to our scheme, the need would be greater for one or another at different stages of reading development.

THE PRECOCIOUS READER

About 16 percent of the school population tests significantly above the norms for their grades or ages. They move through the stages at a pace that is faster than average, but they are not usually as visible in school as are those whose progress is below the norm. Many precocious readers learn to read before formal schooling begins. They learn from parents and other adults, siblings, friends and neighbors, and from TV.[1]

[1]Historically, there have been shifts in attitudes with regard to how reading should begin and how strongly it should be stimulated. From the 1920s to the 1960s, the preference was for a later start and a slower progression through the developmental stages. Since the middle 1960s, there has been a preference for an earlier start. Head Start, *Sesame Street*, and *The Electric Company* are manifestations of the return to a positive view of early reading.

Early reading has long been associated with brightness (Terman, 1925; Fowler, 1971; Smethurst, 1975), but some evidence suggests that average and below average children may also be early readers (Durkin, 1966, 1974, 1975; Torrey, 1973; Smethurst, 1975). Children who learn early, before formal schooling, have proficiency usually in the three major components of reading—language, cognition, and decoding.

The precocious reader may enter school reading on a Stage 1 level, or with enough of Stage 0 characteristics to make rapid progress in Grade 1. Some may already have learned Stage 1 reading and even that of Stage 2 before entering Grade 1. And some children at age 6 can read expository prose for information, a Stage 3 skill (see Bissex, 1980).

The specific instructional needs of these children as they advance through the elementary grades depends on their particular stage of development. A common need of precocious readers is reading tasks that challenge their reading development and motivation. They need to read on levels close to their stage development and within their areas of interest. But since many are reading on levels above most children in their classes, they do not always receive materials in school on their level of development (Westport, 1964; Rubin, 1975). Also important for precocious readers is a wide range of materials and instruction on a level as close to their achievement as possible. In short, it is important not to underestimate their reading ability.

Guidelines for the teaching of fast-developing readers bring one to some of the current issues regarding how best to educate the gifted. Generally, two major approaches have been followed—enrichment and acceleration. Enrichment, for reading, generally means instruction on a level of ability suitable for the "average" or "norm," and much supplementary reading, some of it on the level of the precocious pupil. Accelerated programs try to match difficulty level of instruction to the pupil's level of achievement.

For reading, it seems that both are essential. If only an enrichment approach is followed, it is possible to hold back the early, fast developers by exposing them to too much that is easy and familiar (assimilation) rather than challenging them with some of the new (accommodation). Acceleration is needed to maintain early reading momentum. To keep it up and to keep developing further, the student needs to be challenged sufficiently by material that meets his achievement and intellectual needs. Indeed, a combination of acceleration and enrichment—accommodation and assimilation—is needed for development through the stages not only by precocious but by all readers. If the wide range of abilities in a classroom makes it difficult to give basic instruction at the student's reading level rather than on the level of his grade placement, it becomes even more essential to have plenty of books available on higher levels for independent reading.

At Stage 3, it is particularly important for precocious readers to branch out into all kinds of books and print media. Books help them develop strong interests and curiosities, and curiosities and interests spur them to seek out books. Schools and homes must set an atmosphere favorable for reading at this stage.

What should schools whose pupils average two or more years above the national norm do about basal readers and subject matter textbooks written for a particular grade level—on a reading level below that of their students? Recent studies would suggest more difficult books to match the sutdents' reading levels. (Westport, 1964; Rubin, 1975; Chall, Conard, and Harris, 1977).

READERS WHO PROGRESS BELOW EXPECTATIONS

Who are those who make progress below expectation? Why do they have problems in learning to read and in what aspects of reading do they have difficulty? Do they have greater difficulty at certain stages of development than at others?

The literature on these questions is vast, and it has a long history. The answers are varied, with much difference of opinion. Before discussing the possible strengths and weaknesses found in particular individuals I should like to state again that their difficulties or strengths occur in interaction with their experience—the instruction, stimulation, and background provided by their homes, schools, and communities. So, although

I discuss strengths and weaknesses in individuals, it should be understood that I mean also what was or was not taught to them in their schools and in their homes.

For purposes of understanding the nature of poor reading development and for prevention and remediation, I propose to use the two major components of reading—the medium, or print, and the message, or meaning.

Poor readers tend to have difficulty with one or the other or both aspects. And the difficulties tend to vary with the reading stage. As I noted in Chapters 2 and 5, beginners, those in Stages 1 and 2, have to learn the medium aspect of reading; most can understand the message if they can "decode" it or if it is read to them. Beginning with Stage 3, reading difficulty may be with both the medium and the message. At Stage 3, the language or the ideas may begin to be a source of difficulty because the materials they are expected to read begin to go beyond the reader's everyday experiences. From their own development and environmental stimulation, some readers may have developed greater strengths with the message or with the medium. Generally, those who have greater facility with the message have better language and cognitive development. Language and general cognitive development correlate substantially with reading achievement at Stage 3 level and higher —more than in the beginning stages. But the minimal essentials in language for progress at the beginning are not known, nor are they at the succeeding reading stages.

Difficulties with the medium aspect of reading tend to be distributed more evenly among children of varied backgrounds and cognitive abilities. Their parents may be of affluent, middle, or low income. They may have high or more limited educational attainment. There is a growing consensus that most of the extreme difficulties with the medium, the print (decoding, phonics) side of reading, stem from neurological factors. Some children may suffer from difficulties with both major components of reading. They may have difficulty with both the language/cognitive and with the decoding aspects of reading.

Other causes of slow and difficult reading development also exist, of course. Only a few can be mentioned.

Emotionally based problems in learning may be found among children whose neurological, language, and mental development may be normal. Or emotional problems may be combined with other problems. Some children may have been exposed to a stimulating educational environment, but their motivation and capacity for concentrated attention and work is not adequate for the academic work required. Such children usually have learning problems in mathematics and in other subjects as well as in reading.

Adult illiterates, those who can barely read or write, and those who are functionally literate—who can function in reading only with the simplest "survival" materials such as the reading of signs, labels, and ads—may have had difficulties with the linguistic or print aspects of reading or both. These categories of "problem" readers are not mutually exclusive.

As we later see, although each group lags behind expected progress in reading, individual members of each group have weaknesses and strengths of different kinds at different stages of development. We assume here that most individuals who are delayed in reading have the mental capacity to learn (Bloom, 1976). Is it possible that some poor readers score low on verbal group tests of intelligence because their reading falls below the level required by the intelligence test?

In discussing those whose progress is below expectation, we emphasize Stages 1 to 3, because difficulties with Stages 4 and 5 are varied and can be found among all kinds of students (Perry, 1970).

SLOW LANGUAGE DEVELOPMENT AND THE READING STAGES

Generally, children's language development is related to the degree of stimulation at home and in school. Children who lack a rich linguistic environment may tend to have less difficulty at Stages 1 and 2 than with later stages. It seems possible, therefore, for such children to learn beginning reading quite well, if the methods used do not depend too much on high verbal exchange.

• **Stage 1** For more than 50 years the research correlating language and beginning reading found that language is highly predictive of early reading success. It did not, however, establish the minimal language development necessary for beginning reading instruction. Indeed, there is considerable evidence that not a great amount is needed if the instruction is appropriate (Gates and Russell, 1936; Engleman and Bruner, 1969).

Thus, although children of lower language development will probably be "less ready" than those with more highly developed language, with good instruction in Grade 1, evidence shows that they can learn. This is because in Stage 1 reading students mainly learn the medium—some of the basic phonic elements, insight into decoding, and several hundred words to be recognized. These are finite, specific, and when learned, become self-generative.[2]

Good progress should follow from a program that is based on direct teaching of letter-sound relations and much opportunity for practice in reading connected text. Indeed, such claims are made by some of the reading systems that focus on direct teaching of decoding and word recognition. [See, for example, SRA's Distar (Engleman and Bruner, 1969); the Suppes-Atkinson Computer Aided Instruction Beginning Reading Program (Atkinson et al., 1970); the reading program developed in Israel by Dina Feitelson (Feitelson, 1973); and Ethna Reid's Exemplary Reading Program (Reid, 1980).]

The direct teaching and learning of the medium—decoding—accelerates the learning of Stage 1, particularly for those with limited readiness (Chall, 1967; Chall, 1982). At the same time, it is important to develop children's language through reading to them (Chomsky, 1972, 1978).

• **Stage 2**   The gap in reading for those whose special needs were not met in Stage 1 widens at Stage 2, the stage requiring much reading and predicting of new words. The decoding learned in Stage 1 does not unlock all words. To unlock "new" words, "guessing from context" is also needed. To do this requires confidence, daring, and a good vocabulary and knowledge of syntax. Also required is much practice, under the guidance of those who are more advanced in reading and who love and care for and encourage the beginner.

[2]Chall (1969), after analyzing the recent research in linguistics and reading, proposed two ways to approach reading and language in Grade 1: first, early reading which could lead to faster acquisition of language through the reading of books; and second, early language emphasis before and during beginning reading instruction.

Stage 2 is a time of integrating the skill of converting print into language—and into a message. In a sense, the child learns more assurance in how to read a story for the message—a simply written story, to be sure, but a story which needs to be converted from a still uncertain medium.

Such demands seem to be particularly hard on the children who may have few books to read on their own at home, few adults to smile at them when they read well and when they try. Furthermore, if their language is limited, their "guessing" from context may not be very effective.

For such children, Stage 2 is particularly difficult to achieve by means of school books alone. Such children need to read widely from interesting beginner books, and they should do so orally as well as silently in order to be confirmed in their trials (Chomsky, 1978).

• **Stage 3**   At Stage 3 the language of the textbooks, encyclopedias, and other instructional materials becomes "bookish" and abstract, more removed from the conversational language of most homes. Therefore, the concepts and vocabulary characteristic of these books and the strategies for reading such books need to be taught. While it may be possible for children with rich language experiences to move smoothly from Stage 2 to Stage 3, it is less likely for those of more limited language experience. Not only is their language more removed from their school needs, but their knowledge of the world, which becomes a major factor in reading at Stage 3, may be more limited.

Children with limited language and knowledge, therefore, must be helped more deliberately by the school to make the necessary transitions to and through this reading stage. Because opportunities for such learning are not commonly provided by most homes, it seems essential that the school provide well for them.

• **Suggestions for improving reading of those with limited language experience   At Stage 0:** Children need to be read to at home, in libraries, and at nursery schools. Older children can be taught to read to the younger ones. Children might visit the public library and select books to be read to them.

The home might provide paper, pencils, crayons, blackboard, and chalk for writing.

High schools might experiment in providing courses for future parents on how to prepare the preschool child at home for reading.

At Stage 1: Direct systematic instructions in school might be supplemented by reading to children in the home. Children can begin transition to Stage 2 by reading beginner books independently and to each other toward the end of Stage 1.

At Stage 2: Classrooms need many books for children to read independently and to each other.

Schools can help by arranging a system of home loans of books that parents or older siblings can read to the child or that the child can read on his or her own. Schools can also help by building up the student's confidence and independence in reading, keeping motivation and success high.

At Stage 3: Formal vocabulary and concept development is usually needed, as well as reading in the content areas from a variety of textbooks, encyclopedias, reference books, and the like. There is also need for much independent reading of trade books.

At Stages 4 and 5: Much reading in a variety of fields is needed, and usually direct vocabulary study, study skills practice, practice in efficient reading, and the like.

DIFFICULTIES WITH PRINT (DECODING) AND THE READING STAGES

The basic characteristic of most of those with difficulties in decoding is a discrepancy between their reading achievement and their general cognitive ability. Their general language and cognitive development is usually ahead of their tested reading achievement. Generally, their ability to derive meaning from printed words lags behind their ability to get it from spoken words. Their difficulty is usually not with the understanding of ideas—with the message—but with the medium—the print.[3]

Clinical and classroom experience agree that these children have greatest difficulty with Stage 1, particularly with decoding. They have great difficulty in associating letters with sounds and even greater difficulty with blending sounds to form words. Many also have trouble learning to recognize whole words at sight. But they can learn these with extra care and time.

Those who have these problems with print at Stage 1 usually have trouble with Stage 2, not because the stories they are expected to read are too hard to understand but because their word recognition and decoding are insufficient for the task. Their decoding is not sufficiently fluent and automatic to make concentration on the content possible. Generally, the more severe the problem with decoding, the greater the problem with Stage 1 and Stage 2 (Chall, 1967; Chall, in press).

Compared with others of similar chronological age and cognitive development, the transition of these children from Stage 1 to Stage 2 is more difficult and takes longer. It may take many years before such children are comfortable reading the simplest book. At an age when most move into the fluency of Stage 2, they are either glued to the print or they ignore the print and guess wildly.

The difficult transition from decoding (Stage 1) to fluency (Stage 2) was noted by many of the early investigators of reading disability, among them, Gray, Gates, Orton, and Fernald (Chall, 1967). The problem continues to concern reading researchers. Samuels and his associates have been developing techniques for effecting this transition toward "automaticity" (Samuels, Dahl, and Archwanety, 1974; Dahl, 1975–1976).

An overlong stay in Stage 1 is serious. Aside from the impression these children and others may get that they cannot learn to read, they also fall behind in acquiring the substantive knowledge that others more advanced gain from their reading. Therefore, provision needs to be made for the pupil's contin-

---

[3]Children (and adults) with these difficulties are often classified as having learning disability or dyslexia. Although there are differences of opinion regarding causation, there is growing consensus that the cause is usually related to neurological factors.

ued conceptual and informational development which, in most schools, comes from reading printed materials. If this is not provided while the poor reader is still learning to read and cannot yet use his reading for learning, he or she may also lose out on the knowledge, vocabulary, and concepts needed for further education and also as background for reading at Stage 3 and beyond. Students may become deficient in their cognitive development, although their original problem may have been with decoding alone.

EMOTIONAL BASES FOR READING DIFFICULTIES

When the major reason for poor reading is emotional, the rate of progress through the stages is less predictable than it is for those with language and/or decoding problems. Difficulty may occur at any stage. Because the stages are cumulative, the earlier the problem, the more severely affected are the later stages.

Emotional difficulties may affect reading development through attentional processes that prevent full attention and persistence. Difficulty in concentration may prevent or retard the learning of a variety of reading skills. Difficulties with attention may hamper a child's desire to read books and other materials independently, a requirement beginning with Stage 2. With little skill or practice in this area at Stage 2, and perhaps with little interest in information and knowledge, such children may also do poorly in Stage 3. We should note, however, that some children with emotional problems do learn to read well, and they may, in fact, use reading as a way to escape from their problems.

ADULT ILLITERATES AND FUNCTIONAL LITERATES

Illiterates are people who cannot read or write. By the standards of norm-referenced standardized tests, they would test at about a beginning reading level. Functionally literate adults are those who can read at about a 4th or 5th grade level on a standardized reading test—somewhere toward the beginning of Stage 3. Functional literacy reading skills are sufficient to permit the reading of material that is fairly familiar, material that is within the reader's existing knowledge and meaning vocabulary. This includes the simple, nontechnical parts of some newspapers and application forms, ads, signs, and labels. The use of reading to gain new technical and scientific knowledge or to learn about the past is usually not within the ability of those classified as functionally literate.

Relatively few adults are now classified as illiterate, although as many as 20 million are estimated to be functionally literate. Illiterates tend to be older, and some are foreign born although the majority are native Americans. Functional literates have attended school longer than those classified as illiterate.

Why are so many adults totally and functionally illiterate? For some, the problem probably stems from their limited school attendance, from inadequate schooling, or both. The other reasons are similar to those already discussed with regard to children. These adults, too, may have had early deficiencies in language or in decoding or both. Adult illiteracy is not a condition that happens to the adult, but something that in all probability started during the early and later years of schooling. The gap between an adult's general ability and his or her deficient reading could have been lessened with diagnosis and remedial instruction. It could have been closed or lessened in the elementary school years or in the high school. Generally, the earlier the attention, the more effective the treatment seems to be.

A common scenario for illiterate adults is early difficulty at Stages 1 and 2 (Grades 1–3) and continued struggle with these early reading stages while other children move on to Stage 3. The lag continues, making it very difficult to keep up with the reading requirements in the intermediate and upper elementary grades (4–8). As teenagers, many drop out of high school because they are unable to read and write on a level sufficient to high school needs. Tragically, the level they attain upon leaving school is also inadequate for most work, citizenship, and personal needs. So, from severely retarded readers in the elementary and high schools, they become adult illiterates or functional literates. The process is gradual, and with it comes the child's and later the adolescent's and adult's feelings of inadequacy with regard to all kinds of school and verbal learning.

To teach adult illiterates to read, it is helpful to think of them as either illiterate or functionally literate. In general, adult illiterates have instructional needs similar to those of beginning readers. If they have command of the English language, their main beginning task is usually learning the medium—decoding. Most adults, even those totally illiterate, know some or all of the letters and recognize some common words and signs. But their exact knowledge should be assessed. Why would adults, even illiterate adults, need to start so far back when their language and experience are much beyond that needed for beginning reading? Because their major hurdle in becoming literate is not knowing the printed medium—the printed words and the letters and how they relate to spoken words. They already speak and understand the words they need to read. But since they did not discover them on their own—the printed words and the letters—even though they have lived in a literate world for twenty years or more, they need sympathetic instruction to learn them.

Once Stage 1 is mastered and the letters can be sounded and many common words are recognized, progress through Stage 2 can be rapid because of the adult's advantage over the child in language and experience. The problem with instructing adults on a Stage 2 level is that of finding sufficiently interesting material that is easy and familiar enough. Stage 3 reading should not create undue problems for adults if they have sufficient language and background knowledge for the content materials that are read. If their language and background knowledge is not adequate, they will need, as do younger learners, instruction in the special vocabulary and concepts needed.

The adult illiterate needs greatest practice in Stages 1 and 2, practice in decoding and in gaining fluency. If the first two stages are learned well, Stage 3 reading—reading for new knowledge, the level on which one can educate oneself —should come for many without too much stress.

Functionally literate adults generally start at about a beginning Stage 3 level. Many are still lacking in some decoding skills and in fluent reading of simple materials. If this is so, a review of some aspects of decoding and practice in reading for fluency is needed. But, generally, they require starting at a Stage 3 level, with an emphasis on learning from reading.[4] Stages 4 and 5 for adults are similar to those for children and young people. (See Chapter 5 and Chapter 2 for suggestions.)

READING IMPROVEMENT PROGRAMS IN COLLEGE

College reading improvement programs vary—from a major emphasis on learning skills deficient to date, to applications to varied content needed in college, and, more recently, to combining reading with writing and with study skills. The programs go under various names—from reading efficiency, to remedial reading, to study skills.

The reading instruction in these programs tends to start on a Stage 4 level, emphasizing the need to read with understanding and efficiency materials of varying kinds, viewpoints, and complexities. Some programs may, however, start on a Stage 3 level. Most programs also emphasize rate of reading and the development of general and special vocabularies.

Such programs are not especially different from regular reading programs found in some high schools and even upper elementary schools. In essence, they focus on the reading and related language and study skills to make it possible for college students to use reading (and writing) as vehicles for learning in their regular course work (see Cross, 1981, for a review of such programs).

BILINGUALISM

Bilingualism as such is not considered an inherent deterrent to reading development (Lambert, 1977). It has, in fact, been found that bilingualism has a positive effect on cognitive and linguistic development. And yet the extent of slow reading development among large groups of non-English and bilingual children is considerable.

[4]An example of self-taught reading by an adult reader is found in the *Autobiography of Malcolm X*. While in prison, he taught himself, from a Stage 3 level (study of words in a dictionary), to read at a Stage 5 level, reading classic philosophical and political works and writing papers analyzing and criticizing them.

It is not my purpose here to analyze this situation in any comprehensive manner. Too many unknowns and too many poorly understood factors have been revealed in the various evaluations of federal bilingual programs, none of which has a clear outcome. There is no clear evidence as to whether the bilingual route is most effective for reading development, irrespective of ethnic and cultural considerations.

What, then, can be said about teaching reading to non-English speaking and bilingual children? I offer the following as general observations that fit with existing research and with my proposed reading-stage scheme.

A strong language background is of great benefit to reading development, but it seems to be more essential for later than earlier reading stages. A language strength helps most if it is in the language which is being used for reading, but it also helps if it is in the native language. It would seem that the language structures and concepts transfer from one language to the other. The same is true of word recognition and decoding. Knowing how to read (decode) in one's native language is beneficial when learning to read (decode) the new language.

Thus early listening to stories and early interest in and practice of letters and sounds are beneficial whether in English or in the child's native language.

The factors important to progression through the reading stages are also the same—whether the reading is in the native or in the English language. Some recent research indicates, however, that an optimal time for transfer of reading skills from one language to the other may exist. It seems to be at the end of Stage 2 or the beginning of Stage 3, when reading in the first language has become strong enough to be used for learning other subjects, that reading transfers best to the other language (Pray, 1979; Lambert, 1977).

If this is so, then what might the reasons be for the wide difficulties in reading development found amoung so many bilingual children today as compared to the national norms? Let us start with reading Stage 0, the preschool years. It may well be that some bilingual children come to school with their native languages not as developed as that of monolinguals (Alba, 1980). Stage 1 reading may be quite successful if the instruction is explicit and direct. Indeed, if something is known of the alphabet and word recognition in the native language, few if any real difficulties should appear in Stage 1. But there may be some difficulties with Stage 1 if the child does not recognize the sounded-out words as real words. This problem should pass as the student learns the English language.

Stage 2 may be slow in developing if the command of English is too limited because in this stage both word recognition and facility with language and decoding are needed. Even if the bilingual child's decoding of English is mastered at Stage 1, he or she may struggle in Stage 2 where a broader vocabulary is needed to recognize and sound out more words quickly in order to attain fluency. The end of Stage 2 requires about 3000 words as compared to about 500 at the end of Stage 1. Therefore much reading from "easy" books and much improvement in learning the language must take place.

The transition from Stages 2 to 3 may also be slower if students read less on their own. Without the needed fluency of Stage 2, they will usually have difficulty with Stage 3 which requires almost automatic recognition of words and phrases. Since the content of Stage 3 reading becomes more abstract, more technical, with a heavier load of abstract words and more complex syntax, a new, more technical language needs to be learned as well.

Stage theory suggests several explanations for the lag in reading development of the bilingual child and several kinds of educational programs to prevent and remedy their difficulties. Bilingual as well as monolingual children need to have books read to them years before the 1st grade. They need enriched language programs in their native and/or in the second language. The Stage 1 decoding program should be direct, regular, and systematic.[5] Stage 2 bilingual children need to do much reading of easy books to integrate decoding skill and develop use of context and fluency. Stage 3 reading needs would be similar to those for monolinguals, with the exception that more focus on the English language, both vocabulary and grammar, would probably be needed.

[5]When English reading should be taught is currently being studied. The procedure currently preferred by the federally supported bilingual programs is the learning of reading in the native language first, with reading of English after some proficiency in literacy in the native language. Other procedures have been proposed, including total and immediate immersion in English with some instruction in the native language.

READING OF THE DEAF

Most deaf children, particularly those born deaf, experience in-ordinate difficulty with reading. Although many start formal instruction as early as age 4,[6] by age 18, after 12 or more years of schooling, most achieve only on about a 4th grade reading level, a beginning Stage 3, while the typical hearing student completes Stage 4, or a Grade 12 level, at the same chronological age.

Norms for deaf students from various standardized reading tests reveal dramatically the great struggles that the deaf have with reading. By Grade 5, the average reading achievement is at about the 2nd grade level. At 10, these children are already three years behind the average hearing 5th grader. In terms of reading stages, the typical deaf child in Grade 5 is probably still at Stage 1, still learning the relationship between printed letters and their use in words and still learning to recognize as wholes the common words in print.

Most standardized scores for deaf students show an in-creasing deficit in relation to national norms with increasing age and grade placement. Overall, there seems to be a "ceil-ing" at about 4th or 5th grade reading levels at the completion of high school or beginning college.

The deaf child's general education must suffer from this slow reading development because Stage 3 reading is not de-veloped until the end of high school or college. The back-ground knowledge and vocabulary acquired in Stage 3 and needed for Stages 4 and 5 are delayed further, perhaps until the college years or later.

In terms of stage development, then, development of read-ing takes a much slower pace among deaf students. It takes about five years to learn to decode (Stage 1) and the next six or seven years to acquire the fluency of Stage 2. The average hearing child takes about a year to one and a half years for Stage 1 and one and a half to two years for Stage 2.

Why the "ceiling" at the 4th–5th grade level for the deaf? Part of it can be explained by the long time it takes to advance through Stages 1 and 2. Stage 1, which focuses on learning the connection between the visual and auditory forms of letters

[6]A group of teachers in France starts deaf infants on reading at 6 months of age.

and words, a great hurdle to many hearing children, is particularly difficult for the deaf. A few hours' visit to a school for the deaf makes clear how great an effort is needed to learn to associate printed with "spoken" words. While hearing children know the meanings and sounds of words and have to learn only the printed words and letter-sound relations, for deaf children almost all of this is new. They are behind at age 6 in the words they can speak, in the separated sounds, and in their printed equivalents. The same is probably true for Stage 2. The deaf child continues to struggle with language even after recognizing words and mastering some decoding skills. When deaf children are ready for Stage 3, they experience additional difficulty because they have neither fluency nor the skill of checking words with speech and previous knowledge. If the acquisition of new information is to take place as needed for Stage 3, the decoding skills of Stage 1 and the fluency of Stage 2 need to be so automatic that full attention can be given to the challenges of Stage 3 reading—new ideas, new words, new feelings.

Stage 3 creates still further problems for the deaf. One of the linguistic characteristics of reading materials at the readability levels of Grades 4–8 is the increasing use of difficult unfamiliar words, words that are beyond the concrete and elemental, longer words that are technical, literary, and of low frequency. Such words are difficult for the hearing to learn and more difficult for the deaf because they are usually not picturable, infrequently encountered in speech and print, difficult to explain, and increasingly more abstract.

Most materials on a 4th grade readability level assume that the reader can recognize (or sound out) and understand about 3000 familiar words—elemental, high-frequency words in the English language known by 80 percent of 4th graders. Materials above 4th grade level contain higher percentages of difficult words—words that are more rare and less frequent than the familiar 3000.

If this analysis is valid, it suggests teaching procedures for the deaf that would make best use of their strengths as well as their weaknesses at the different stages of their reading and language development. While there have been attempts to improve their learning to decode, current interest appears to focus on developing their ability to communicate through sign-ing. While signing may develop language earlier, no evidence suggests a beneficial effect on reading.[7]

In this context, I would propose that the readers for the deaf be more appropriate for them. The picture/reading mate-rials of Christine Gibson and I.A. Richards (1963), written orig-inally for teaching English as a foreign language, might be more suitable for the deaf than the basal series that many schools use. Most schools use the books written for hearing children which have many idioms, exclamations, and "speech-like" forms. Considering their needs, materials with more regular syntactical and semantic structures seem more appropriate, along with materials that are more picturable.

There is need, too, for developing better methods for teaching fluent reading in Stage 2. Improvements in methods, materials, and procedures at Stage 2 would also contribute to more adequate progression through the reading stages. It seems necessary to develop the procedures, materials, and de-vices that will help the deaf to become more self-generative earlier in their language use and in their reading and writ-ing. Also, it would appear that the computer, TV disc, and other electronic media may be useful as self-teaching devices for acquiring the recognition and meaning of the commonest 3000 words.

And then, of course, there is the need to break the Stage 3 barrier, to find effective, interesting, and amusing ways for the deaf to learn the less frequent, abstract words that are both necessary for reading beyond a 4th grade level and for acquir-ing advanced knowledge by means of more mature reading at Stages 4 and 5.

The reading gaps of the deaf as compared to the blind seem almost a contradiction. Common sense tells us that the deaf would be the better readers because they can see the print. Yet the blind are the better readers. This happens be-cause reading is closer to hearing than to seeing. Indeed, read-ing from the start is based on language, and it seems to depend more and more upon language as it becomes more mature and complex.

---

[7]An informal survey by Zorfass (1980) found little difference in reading achievement among those children who learned to speak and those who learned to sign.

But none of this is irreversible. The more we understand the process of reading and how it develops in most people and in those who have handicaps, the more possible it is to make the needed adjustments for those with problems.

CHAPTER 7

READING STAGES: THEN AND NOW

T HIS CHAPTER PRESENTS an overview of reading stage theory in the past. Three of these are by leading reading scholars and researchers, W. S. Gray, A. I. Gates, and David Russell. Frances Ilg and Louise Bates Ames of the Gesell Institute contributed the fourth scheme. A fifth comes from two linguists, P. Rozin and L. Gleitman. I include here the findings of a survey on current views of reading stages and conclude with a brief section on other widely known developmental stage schemes of the past and present. The technical and more detailed reports on each are presented in Appendixes B and C.

READING STAGE SCHEMES

• **Gray's Reading Stages** The first reading stage scheme, by William S. Gray, was published in the 1925 *National Society for the Study of Education Yearbook,* "Report of the National Committee on Reading." Gray, the chairman of the committee, stated that "a careful study of the progress of children in reading shows that they pass through different stages of development in acquiring mature habits" (p. 21.) Reading instruction, he noted, should be planned with these stages in mind. He proposed five periods, or stages: (1) preparation for reading (preschool, K, and sometimes early Grade 1); (2) the initial period of reading instruction (Grade 1); (3) the period of rapid progress in fundamental attitudes, habits, and skills (Grades 2 and 3); (4) the period of wide reading to extend and enrich experience and to cultivate important reading habits and tactics (Grades 4–6); (5) the period of refinement of specific reading attitudes, habits, and tastes (junior high, senior high, junior college).

These were again discussed in the 1937 *NSSE Yearbook,* as "five important stages of development in reading" (p. 76). For each of these periods, or stages, Gray also specified the overall aims and levels of achievement acquired at the completion of the particular stage. Thus, for Stage 2, "initial guidance in learning to read" (Grade 1), the first two of the five goals listed were "to develop an interest in reading" and "to develop a thoughtful reading attitude" (p. 76). The first three of ten achievements at the end of the stage were: "reads simple material with interest and absorption," "has desire to read independently," and "is able to read silently with limited or no lip movements" (p. 76).

Stage 3, "rapid progress" (Grades 2 and 3), has as specific aims the reading of "the world's greatest stories for children" (p. 101) and a variety of other informational materials, stimulating rapid growth in comprehension and intelligent interpretation, and developing speed of silent reading and fluency in oral reading. The achievement levels at the end of the stage included the habit of independent reading, and reading silently more rapidly than orally, among others.

At Stage 4 (Grades 4–6), the goals were greater emphasis on reading in the content areas and "better forms of literature" (p. 112). At Stage 5 (Grade 7 to junior college), the goals were the broader use of books, newspapers, and periodicals.

Although Gray presented many detailed descriptions and goals for each stage, the distinctions between them are not always clear. Similar goals appear at each stage, although they are more fully developed at the higher stages. The aims usually concern what Gray called the various "phases" of reading—word recognition, oral reading, silent reading, comprehension, and interpretation. For example, the description of goals for word recognition are almost the same for Stage 2 (first reader), "to develop increased independence in the recognition of new words"; Stage 3 (Grades 2 and 3), "to promote continuous development in accuracy and independence in word recognition" (p. 101); and Stage 4 (Grades 4–6), ". . . greater accuracy and independence in word recognition . . ." and "accuracy and independence in pronouncing increasingly difficult words" (p. 113).

A similar lack of distinction appears with regard to oral reading and with regard to an emphasis on meaning and a thoughtful attitude toward reading. Thus, even for Stage 2 (Grade 1), initial guidance, the first goal out of five for the primer period (the middle of Grade 1) was "to learn to anticipate the meanings of words and to use context in recognizing words."

In spite of the tendency to emphasize "meaningful reading" at all stages and his concern for early silent reading, Gray was definite that differences existed between beginning and mature reading. He noted that beginning with Grades 4–6 (his Stage 4) reading in content areas should receive attention and that Stage 5 (junior and senior high, junior college) is to focus on meaning, vocabulary, and wide reading in a variety of books and other print media.

Gray cited research results from his own studies and from Buswell as evidence for emphasizing given aspects of reading at particular stages or grade levels. He also tied his stages to the increasing complexity of the reading materials and standardized reading tests published for the various grades.

• **A. I. Gates's Reading Stages** Arthur I. Gates published his theory of reading stages in *The Improvement of Reading* (1947), noting that the concept of reading stages would contribute to an understanding of the nature of reading. "The Stages . . . are selected for the purpose of illustrating some of the more important techniques and limitations shown by the typical pupil as he progresses through the elementary school." Gates's scheme included eight periods, from the "prereading" period to the "mature reading" period. Gates's periods are more numerous for the early elementary years, with two prereading periods and four periods of reading covering the primary grades.

The Gates scheme is similar in many respects to that of Gray. Both view beginners as acquiring first a sight vocabulary and as reading simple, connected text, usually word by word. Then, gradually, they develop some skill in pronouncing unknown words, first by "guessing" from context and then by noticing similar letters, syllables, and phonograms.

Gates differs from Gray in allowing for a longer period in which word recognition is acquired. According to Gates, at the end of Grade 1 and beginning of Grade 2, children still read "word by word" and make errors in word recognition that may prevent them from getting the full thought of a passage. For the same period (end of Grade 1), Gray has typical children "reading orally in thought units, rather than word by word."

Gates also tends to place similar materials as appropriate for later grades. Gray includes as an aim for Grade 1 the reading of different kinds of materials (story, information, study), and interpreting them intelligently, for different purposes. Gates does not present these as goals until later.

Crucial to the Gates scheme is his "transition period from primary to intermediate reading" (Grades 2 and 3) when the typical child will begin to shift from a primary type of reading to a higher level of reading ability which we shall call "intermediate reading."

. . . .During this period marked changes are going on under the surface even though the curve of growth in rate of reading and in other aspects shows a · continuous, unbroken advance (p. 33).

Also noted for this transition period was that

. . . a higher level of perception becomes possible. The pupil will begin to recognize certain phrases and word combinations at one glance quite as readily and quickly as he previously recognized each of the single words in the thought unit (p. 34).

This refined perception enables the pupil to read with greater smoothness and speed, to make fewer fixations, and to organize the material better. By the end of Grade 3, Gates saw the typical reader as advancing from "word-by-word reading to reading by thought units," or "from the stage of 'reading by talking' to the stage of 'reading by thinking' " (p. 34).

The "intermediate period" (Grades 4–6) emphasizes reading for content. Gates's explanation for this important shift is that "word recognition in reasonably familiar material has now become so effective that the pupil can and does give his mind more fully to the thought" (p. 34). It is a time, according to Gates, of "differentiation and versatility" in reading a variety of materials and with different comprehension skills. It is of interest that Gray mentioned these goals for an earlier stage, as early as Grade 2.

Gates characterizes "mature reading" (beyond Grade 6) as a period of refinement and perfected skills, more versatile in adapting to the varied reading tasks. He focused this period more and more on thought: "As he becomes more proficient, the pupil can give more of this attention to thinking about, evaluating, comparing, organizing, or otherwise using the content during the actual process of reading" (p. 39).

DAVID RUSSELL'S READING STAGES

The reading stage scheme of David Russell (*NSSE Yearbook*, 1949) took a somewhat different turn. His main concern seemed to be with the implications of child-development research for the teaching of reading. Toward this end, he listed some of the child development characteristics for three age groups: 6–8 (Grades 1–3), 9–11 (Grades 4–6), and 12–14 (Grades 7–9). Next to them, he listed corresponding implications for reading.

For Grades 1 to 3, the first child-development characteristic listed was "interested in here and now of immediate environment." The corresponding "possible implication for reading" was "reading materials should be centered mainly around objects or events in the immediate environment" (p. 13).

Russell also presents six reading stages (or periods) which tend to resemble Gates's more than they do Gray's. Similar to Gates, he had a separate transition period between primary and intermediate reading. Although Russell's child-development data and his reading stage scheme seem to have much in common, it is notable that he did not explain how they were actually related.

We should not, therefore, be surprised to find that Russell's article on reading in the 1961 *NSSE Yearbook* gave little attention to reading stages. He referred to the 1937 and 1949 yearbooks and presented his reading stage scheme from the 1949 yearbook, noting that

> Research and teachers' experience indicate that school children normally go through a sequence of stages in their development of reading abilities. . . . The committee for the present yearbook believes that such descriptions are still valid but wishes to point out that, at best, they are general descriptions, giving rough approximation of a child's reading status (p. 229).

The notion of reading stages seemed to give way, in the 1961 yearbook, to the reading skills to be taught at the primary, intermediate, junior high, senior high, and college levels.

The reading stage schemes above (see also Appendix B) have much in common. All have a prereading, a beginning reading, an intermediate, and an advanced reading stage. All agreed on the method by which the beginners are to be taught: by the introduction of "sight words," the early reading of connected text containing the sight words learned, and the gradual acquisition of word-analysis techniques. This was, in fact, the general consensus from theory, research, and practice from the 1920s to the early 1960s, and it was incorporated in most basal readers of that time (Chall, 1967). Beginners were depicted as having little skill in sounding out unknown words for the entire first year (Russell, 1949). It was not until Grade 2 that Russell saw the child as being able to work out new words on his own. Gray seemed to place even less emphasis on the development of word analysis in Grades 1 through 3. Gates, more than the others, described the growing abilities in word analysis and the beneficial effects its development had on "reading for thoughts." The particular methods in use at the time may have affected the reading characteristics of the children as well as the theoretical conceptions of how reading develops.

All three of the reading schemes agreed even more on the aims and characteristic features of the intermediate grade period. Such reading comprehension skills as finding the main idea, locating information, summarizing, and outlining are included in all three schemes. Here, too, one may ask if these are general characteristics of the intermediate period or if they are found because they were taught? All three authors refer also to higher intellectual functioning during this stage. Gray refers to depth of comprehension (comparing and evaluating ideas, understanding implications). Gates stresses the need for "differentiation and versatility" (reading in different ways for different purposes). Russell refers to "comprehension of more accurate, advanced, and subtle forms." All agree that at the completion of this stage (end of Grade 6), adult reading matter is within the comprehension level of students.

The "advanced level" (beyond Grade 6) for all three is a period of refinement, with greater variety, diversity, and depth of thought.

The differences tend to be mainly at the beginning stages, specifically with regard to word recognition and word analyses, their course of development and their role in mature, meaningful reading. Indeed, these are the same issues that have been debated again and again over the decades and centuries (Chall, 1967; Balmuth, 1981; Chall, in press).

THE ILG AND AMES READING GRADIENT

Frances L. Ilg and Louise Bates Ames were members of the Gesell Institute at the Yale School of Medicine. Ilg was an M.D., listed in *Who's Who* as an educator; Ames was a developmental psychologist. Their scheme was published in two parts. The first, in 1950, covered the years 15 months to age 9. The second part appeared in 1956, in Gesell, Ilg, and Ames, *Youth: The Years from Ten to Sixteen.*

Their "reading gradient" varies from the previous schemes in several respects. It published much of the rather extensive data collected through observations and tests of hundreds of children aged 15 months to 9 years. Overall, they found a rich amount of exposure to reading in the preschool years and much learning about reading by the children they observed during the preschool years. Their gradient, more than the previous schemes, presented much rich detail, by sex, on the development of abilities in word recognition, word analysis, the oral reading errors, and the average oral and silent reading scores over many years.

Similar to the other reading schemes, they found a progression with age toward greater precision in word recognition and decoding which culminates in the ability to read thoughtfully varied materials in the content areas by age 9.

For the 10- to 16-year-olds, the developmental changes for reading are presented together with other changes in school life, in TV watching, radio listening, and other activities. (These are found in Appendix B.)

It is to be noted from the table that the data presented for ages 10–16 consists mainly of the changes in the number and kind of books read "outside of school." No data were presented for changes in skills and abilities as they were for the years up to 9. According to the Ilg and Ames reading gradient, at age 10, 5 books a week are read, and the 10-year-olds prefer reading about animals, adventure, and mystery. At age 14, from 0 to 15 books a week are read, including adult books and those by preferred authors.

THE ROZIN AND GLEITMAN READING SCHEME

Intended for use in the very earliest years, this scheme (1977) is based on the historical development of written language, from pictorial representation to logographic characters (abstract diagrams), phonetization (focusing on sound rather than meaning), syllabary, and the alphabet—the most economic, and most abstract representation. "The developing child seems to traverse, in his conscious discovery of properties of his own speech, the road traveled in historical time by those who designed successful writing systems" (p. 111).

In light of their scheme, Rozin and Gleitman recommend an historically oriented reading curriculum: (1) starting the child on learning that meaning can be represented visually (pictorially); (2) giving each word its own logographic representation; (3) teaching phonetizaton notions (e.g., sound segmentation); (4) syllabic reading; then (5) teaching phonemes.

Appendix B presents a chart from Rozin and Gleitman (1977, p. 112) giving more detail on these stages, particularly with regard to suggestions for teaching.

CURRENT VIEWS ON READING STAGES

More than five decades have passed since the first of these theories of reading stages was first published. Are they still considered in the teaching of reading? I sought answers to this question through a content analysis of widely used professional textbooks on the teaching of reading. I assumed that if an idea were important, in theory or in practice, it would be included in introductory textbooks designed for prospective and practicing teachers.

I selected for analysis 25 widely used textbooks on methods of teaching reading published during the 1970s. (Appendix C contains the references to the textbooks, the questions posed, the methods of analysis, the findings, and the interpretations.) The following section presents the highlights of the findings.

To assure finding any existing coverage of the reading stages in the professional textbooks, we searched for seven possible categories: *reading development, developmental reading, development, growth, reading growth, reading stages,* and *stages of reading development.* Others were also used if they might lead to a discussion of reading stages.

Of the 25 textbooks analyzed, nearly half contained listings under one of the seven categories. Seven referred to the category *developmental reading* as reading instruction for pupils who progress normally as distinguished from those needing corrective or remedial reading. The categories *growth* and/or *reading growth* were found in two of the textbooks but were used mainly for discussing the influence of physical, mental, and emotional growth on reading. In none of the textbooks did an entry under *growth* refer to reading growth or reading development.

When reading growth was discussed under such terms as *reading development, reading growth,* and *reading stages,* it generally referred to the scope and sequence of reading skills to be taught or to the necessity of individual instruction inasmuch as individuals develop at a different rate. Overall, we found little attention paid in these 25 widely used professional textbooks to changes in the individual readers, in what they can do, and in what they are expected to do as they develop in reading ability.

To determine why so little attention was paid to reading development in the textbooks published in the 1970s, we compared "younger" with the "older" textbooks. The "younger" were those texts copyrighted originally in the 1970s; the "older," those first copyrighted before 1970 and in their second or later editions in the 1970s. Ten of the 25 were classified as "older" texts, 15 as "younger." Of the 10 older texts, 6 contained references to *growth, reading stages, developmental reading,* and the like. Even among those "older" books, the earlier the original copyright date, the greater the probability of their mentioning reading development. The "younger" textbooks as a group had fewer references to reading development. Only 2 of the 15 "younger" texts had listings under one or more of the seven categories. One of these 2 textbooks referred to the relevance of Piaget's cognitive stages to reading readiness, particularly readiness for decoding. Only one of the 15 newer textbooks referred to any of the early reading stage schemes.

As a group, then, the older methods textbooks devoted more attention to reading development and reading stages than the younger ones. Generally, however, they too reveal a growing caution, over time, about the value of stages. Most of them see the value of stage theory for sequencing the skills to be taught, but they show concern that the stages may not be helpful for individual readers whose course of development differs from the expected and that a stage scheme might also encourage lock-stepping of children through reading instruction.

Why were the younger textbooks less favorable toward stages than the older ones? And why does there seem to be a growing cautiousness toward the possible misuses of reading stages by the older textbooks as well?

Many factors are no doubt involved. One is the "absorption" of some of the aspects of the reading stages into existing practices—particularly sequences of skills. Since the authors of the three major reading stage schemes were also the senior authors of the most widely used basal reading series of their time, it would seem reasonable to assume that the reading series with which they were associated (Gray: Scott, Foresman; Gates: Macmillan; and Russell: Ginn) would adopt their reading development schemes. Indeed, since these three reading series were popular, it also seems reasonable to suppose that other reading series would adopt their skill sequences. Thus, the wide acceptance of the skill sequences, one aspect of the reading stage schemes, may have dominated the other aspects. The concern for what should be taught, when, and how it should be taught, took over the developmental concerns of what is generally learned, when, how, and why.

Another explanation may be the growing interest of many reading researchers in child development and its relation to learning to read. There was interest in the 1940s and 1950s, for example, in the correlation of skeletal development and reading achievement (Olson, 1961). There was growing interest in the relationship between emotional and social development and reading. More recently, there has been interest in the relation between Piagetian cognitive stage development and beginning reading (Elkind, 1976). In this manner, reading development began to be viewed not as a process that grows and changes but as a correlate of other aspects of child development.

The term "reading development" also took on different meanings after 1950. One was the distinction of developmental reading from remedial reading, and later from recreational reading. Developmental reading thus began to refer to regular reading instruction as distinguished from remedial reading, particularly at the secondary level. Both were distinguished from recreational reading, which was used to refer to reading for pleasure. The developmental remedial reading distinction may strike one as strange because a case can be made for remedial reading requiring even more attention to the developmental needs of the student than regular reading.

The concept of reading development shifted around the 1950s from the typical characteristics of reading at different ages or grades to a study of the ways the child develops —cognitively, emotionally, linguistically, and more recently neurologically—and how these relate to reading. What seems to remain in the current professional textbooks of the original concept of reading development is the detailed scope and sequence charts of specific reading skills thought to be essential at the different grade levels. The broader aspects of reading development have unfortunately been underplayed. The reasons often given in these texts is fear that they may be used prescriptively and rigidly to hold some children back and force others to move faster than they are able to. It is somewhat ironic that this danger is not expressed for the specific skill sequences for each of the grade levels.

CHAPTER 8

HISTORICAL AND CULTURAL INFLUENCES

UNIVERSAL LITERACY IS a recent phenomenon, and it exists in only half of the world today. Up until about a hundred years ago, most people were completely illiterate.

The growth in the number who are literate and in the extent and quality of their literacy can be appreciated in terms of the broad historical changes that social scientists see. According to many, modern civilization has gone through three great revolutions[1] which human beings brought about and which in turn changed them forever.

I propose that we view the spread of literacy—as well as its levels and quality—in relation to these great revolutions. The agricultural revolution probably brought an increase in the numbers of literate people who could keep simple records and read them. By our stages scheme, this would require proficiency at about a Stage 1 or Stage 2 level—the ability to read what is familiar and already known. Such a level of proficiency would also be useful for most religious purposes—for reading prayers and psalms that have already been learned orally and have largely been memorized. Thus, although most people were totally illiterate, I suggest that during the agricultural age those who were literate reached a level of reading approxi-

[1] Alvin Toffler (1980) calls them "waves."

142

mately equal to the 3rd grade reading level—functional literacy—or reading achievement at Stage 2.

With the industrial revolution, the ideal level of reading rose to Stage 3, which meant the ability to read and learn from unfamiliar texts. With the knowledge revolution, and perhaps because of it, most people in the technologically advanced, developed countries need a higher level of reading—Stage 4—the reading of difficult, unfamiliar texts analytically. Such reading levels are generally acquired in secondary schools.

In my view, most of the reading (and writing) in simple agricultural societies, with the exception of the rulers, scribes, philosophers, physicians, and scholars who no doubt read at Stages 4 and 5, was limited to the lower reading stages—to Stage 1, which consisted mainly of writing one's name, and Stage 2, which consisted of reading text that was familiar and known. Such reading was consonant with an "oral tradition." It served mainly as a reminder about items bought, sold, and borrowed, and as a vehicle to ritualize knowledge previously obtained through listening, chanting, and so on.

Stage 2 proficiency was particularly consonant with the needs of a society that kept only simple records, and because life was stable, it required no really new vocabulary and concepts. It was also useful for religious prayers, which were no doubt read aloud or with moving lips.

Stage 3 reading, the reading that is "for the new," the reading achieved by most children today during the middle and upper elementary grades, is a relatively recent advancement in the evolution of reading. It brought with it the capacity to acquire one's own new knowledge and to experience the esthetic-affective reaction through reading. Thus one can further one's own continued learning and expand one's own views—abilities valued during an industrial period. Its great power was that it permitted independence in the reader. Stage 3 was usually the beginning of silent reading, and thus it permitted a privacy and kind of secrecy to the reading not possible with proficiency in Stage 2 reading.

Stages 4 and 5 became more prevalent as the need for such expertise in industry, in government, and in the professions grew and as greater proportions of the population attended high school and college. The knowledge revolution required greater numbers proficient in reading stages 4 and 5, as scientific and technical work became more complex and more extensive.[2]

I have painted all this with a broad brush. Within any time period, and in any country, wide variations in literacy were no doubt found. Indeed, in the United States today, while about half of the population can read at Stages 4 and 5, about 20 million are estimated to be only functionally literate. Most developing nations are still predominantly illiterate or at Stages 1 and 2, with minority populations at Stage 3 and above.

Generally, in the most advanced nations, adults can be found at all stages of reading development—from illiterate to the most advanced. And while in earlier generations it was mainly the foreign-born and those who had not attended schools who were illiterate, it is more common today to find native-born high school graduates who read below a 4th–5th grade level even when the expectation for high school graduates is a 12th grade level.

We can look at these historical changes in reading development from still another viewpoint. While the highly educated few in each culture probably reached levels equivalent to those of the highly educated today, the average were on a lower stage than the average are today. Over the historical existence of literacy in a nation, typical, average, adult readers have changed greatly in how they read, in what they can read, and in the uses to which they put reading.

For most of recorded history, those who could read at all could read only on a limited level. They could read what they already knew, about the thoughts and experiences they already had. This they did mostly by reading aloud, usually in unison with others.[3] The texts and scrolls available for reading were few in number and difficult to come by for most with limited means.

The invention of moveable type and the wider availability of books and texts also contributed to the development of Stage 3 reading. The practice of silent reading, more possible

---

[2]Recent figures on "first job" employment trends indicate that technical jobs are increasing while nontechnical, routine jobs are declining.
[3]At the beginning stages, oral reading is easier than silent for most readers.

at Stage 3 than at Stage 2 level, brought additional advantages to those who could read at that level. Compared to the oral, unison reading of earlier times and of Stage 2 readers, silent reading permitted independence in one's reading. Prior to the time of Stage 3 reading, most reading was open, communal, and shared.

The concern for silent rather than oral reading became particularly strong in the United States starting in the 1920s when the average school grade reached by most adults was an 8th grade level and larger numbers were entering high school. In the 1960s and 1970s, the great increases were in high school graduates and college attendance (according to the National Center for Educational Statistics, as of October 1980, about 75% of those in high school graduate, and about 35% of the college-aged population are in college), thus raising the average reading level. The growing popularity of speed reading, with courses at colleges, franchised schools, and home programs, is further evidence that typical literacy has moved to Stages 4 and 5, with more people seeking more proficient reading.

There is also a relationship between the average reading stage of a nation and the amount of knowledge in print that is readily available. When the predominant level of literacy in a society is on a Stage 2 level, the extent of knowledge in print is relatively small. When it rises to Stage 3 and higher, the amount of material rises.

The rise of Protestantism apparently brought with it a rise in Stage 3 reading. Following the Protestant Reformation, and particularly when the Bible was translated into various languages, each person felt the need and had the opportunity to read and interpret the Bible for himself or herself. Although oral reading still continued in church worship and in family reading of the Bible, individual study and worship required silent reading and interpretation.

Among English-speaking peoples, the other book of prescribed and total knowledge was Shakespeare. Similar to the Bible in the vernacular, Shakespeare was probably read most on a Stage 3 level for the purpose of gaining new experience and knowledge—silently for private uses and orally for family reading.

Compare the time in the English-speaking world when

texts were limited to the Bible and Shakespeare to contemporary times in advanced technological nations with their profusion of newspapers, magazines, books, paperbacks, manuals, textbooks, ads, etc., etc. The "reading" task faced by the adult in such nations is limitless, as is the task of the child learning to read and to cope with these materials.

The problem of reading and literacy for today is that higher levels of reading are needed by more and more people in every country. The stage of reading development needed today to do the jobs available is the highest ever. And yet while the developed nations are striving to have more people reach Stages 4 and 5, the developing countries are striving for attaining Stages 2 and 3.

An index of the average reading stage reached may be useful as a sociological and educational description of a nation at a given historical period. This index would, I believe, be useful for comparisons over time, and for comparisons across nations. It might also be useful for making comparisons in terms of economic conditions, industrial production, the rise and fall of numbers in given occupations, and the like. Interesting comparisons could also be made between generations and over broad historical periods.

Such a reading stage index would be similar to but different from the census data on last grade reached. The stage index would give a more accurate view of achievement level because, increasingly, the last grade reached correlates less well with achievement. (We have already noted that high school graduates range from a 4th grade to a 12th or higher grade reading level.) Since the reading stage index would more closely approximate achievement level, it would be useful also for recording how many people can read at what broad stage levels. This might also have more meaning than an index of last grade reached for matching readers' proficiency to the level of their academic and work tasks.

The National Assessment and other surveys also indicate that achievement ranges from near illiteracy to college level and above after 12 years of schooling. The international study of reading (Thorndike, 1973) found that when the same text was translated into 15 languages, at age 17 the students educated in the developing countries had achieved only about one-half to two-thirds of the reading achievement of students in advanced countries after the same number of years of schooling. For comparisons that meet international needs, broad standards like those of the reading stages might be useful.

I think that educational planners, economists, sociologists, and other social scientists could benefit from knowing how many people of different ages are able to function on the various levels of reading development. For example, to speak of 95 percent literacy in the United States is not sufficiently descriptive because it includes literacy at Stages 1 through 5. It would be helpful to know where most people, age 25 and over, rank in terms of the reading stages. How many would be at Stage 1? Stage 2? Stage 3? And it would be useful to know what stage of reading various jobs require. Sticht (1975) has found, for example, that army cook's manuals require an 8th grade reading level (end of Stage 3) and that technicians in the Navy require an 11th–12th grade level (Stage 4) to read most technical manuals.

An index based on reading stage levels might prove to be more sensitive for estimating the literacy functioning of various subgroups within the population. And it could be associated with various economic factors, further education, and other aspects of the quality of life.

Some interesting questions could be asked. What happens, for instance, to those young people and adults who graduate from high school reading at the lowest end of the stage continuum—at Stage 1 or 2—in a country that is predominantly at Stages 4 and 5? In one that is predominantly at Stage 3? The malpractice suits of some five and six years ago apparently were manifestations of this phenomenon. In the Peter Doe vs. the San Francisco school system case, Peter's mother brought action because Peter, after graduating from high school, was able to function only on a 5th grade reading level (beginning Stage 3) which, his mother claimed, was insufficient for holding a job, for filling out a job application, and for reading a driver's manual. Would such an action have occurred in the seventeenth century when the average reading achievement of adults was probably below Peter's, at about Stage 2? Or in developing countries where the average stage level may be 1 or 2?

This is perhaps the first time in the history of the United States, and of the world, that so many adults have been able to read at so high a level. Those at the two upper stages of literacy will shortly be in the majority in the United States. For the first time, then, those reading on the lowest stages will be in the minority. Will this phenomenon bring with it a change of tastes in reading matter? Can we say that this change has already occurred in magazines—with decreasing circulation of the "pulps" (Stages 2 and 3) and increasing circulation of the digests (Stage 3 to 4)? Is it possible that the growing popularity of news magazines (Stages 4 and 5) can be viewed in terms of the increase in the numbers who can read at Stages 4 and 5? Can the closing of the *Saturday Evening Post, Life,* and *Look* reflect the advance in the nation's reading development? All three were geared to about a Stage 3 reading level, and all three magazines, highly successful for 30 years or more, ceased publication. Meanwhile, *Time* and *Newsweek* (requiring Stage 4–5 reading) and other such magazines have increased in circulation.

The general shift upward in reading achievement has caused problems for those who have been unable to meet these standards. The states are currently trying to require minimal standards (minimal competencies) for reading and other basic skills. An analysis of the reading development required by eight minimum competency tests in reading—four state tests and four commercial—found that the required reading grade levels range from about the 5th or 6th grade level to about the 11th or 12th grade levels—Stage 3 to middle Stage 4. Most required a reading stage of 3, about that typical at the completion of the 8th grade (Chall, Freeman, and Levy, 1981).

More remedial reading is also available to high school and college students whose reading falls short of the level they need for their studies. Efforts to promote basic adult literacy have also increased, with more adults getting literacy training in industry, in schools, and in various federal projects.

It would be interesting to relate the numbers of young adults at different reading stages with the numbers of jobs requiring these levels of reading development. The relation between the two should show discrepancies in fit, and it might indicate the expected unemployment rates for those whose literacy development is too low. It would also be useful to relate the reading stage development required on the entrance examinations for different jobs with the minimal reading level required for doing the jobs.

What kind of life would a people predominantly at reading stages 4 to 5 have? What would the intellectual and social climate be like? Political and social surveys have found great differences among groups by educational attainment (Hyman, Wright, & Reed, 1975). The more educated are less violent, generally, more liberal in politics, and more tolerant of others' views. They also have higher incomes and their children have higher educational attainments. Do they also make stronger demands on their children and on the schools?

What about those who do not and cannot reach the typical Stage 4 to 5 level? Won't the gap be felt with greater pain, deprivation, and shame than in the past? In Chapter 6 we saw that many children and adults have handicaps that may make it difficult to reach these high levels without special assistance. Special help will ease their problem, but it may not solve it altogether. Their feelings of incompetence can be severe, for in their own eyes everyone else does easily what they do with great effort.

The pain of being behind was probably not as great as when the average educational attainment was lower (e.g., the 8th grade in 1940) and when many who dropped out of school could find jobs. Also, because students with difficulty in reading left school earlier, they had fewer years in school in which to be ashamed of their difficulty and suspected stupidity. I suggest that there will be profound changes in those "left behind" as we become a nation of higher reading attainment. We need to plan for the possible consequences very soon.

Those not going on to college seem to fear that the world has little to offer them, particularly when attending college is the next step after high school for the great majority. An excerpt from Studs Terkel's *Working* gives an insight into the conflict felt by a steel worker toward those of more education:

"I want my kid to be an effete snob. . . . I want him to tell me he's not gonna be like me." His fellow workers laugh at him for reading and trying to think seriously; the college kids he meets patronize him—or, what is even worse, romanticize him." (*New York Times Book Review,* March 24, 1974).

READING STAGES: A CROSS-CULTURAL VIEW

We compare here current practices and views of reading development with those of older, more traditional societies—Koranic schools, Hebrew schools, and the religiously oriented schools of early America.

All of the traditional schools, as well as modern schools, have as their first objective teaching to read and developing in students the abilities needed for more advanced reading. Anthropologists have long held that we can learn more about ourselves by becoming immersed in the cultures of others. It is in this spirit that I present some comparisons with other cultures and other historical periods. I do not think it essential for us to know how Colonial children learned to read, but the knowledge is of value if it unglues us at least temporarily from the views we have of ourselves. The cross-cultural comparisons are made in broad terms, juxtaposing older traditions with current Western ones. The comparisons also utilize the stages scheme.

Probably the greatest distinction between the older, traditional schools and our modern schools lay in how reading was valued. Reading, that is, reading the Book that formed the core of the culture, had the highest possible value. This book was highly valued by the family and by the child, even before he or she entered school. The families who valued their children's learning no doubt taught them stories and perhaps letters that prepared them to learn to read. Attendance at worship services also helped the children learn.

From an emotional commitment and from a cognitive standpoint, therefore, the families and the community prepared the children with the entry skills they needed for reading.[4] The modern child, particularly of college educated parents, is also prepared for school at home. The child is read to, learns the letters, and also learns that it is important to learn. But such preparation does not have the single purpose that it does in religious communities. Motives vary—some stressing interest, some competence and independence, some competition.

[4] In traditional eastern European Jewish communities, boys were sent to Heder as young as age 3.

During Stage 1, in the traditional schools the alphabetic principle was usually taught as a separate, first step in reading. In Hebrew schools, learning the alphabet and sounds took place in a separate school, the Heder, usually when students were younger than 5 or 6. Early American primers were also strongly oriented to teaching the letters and syllables first, then short words, and often short sentences for practicing the letters and word parts learned. The New England primer demonstrates that simple sayings were also read while the alphabet was being mastered.

We tend today to view the learning from these primers as having been all rote, with no opportunity to read for meaning. I take a different view. Most of the rhymes (see page 155) and sayings came directly out of family and cultural tradition, and the chances are great that children were already familiar with the content and their meaning. This means that learning to read for them was like learning to read today: they read for meaning as soon as they could break through the code.

At Stage 2, in the traditional schools children began the actual reading of the holy text, or part of it, with some interpretations. As soon as decoding was mastered in Stage 1 (although Koranic schools seem not to have had a formal separate period for learning the alphabet), the child read and learned from adult texts. This contrasts sharply with practice in modern schools which stress the reading of stories and other selections whose content and language are selected to be familiar and appealing to the children.

How can adult texts be effective? The psychological factors of familiarity and importance are central. For children in traditional religious schools, the adult language—although archaic—was already familiar to the child. Further, parental and community support made it worthwhile to expend the effort. By the time the child reached Stage 2 at age $7\frac{1}{2}$ or 8, the language of the Bible or Koran was sufficiently familiar to make possible the recognition of words, phrases, and sentences through the use of context as well as through word recognition and decoding. Chanting and unison oral reading also helped in learning the extensive vocabularies, only a fraction of which would be considered suitable for the texts for 2nd and 3rd graders in modern American schools. Stage 2 reading was mastered in traditional religious schools by means of strong linguistic familiarity with the text, and the text and content were highly meaningful to and respected by the culture. The child realized early that reading is about matters of great importance to his parents, siblings, and to the adults in the community (Bettelheim and Zelan, 1981).

Modern reading textbooks for Grades 1, 2, and 3 (Stages 1 and 2), when compared with traditional texts, are completely child-centered. They are written specifically to appeal to the child's interests while he or she learns the reading skills. Although some of the texts for Grades 2 and 3 are quite appealing, it would be difficult for anyone to claim that the content is important or instructive. Nor would authors and publishers make such a claim. If any claims are made, they are that the material is interesting, pleasurable, and fun. Indeed, that is the motive most often heard in classrooms and in teacher training.

One wonders how it came about that the strongest incentive offered to the child for learning to read is fun. It came no doubt before the universal availability of TV because TV provides an easier way for the child to get the same content. Indeed, it takes most children until the end of Stage 3 (Grade 8) for reading to be as efficient as listening. One might well ask whether the major focus of the beginning readers of today should be on fun.

During Stage 3, the reading tasks of the modern and traditional religious schools become more similar. Both are concerned with the child's learning to read and to understand the basic, valued knowledge of the culture. The basic knowledge is different, of course: religious schools stress the main religious writings; modern schools stress scientific and historical information. There has been a lessening of serious content in modern readers at the Stage 3 level, however. The texts of the traditional religious schools are more serious and also more difficult. The texts in modern schools are considerably easier.

Both traditional and modern schools move toward more silent than oral reading and toward greater independence. Generally, the traditional schools in early America and the Hebrew and Koranic schools engaged in more oral reading at this stage than modern schools ask children to do. In traditional schools, reading practice at Stage 3 was seldom referred to as intruction in reading. It more often focused on the content—its history, its legal aspects, its ethics, and the like.

Modern Stage 3 reading has been taught by "reading lessons." The content texts in history, geography, science, and literature are taught separately as subject areas. A recent movement has begun to bring reading instruction to the content areas. There have also been some requests that we bring expository writing back into the basal readers (Venezky, 1981).

Stages 4 and 5 are similar in modern and traditional schools. They do differ in the breadth of content that modern schools try to teach and in the difficulty level. At Stage 4, the difficulty of the religious texts seemed much greater than that of the modern texts. Yet in one area at least—the variety and amount of reading matter—it may have been easier to achieve Stages 4 and 5 in traditional schools than in modern high schools and colleges. The written sources of religious learning are finite when compared to what is written about the modern sciences, for example. Although religious interpretations continue to appear, these are quite limited compared to the constant flow of publications in any area of modern study. The data from which the traditional religious student drew his interpretations were more stable and less open—and less confusing.

In sum, traditional religious schools started children earlier on Stage 1, with greater formal separation from connected reading. Reading of adult text (the Bible, the Koran) began early, at Stage 2. This reading was done aloud, together, and sometimes chanted. Modern schools expect more individual and more independent reading at Stage 1 and particularly at Stage 2. At Stage 3, modern and traditional schools begin to resemble each other, but the difficulty of the reading texts in the religious schools still seems higher. There is also more oral reading and, in some schools, more oral interpretation of the text. Stages 4 and 5 seem to be more similar among modern and traditional schools, but the breadth of content is greater in modern schools than in the traditional ones.

Traditional schools also seem to have a faster pace. Early American reading texts for a given grade are much more difficult than modern ones designated for the same grade. Perhaps the texts were read by older students. But it seems that level for level the books were harder than they are today.

The following pages illustrate the kinds of selections included in readers for children who have gone beyond the beginning stages, then and now.

We present pages 216 and 217 from Wilson's Fifth Reader *(Harper and Brichas, 1861), Gil Blass and the Archbishop, or the Danger of Giving Advice.*

Generally, these selections illustrate what various studies have shown—that the modern readers contain more stories (narrative) that are child-oriented. Compared to the older readers, there is little of adult literature and little of expository writing of content valued by adults, and that children are expected to learn. They are written in a style that is significantly easier than in earlier years. Chall, Conard, and Harris (1977).

I include also p. 100 from a third reader, "The Truthful Little Persian" from Stepping Stones to Literature *(Silver, Burdett and Company, 1897). This story and others in this reader and in other readers like it were more mature than most stories of current readers at even a Grade 5 level. They seem more suitable for reading at a Stage 3 level, "reading to learn the new," than are many modern readers for Grades 4 to 8.*

3. A sweeter bloom to Eva's youth
   Rejoicing Nature gave;
   And heaven was mirrored in her truth
   More clear than on the wave.

4. Oft to that lone, sequester'd place
   My boyish steps would roam;
   There was a book in Eva's face
   That seem'd a smile of home.

5. And oft I paused to hear at noon
   A voice that sang for glee;
   Or mark the white neck glancing down,
   The book upon the knee.

6. Years pass; the same the peaceful vale,
   The jasmine round the door,
   The hill still shelters from the gale,
   The brook still glides before;

7. Still sweet the jasmine's buds of snow;—
   But 'neath the yew-tree's shade,
   Where silver-clear the waters flow,
   Her holy dust is laid.—BULWER LYTTON.

LESSON II.—GIL BLAS AND THE ARCHBISHOP, OR THE DANGER OF GIVING ADVICE.

Archbishop. WHAT is your business with me, my friend? *Gil Blas.* I am the young man who was recommended to you by your nephew, Don Fernando.

Arch. Oh! you are the person of whom he spoke so handsomely. I retain you in my service; I regard you as an acquisition. Your education, it would seem, has not been neglected; you know enough of Greek and Latin for my purpose, and your handwriting suits me. I am obliged to my nephew for sending me so clever a young fellow. So good a copyist must be also a grammarian. Tell me, did you find nothing in the sermon you transcribed for me which shocked your taste? no little negligence of style, or impropriety of diction?

Gil B. Oh, sir! I am not qualified to play the critic; and if I were, I am persuaded that your grace's compositions would defy censure.

Arch. Ahem! well, I do flatter myself that not many flaws could be picked in them. But, my young friend, tell me what passages struck you most forcibly.

Gil B. If, where all was excellent, any passages more particularly moved me, they were those personifying hope, and describing the good man's death.

Arch. You show an accurate taste and delicate appreciation. I see your judgment may be relied upon. Give yourself no inquietude, Gil Blas, in regard to your advancement in life. I will take care of that. I have an affection for you, and, to prove it, I will now make you my confidant. Yes, my young friend, I will make you the depositary of my most secret thoughts. Listen to what I have to say. I am fond of preaching, and my sermons are not without effect upon my hearers. The conversions of which I am the humble instrument ought to content me. But—shall I confess my weakness?—my reputation as a finished orator is what gratifies me most. My productions are celebrated as at once vigorous and elegant. But I would, of all things, avoid the mistake of those authors who do not know when to stop—I would produce nothing beneath my reputation; I would retire seasonably, ere that is impaired. And so, my dear Gil Blas, one thing I exact of your zeal, which is, that when you shall find that my pen begins to flag and to give signs of old age in the owner, you shall not hesitate to apprise me of the fact. Do not be afraid that I shall take it unkindly. I can not trust my own judgment on this point; self-love may mislead me. A disinterested understanding is what I require for my guidance I make choice of yours, and mean to abide by your decision.

Gil B. Thank Heaven, sir, the period is likely to be far distant when any such hint shall be needed. Besides, a genius like yours will wear better than that of an inferior man; or, to speak more justly, your faculties are above the encroachments of age. Instead of being weakened, they promise to be invigorated by time.

Arch. No flattery, my friend. I am well aware that I am liable to give way at any time, all at once. At my age, certain infirmities of the flesh are unavoidable, and they must needs affect the mental powers. I repeat it, Gil Blas, so soon as you shall perceive the slightest symptom of deterioration in my writings, give me fair warning. Do not shrink from being perfectly candid and sincere, for I shall receive such a monition as a token of your regard for me.

Gil B. In good faith, sir, I shall endeavor to merit your confidence.

Arch. Nay, your interests are bound up with your obedience in this respect; for if, unfortunately for you, I should hear in the city a whisper of a falling-off in my discourses— an intimation that I ought to stop preaching—I should hold you responsible, and consider myself exempted from all care

K

THE TRUTHFUL LITTLE PERSIAN.

FAR, far across the ocean, thousands of miles away, lies a country called Persia. Hundreds of years ago there lived in Persia a wise man who was so good that his people called him a saint. When he was a boy, it is said, he desired to give himself to learning what was right, and to doing what was good, and he asked his mother if he might go to Bagdad to obtain this knowledge.

His mother gave her consent; and, taking out eighty pieces of silver, she told him that, as he had a brother, half of that money would be his whole inheritance. She made him promise solemnly, when she gave it to him, never to tell a lie, and then bade him farewell, exclaiming, "Go, my son! I give thee to God! we shall not meet again till the day of judgment!"

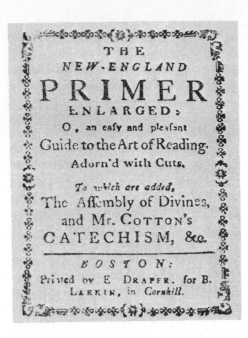

Excerpts from the New England Primer: *It illustrates the use of serious content—religious and the importance of learning to read—in the child's first text for reading instruction.*

The BUTTERFLY.

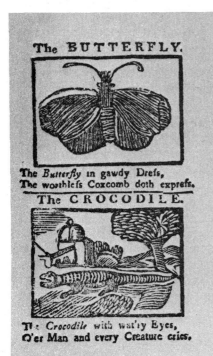

The *Butterfly* in gawdy Dress,
The worthless Coxcomb doth expref's.

The CROCODILE.

The *Crocodile* with wat'ry Eyes,
O'er Man and every Creature cries.

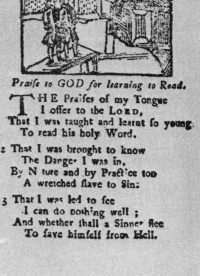

Praise to GOD *for learning to Read.*

THE Praifes of my Tongue
  I offer to the LORD,
That I was taught and learnt fo young,
  To read his holy Word.

2 That I was brought to know
    The Danger I was in,
  By Nature and by Practice too
    A wretched flave to Sin:

3 That I was led to fee
  .I can do nothing well ;
  And whether fhall a Sinner flee
    To fave himfelf from Hell.

TABLE XXXI.
Familiar Lessons.

HENRY is a good boy. Come here, Henry, let me hear you read. Can you spell easy words? Hold up your head; speak loud and plain. Keep your book clean; do not tear it.

John, keep your seat, and sit still. You must not say a word, nor laugh nor play. Look on your book, learn your letters, study your lesson.

Charles, can you count? Try. One, two, three, four, five, six, seven, eight, nine, ten.—Well said; now spell bird. B-i-r-d. How the birds sing and hop from branch to branch among the trees. They make nests too, and lay eggs; then sit on their eggs, and hatch young birds. Dear little birds, how they sing and play. You must not rob their nests, nor kill their young: it is cruel.

Moses, see the cat, how quiet she lies by the fire. Puss catches mice. Did you ever see puss watching for mice? How still and sly! She creeps along, fixing her eyes steady on the place where the mouse lies. As soon as she gets near enough, she darts forward, and seizes the little victim by the neck. Now the little mouse will do no more mischief.

See the little helpless kittens. How warm and quiet they lie in their bed, while puss is gone. Take them in your hands, don't hurt them; they are harmless, and do no hurt. They will not bite nor scratch. Lay them down softly, and let them go to sleep.

George, the sun has risen, and it is time for you to rise. See the sun, how it shines: it dispels the darkness of night, and makes all nature gay and cheerful. Get up, Charles; wash your hands, comb your hair, and get ready for breakfast. What are we to have for breakfast? Bread and milk

This is the best food for little boys. Sometimes we have coffee or tea, and toast. Sometimes we have cakes.

James, hold your spoon in your right hand; and if you use a knife and fork, hold the knife in your right hand. Do not eat fast: hungry boys are apt to eat fast, like the pigs. Never waste your bread; bread is gained by the sweat of the brow. Your father plants or sows corn; corn grows in the field; when it is ripe, it is cut, and put in the barn; then it is thrashed out of the ears, and sent to a mill: the mill grinds it, and the bolter separates the bran from the flour. Flour is wet with water or milk; and with a little yeast or leaven, it is raised, and made light; this is called dough: dough is baked in an oven, or pan, and makes bread.

THE SISTERS.

Emily, look at the flowers in the garden. What a charming sight. How the tulips adorn the borders of the alleys, dressing them with gayety. Soon the sweet pinks will deck the beds; and the fragrant roses perfume the air. Take care of the sweet-williams, the jonquils, and the artemisia. See the honey-suckle, how it winds about the column, and climbs along the margin of the windows. Now it is in bloom. how fragrant the air around it; how sweet the perfume, after a gentle shower, or amidst the soft dews of the evening. Such are the charms of youth, when robed in innocence; such is the bloom of life, when decked with modesty, and a sweet temper.——Come, my child, let me hear your song.

The Rose.

The rose had been wash'd, lately wash'd in a show'r,
That Julia to Emma convey'd;
A plentiful moisture encumber'd the flow'r,
And weigh'd down its beautiful head.

G 2

CHAPTER 9

READING
AND SOCIAL POLICY

F OR MORE THAN A DECADE, through one federally funded program after another (Right-to-Read, Upward Bound, Basic Skills, Head Start, Reading is Fundamental), we have been made aware of the existence of a serious reading problem. Twenty million adults have been reported to be only functionally literate. Seventeen-year-old students have been found by the National Assessment of Educational Progress to have declined in reading comprehension, particularly on the higher level skills of interpretation and critical reading (NAEP, 1981). The decline in verbal SAT scores over the past 15 years has also been used as an index of decline in reading at the higher levels.

In this chapter I consider whether these reading problems are indeed serious. If they are, what are their social implications?

Before discussing the seriousness of the problem, it is important to note some constructive developments. More people have achieved more years of schooling and hence a higher reading development than ever. Indeed, according to the 1940 U.S. census, the average school grade completed by adults of 25 years and over was 8th grade. Today the average level would be close to 11th or 12th grade.

The drop-out rate from high school has also decreased markedly. Today about 80 percent of those who enter high school graduate. And the increase in entrance into college is equally impressive. About half of high school graduates are enrolled in some form of college or post-secondary education. So, there is evidence both of great success and of serious failure.

One can see the failure as part of the success. As the average achievement goes up, the range increases. This was shown for the first four grades by Ilg and Ames (1950). On the Gray Oral Test, 7-year-old boys averaged 2.9, and ranged from 1.6 to 3.7; 8-year-olds averaged 3.4 and ranged from 1.9 to 6.1; and 9-year-olds averaged 4.0 and ranged from 1.4 to 8.0. This seems to be consistent throughout: the higher the grade, the higher the average achievement and the wider the range and variation. The higher achievers seem to keep rising, and those at the bottom seem to make little progress.

There are tragic aspects to this phenomenon—for society and for the individuals who are not developing according to expectations of national norms or expectations based on their own cognitive abilities. The statistics from the Office of Basic Skills, formerly Right-to-Read, paint a very sad picture of severe gaps in reading achievement, most of which cannot be attributed to deficiencies in cognitive development. The variety of causes behind such gaps between achievement and ability have been documented by presidential and other federally appointed committees (National Academy of Education Reading Committee; Carroll and Chall, 1975; National Advisory Committee on Dyslexia and Reading Disorders, 1970).

Many say that those who react strongly to these failures overlook the fact that half of any group has to be below the average. Indeed, there have been criticisms of remedial reading teachers for their strong drive to make everyone literate, in spite of the great difficulties many students have in learning. Why not relieve such people of the agony of learning to read and educate them instead by TV and the other electronic media (Postman, 1970). But in his book *Teaching as a Conserving Activity* Postman seems to reverse himself. In one chapter after another he asserts that TV and other such media are not legitimate means for educating people. Indeed, his argument for reading and against TV goes as far as stating that reading develops the brain and TV does not (Postman, 1979).

Some day it may be possible to be fully educated although unable to read. But not as things stand now. Complete courses of study on TV discs or tapes do not yet exist.

What is considered a serious reading problem depends now upon who defines it, and, perhaps even more, for whom it is being defined. I suggest, therefore, that reading is a social policy issue of the highest importance—not only to schools but to business and industry, and, of course, to the person who has the problem, who is below the average and below where he or she can be intellectually.

Two basic questions are important here.

First, how much reading ability is presently achieved by the average student upon graduating from high school, the most typical (average) school level?

Second, how much variation at the lower end can be acceptable? And how much of a gap is detrimental to the person and to society?

1. What is the average reading level now? From best estimates, the average for high-school graduates is probably around a 12th grade reading level. This means, in general, the ability to read materials up to a level of difficulty of *The New York Times, Time,* and *Newsweek,* and the serious news in local newspapers. This level (see Chapters 2 and 5, for descriptions of Stage 4) means, on the whole, skills sufficient for the first year of college. With a 12th grade reading level, students can move on to further education if they choose to do so— reading well enough to cope with textbooks in the first year of a 4-year college, junior college, or a post-secondary technical school.[1]

2. How great a reading gap can be tolerated—by the person and by society? This does not have clear-cut answers, because answers here cannot be totally objective. But for children and young people in school, as well as for adults who have completed school, it would seem that the larger the reading gap, the more troublesome it is for society and for the person.

For those in school who are still learning to read as well as learning academic and other subjects, several criteria are essen-

[1]With assistance from a college remedial program, students with low reading levels have been able to raise them (Cross, 1981).

tial for judging the seriousness of a reading gap and the need for special help.

a. How far is the achievement below the student's grade placement and the expected score based on national norms?

b. How far is the student's achievement below his or her mental ability?

c. How far is the student's reading level below the level of the textbooks used in various subjects?

Most reading specialists agree that two years below grade level is a significant gap. And a full reading stage below expectation can be used as an index of retardation serious enough to interfere with the student's general educational development as well as his or her further reading development.

There is need for help, therefore, when people are as much as one stage below where they should be by chronological age, grade, and ability. If they should be at Stage 2, and are still at Stage 1, it can be extremely difficult for the child and for the teacher. The student will not be able to function adequately in content learning, although inherently talented and even gifted intellectually.[2]

An even greater gap exists in the intermediate grades where Stage 3 reading is needed to study the content subjects. A child lagging behind on a Stage 2 level of reading with only the skills to read easy familiar text will have difficulty in reading any of the science and social studies textbooks assigned to these grades. Indeed, this is one of the reasons for the critical nature of the 4th grade. It is at this grade that many children who have not until then been picked up as having reading problems are first noticed. The reading problem then is very serious, because reading is so heavily used for learning. Similarly, if school assignments require textbooks at the Stage 4 level and a student can read only up to a Stage 3 level, he or she will have difficulty.

For adults, the criterion of difficulty and need for help

---

[2]Even with the greater availability of remedial services for children with reading and learning disabilities in schools during the past decade, there has been no real breakthrough in how to educate these children while they are learning how to read, i.e., they are not receiving an education in the content subjects as are others of their age. The children whose parents read to them from literature and their textbooks have a better chance. The Kurzweil reading machine for the blind, which reads books by computer (1978), may be an important source.

would be based first on work needs, i.e., sufficient reading development to meet job requirements. The minimal level seems to be growing as work becomes more technical and skilled. Studies of the readability of work manuals in the armed forces have found the easiest material to be the Army cook's manual requiring approximately a 7th–8th grade reading level (Sticht, 1975). Most Navy technical manuals require an 11th–12th grade reading level.

Two other criteria are important for judging essential reading needs of adults: civic needs, such as the ability to read income tax forms and instructions, applications for health services, and so forth, as well as to read about world, state, and local events from newspapers and magazines; and personal needs, such as writing letters, reading to one's children, and reading what most others read.

The student in elementary and high school also has civic and personal needs for reading. Should his achievement be too low to satisfy them, he may have problems with personal and social adjustment (Meyer, 1977).

Table 9-1 helps pull some of these criteria together for children and adults. It can be used for estimating the need for special help for both students and adults because, essentially, both share the same problem, the gap between their achievement and their needs. The various columns should be filled in as fully as possible for each person who is having difficulty.

For estimating achievement, one of these two sources is suggested: grade equivalent score on a standardized norm-referenced test, or the grade level (readability) of materials the person is able to read. If not available, use what is available to estimate an approximate level of functioning. The grade level is then translated into stage level (see Table 5-3, page 92, Chapter 5). The second estimate of achievement based on the readability level of the materials the student can read should also be converted into a stage level.

Four estimates of reading needs are suggested—at school, at work, for citizenship, and for personal needs. Either grade level or stage level may be used for estimating, although we suggest stage levels because they are broader and should be easier to deal with. For school needs, we suggest that if the students are in a program where they are functioning on na-

Table 9-1
ESTIMATING GAPS BETWEEN READING NEED AND ACHIEVEMENT

| NAME | ESTIMATED ACHIEVEMENT | | | READING NEEDS | | |
	NORM-REFERENCED STANDARDIZED ACHIEVEMENT TEST (1)	READABILITY LEVELS OF MATERIALS THAT CAN BE READ (2)	AT SCHOOL (3)	AT WORK (4)	FOR CITIZENSHIP (5)	FOR PERSONAL REQUIREMENTS (6)
	Stage level	Grade level	Reading stage	Reading stage	Reading stage	Reading stage
	Grade equivalent	Stage level				

163

tional norms, the national norm should be used as the school need. For such students, it can, in all probability, be expected that the textbooks in the content areas would be on a level appropriate for the "average" student who tests on national norms.[3]

The estimate for "at work" may be the reading level or stage level needed for the job held or job anticipated or desired. An estimate of reading level requirements for particular jobs may be made by making a readability check of the reading required on the job (Sticht, 1975).

Citizenship needs include reading of materials for informed voting, filling out government forms, reading signs in public places, newspapers, and so on. These are the same for all individuals, and as things stand now, these forms average out at about 11th–12th grade level, or Stage 4 reading. Personal needs include reading letters, the TV guide, books to children, newspapers and magazines, and so on. Overall, these materials require about a 9th–10th grade level, also Stage 4.

After the various columns are filled out, a judgment can be made as to whether the gap between needs and achievement is serious in one or more areas of need.

These gaps, if not alleviated, can cause great hardship. For the person it means employment difficulties, and feelings of inadequacy and incompetence that grow if not taken care of. When the gap is lessened, the person becomes more confident and can achieve in general academic areas on a level equivalent to intellectual potential. When the reading problem is not taken care of, many kinds of difficulty can ensue, ranging from difficulty in obtaining a job and being promoted to difficulties with emotional and social adjustments.[4] All agree that there are usually losses in further education, in work, and in the quality of life.[5]

Remediation is expensive, and the later it is undertaken, the more expensive it is. Prevention through improved pro-

---

[3]Where the average reading scores are a year or more above the national norms, the gap for those with reading problems will be greater.

[4]Many studies have shown that a significantly higher proportion of reading disability problems are found among young delinquents and adults in prisons.

[5]Lloyd (1976) has documented that early reading failure, if not treated, leads to continued reading failure, failure in academic subjects, and early dropping out of school. [See also Bloom (1976) for similar correlations.]

grams would be the best solution to the problem. But remedial treatment cannot be totally avoided because problems in reading are similar to problems of health. Prevention does much, but it does not eliminate all problems.

Prevention plans need to be broadbased and include improvements in classroom instruction in methods and materials suitable for all kinds of students at all levels. Books must be highly accessible to children in school and at home, and time must be set aside for reading them. Regular assessment and careful testing must be available for those falling behind. The earlier a problem is found, the more effective its treatment, and the more cost effective.

In summary, learning to read is not like learning history. It is not disastrous to be doing poorly on certain historical periods in a particular grade. Reading is a complex skill, each level building upon the previous one, and most other learnings depending on it.

Reading is pervasive in its influence and its effects, and when people fail in reading, it becomes a personal tragedy as well as a societal problem. Ironically, the number of reading failures is growing because more students stay in school longer and are expected to achieve more. When more students dropped out earlier, and when jobs were available for those without diplomas, poor readers suffered less. But that time is gone.

CHAPTER 10

CONCLUSIONS AND RECOMMENDATIONS

MARCEL MARCEAU, the great French mime, does a 1-minute work on the stages of man. For that brief time, a haunting quiet settles over the audience, as Marceau transforms himself from babbling infant to child, youth, adult, middle-aged, and finally old man.

Stage development schemes are deep in our culture. The most famous, of course, which probably also takes a minute to recite, is Shakespeare's "ages of man." Most of the modern schemes would probably take no more than a minute to summarize. In psychology, there is the developmental scheme of Freud, biologically based and encompassing the emotions and the intellect (Wolff, 1960). Gesell's stages of development (Gesell, Ilg, and Ames, 1956) were concerned with social, emotional, and academic changes based on observations of thousands of infants and children; Robert Havighurst's scheme (1972) stressed developmental needs, and Erik Erikson's (1964) stressed changes in identity.

Probably more than any others, the scheme of Jean Piaget covering stages of cognitive development has had the greatest current impact. His scheme influenced Lawrence Kohlberg's (1969) theory of moral development as well as many others. But, oddly, although the work of teaching is essentially con-

166

cerned with development, little of Piaget's scheme has been applied to education and reading.

Stage development schemes for reading were published by Gray, Gates, and Russell, all reading specialists; and by Ilg and Ames, a medical doctor and a child psychologist; and by Rozin and Gleitman, linguists (see Chapter 7 and Appendix B).

In a real sense, many of the important concepts and terms in reading are developmental. We talk of retarded readers and precocious readers. We talk of beginning reading as distinguished from later reading. Good readers make fast progress and poor readers progress slowly. The earliest books were called primers, until pre-primers were invented. For more than 100 years, reading textbooks have been graded from 1 to 8 for the 8 years of elementary school. More recently, grades have been turned into levels, with as many as 15 levels for the 8 grades.[1]

Developmental concepts are used also in standardized reading tests, particularly in norm-referenced tests. The standardized scores are converted into various measures of development, e.g., grade equivalent, percentiles, and stanines. The items selected for the tests for children of different grades also follow a developmental progression—from simple picture-word matching for Grade 1 to interpretive questions on abstract, technical, and literary selections for the upper grades (Auerbach, 1971; Popp and Lieberman, 1977).

The concept behind the readability measurement used to estimate the difficulty of textbooks is also developmental. It assumes that the higher readability scores generally represent greater difficulty and that texts with such high scores require more mature reading ability.

In spite of all of these different aspects of development, we seem not to have an overall picture of what it means for a reader to advance from one level of reading to the next and on to the highest levels of mature reading. I have sought such a picture through the proposed reading stages scheme. I hope that it helps teachers and researchers to understand what it means to read like a 1st grader, a 4th, or a 6th, or a 12th

[1]A publisher of reading textbooks has made this translation available from grade levels to levels.

grader. What is the difference in the quality of the reading, in the books that can be read, and the uses to which reading can be put at successive points of development? It seems to me that a developmental scheme for reading, in the tradition of Piaget and other developmentalists, would be of use also in understanding those whose reading development is significantly below or above the present norms.

I assume that teachers who have a clear concept of reading at the different stages can provide the appropriate instruction, whether the student is older or younger, ahead or behind expectation. By relying upon broader, qualitative characteristics, I think it possible to interiorize the stage distinctions. A deep knowledge of these can lead to more effective testing and teaching. I do not intend that the finer differentiations now used for testing, grading of textbooks, and for materials selection be discontinued, only that the stages be added to our thinking in order to bring a broader view to reading instruction, one that encourages a deeper understanding of reading and how it develops.

I present the reading stages scheme primarily as an aid to teachers, textbook publishers, test developers, and reading researchers. Although the scheme has paralleled findings from psychological and linguistic research, from research in the neurosciences, and from educational research and practice, it should serve mainly as a metaphor and as an aid to theory and research. I hope it will become a useful guide for what to teach when, as well as for what and when to test. It should not be used for setting inflexible standards for children at given ages.

Generally, it does not mean that children should be expected to read only at one stage level at a time. While their major instruction may be at their developmental reading stage, they will generally find it useful and instructive to do some reading below and above this level.

Indeed, it should be remembered that in using this developmental scheme, as all developmental schemes, it cannot be used inflexibly. Generally it should be emphasized that there is more than one way to reach any given reading stage. The same stage level can be reached by using different processes. Some individuals may, when confronted by a difficult reading task, function on a lower stage than is normal for them. And all people at a given grade or age should not be expected to be on the same reading stage level, nor should we expect all to be at the age and in the grade that characterize the stage.

I would hope that the scheme and its elaborations—the tables, figures, and illustrations—serve to give teachers, researchers, and others concerned with reading development the sense of being part of the building of a magnificent structure. In a sense, each teacher adds by putting a brick upon another brick in a child's reading development. And together all build a great structure.

RECOMMENDATIONS

I will not repeat here all the recommendations for research and practice made in the previous chapters. Instead, I will mention only a few and concentrate on some major issues.

1. The first problem needing research is the effects of the great increase, in only 40 years, of the average educational attainment and reading achievement from an 8th grade level to about a 12th grade level. We need to know more about what such an average gain brings to those who make it and to those who do not. What hardships befall those who are below the average, and what blessings accrue to those on the level and above?

Is it possible to bring up the bottom end of the normal curve for those now below the average? Is it possible, for example, to have not 50 percent of the population below the present reading average of 11th–12th grade level, but less —closer to 20 or 10 percent or somewhat below? Benjamin Bloom and his associates (1976) claim that with mastery learning (special help as soon as needed) about 80 percent can learn to a level of the A and B student. Does this include the highly demanding Stage 4 reading?

My experience with problem readers at all levels has led me to conclude that with appropriate testing and individual remedial teaching, almost all can learn to read to their potential (their mental ability) or near it. As a matter of social policy, we must ask the cost of leaving this great variation as it is. Can we afford to have so many young people reading so poorly that they cannot be educated in academic subjects? Can we afford to have so many adolescents who read so poorly, who cannot get and hold jobs, and who remain unemployed? Can we afford the growing proportion of illiterates in the volunteer army? Can we afford to have significantly higher numbers of poor readers in prisons and correctional institutions? Although few people claim that poor reading leads directly to delinquency, many studies show that offenders have significantly lower reading scores than comparable adults although their general mental ability is the same as the wider population.

It would seem that investigation is needed into why some people's reading lags behind while the general educational and reading level of the population improves. In all probability, this is a source of despair and hopelessness, particularly because reading gaps are found more often among the less privileged—among minorities, among ethnic Americans, and among those of lower socio-economic status.

2. The matter of pacing and progression needs study and analysis. If so many must go so much farther, then the benefits of an earlier start and a faster progression need to be examined more seriously. There has been a trend away from a later to an earlier reading start during the past decade. Parents have also been accepted as partners in teaching reading, when only 10 years ago they were discouraged from teaching their children to read. The effects of an earlier start need study, particularly since most of the research available indicates that it is beneficial, even when comparisons are made in the 6th grade (Smethurst, 1975; Durkin, 1974–1975; Fowler, 1971).

Some evidence also suggests that the declining difficulty of reading and subject matter textbooks over a 30-year period has contributed to the decline in verbal scores on the SAT (Chall, Conard, and Harris, 1977). The problem of optimal difficulty for students at different grades needs to be studied. The continued decline in difficulty of subject textbooks for at least the past three decades at the upper elementary and high school years makes the need for investigations of the issues even greater.

3. What should children read at different stages of reading development? How much reading do they need to do to progress optimally from stage to stage?

Reading textbooks (basal readers) have tended to focus on reading method, i.e., what skills to teach at certain points, and readability (the vocabulary and syntax) of selections. Less attention has been paid to selections to be read and when they should be read for optimal development.

Our analysis of the course of reading development indicates that we need to be more concerned about what children read. Indeed, it would appear that the present preference for narrative in the basal readers throughout the elementary school grades may not enhance fully the development of the successive reading stages. At the intermediate grades, when the emphasis in most reading programs is comprehension (Stage 3), it seems that expository materials are also needed for practice.

Would the use of authentic, adult literature, introduced earlier, give students a sense of the seriousness of reading? Have we perhaps put too much emphasis on fun as an incentive for reading? Perhaps children's readers might do better to offer a contrast from the "fun appeal" of most TV and provide, instead, literature of enduring value.

4. Investigation is needed on the effects of reading on writing and composition and of writing and composition on reading. A growing body of literature suggests that one enhances the other and the dynamics of the interactions need further investigation.

5. Who should teach reading?

For the preschooler and beginner, should it be the parents or the school? Or both? For the middle grades and high school, should it be reading teachers, the English teachers, or subject matter teachers? And when there is trouble, should the reading specialist or the learning disability specialist be called in?

Most of the research seems to indicate that parents contribute considerably to reading development by reading to their child and otherwise encouraging his or her interest and skill. What we need to know is how to help parents do this.

There is a need for clarifying the role of content teachers

with regard to their responsibilities for reading and also for writing. In middle and upper grades, there seems to be a lack of clarity about the role of books and other print materials in the learning of content subjects. There is even less clarity about the role they should play in the development of general reading ability, particularly at Stage 3 and above.

Less confusion now exists about the roles of reading- and learning-disability teachers than there was a decade ago (Chall, 1978), but it has not cleared altogether. Both reading- and learning-disability specialists seem to need more opportunities for collaborating with classroom teachers. Different kinds of specialists are needed to teach and guide students in the long developmental progression. It would be worthwhile to plan for the collaboration of various specialists needed at particular stages of development for the class and the individual student.

6. Are we perhaps having students do too much of their reading by examination?

From the very start in Grade 1, children seem to be answering questions in worksheets and workbooks by circling, drawing lines, and selecting alternative answers to questions following pictures, sentences, and passages. Even when they do not have to mark their answers in workbooks or on worksheets, they are asked question after question orally by the teacher if she follows the teacher's manual of the series. Meanwhile the children read lines and then pages silently in their readers.

This is a fairly modern phenomenon which stems from several historical roots. First was the discovery in the 1920s that accuracy in oral reading does not assure proficiency in silent reading comprehension (Thorndike, 1917). This began the press to read silently for meaning from the beginning. (See in this connection the reading stages schemes of Gray, Gates, and Russell in Appendix A.) In the 60 years since, the preference for early silent reading has changed little.

Second came the press for individual and small group instruction within the same class as a way of adjusting to the range in individual differences. This also encouraged the use of worksheets and reading exercises as a way of having some children working independently while the teacher worked with a group. Third, factor analyses of reading comprehension have pointed to the existence of different kinds of comprehension (main idea, details, inference, and so on) which brought more and more varieties of questions attached to reading selections to assure the acquisition of these comprehension skills (Davis, 1968; Thorndike, 1973–74).

One may ask whether many students don't come away from several years of this with the idea that reading is doing worksheets and getting the right answers. Indeed, Joyce Maynard, in a revealing article in the *New York Times Magazine* when she was about 20, said that her reading as a student consisted mainly of working in one of the most widely used reading kits. She tried to finish "purple" before her friends did. After a while she answered the questions, she said, without reading the selections. She had never been asked to read a book in all of her high school years.

An ethnographic study of reading in selected 5th grade classes found that the best results came from classes where there were larger groups discussing selections that they had read (MacDonald, 1976). Other studies (Durkin, 1979; Stallings, 1975) have questioned the value of so many individual worksheets. While originally a creative response to a real need, should we not now ask whether we have perhaps overdone and overused the individual short selection with questions, the reading quiz sheet?

The respect for and the love of reading must be built from the cradle on. We add much to the enduring habits of reading by giving more realistic experience with reading, that is, the reading of fascinating stories, accounts, biographies, poetry, science, history, and the like.

7. Our final dilemma is how best to deal with individual variation, how best to assure the development of all students, those moving faster and those slower, through the reading stages.

Most classrooms vary considerably in the reading abilities of their students. Adjustments are generally made within the classroom for meeting the varied instructional needs. In the elementary grades, the usual pattern is to have three groups using different levels of readers and workbooks. Further differentiation may be made with individual worksheets. In junior and senior high schools, adjustments are made by program variation, i.e., homogeneous grouping by classes and by curriculum.

Because some teachers have found it difficult to instruct several groups and large numbers of individuals in the same class, interest has been developing in procedures for teaching larger groups and an entire class.

Some recent research suggests that teaching larger groups with greater use of oral reading has beneficial effects (Stallings, 1975). Should we perhaps try experimentally to have the slowest group with the rest of the class, or at least with the average? I have on many occasions found that the slowest learn about half of the words in the top group's stories, without direct teaching. They seem to do this by watching and listening to the top group instead of concentrating on their own work.

Can the best readers in the top groups work with the others, adding spark and zest to the slower developing readers? How can we assure that the "slow" are not accepted as slow throughout their school careers, that they are given intense instruction when they need it, in order to complete the full course of their reading development? How can we assure that those who are below the norm do not fall through the cracks? Is it possible to make the various prevention and testing programs work, to find early those who have difficulties, and to treat them without instilling an undue sense of failure?

EPILOGUE

I SHOULD LIKE TO DRAW my thoughts together, but not too tightly because essentially this work must be left unfinished. I offer here no new conclusions, only a few concerns, a few cautions.

My first concern is that the age and grade ranges for the successive stages not be viewed as prescriptions. They are meant to be only rough estimates of expected progress for typical individuals—not for all individuals, nor for all times. I considered omitting them, relying only on the stage sequences. But I decided against it because teaching reading, more than any other responsibility of the schools, has from earliest times relied on grade level designations. Their use, then, could help clarify the reading stages. I hope that the stages and their estimated grade ranges will serve in a manner similar to height and weight charts, as rough criteria in the knowledge that different individuals reach them at different times, but helpful as confirmations of adequate or inadequate development.

My second concern is with the role of emotions and human interactions in reading development. We can all appreciate the beginner's fear of failing to learn, and therefore we can agree that the child's first teachers must be good and gentle. But risks and fears exist at all stages of reading development. Each reading act is a new act. It requires a new integration, a new understanding. The tasks change with successive stages, but each is challenging for the reader at that particular level of development. Therefore, it is important for readers at all stages to feel free to try, to make mistakes, to try again, and to know that help will be given generously when their own best efforts fail. Students at the highest stages need understanding teachers and mentors just as first graders reading their first primers do.

My final thought concerns the limits of reading development. Is the range proposed here too optimistic for most? Can most people reach Stage 5?

These questions cannot be answered now, for we have not yet provided the optimal medical and environmental conditions that research has shown to be beneficial for highest reading development. But even if such conditions can be made available universally, will there not be limits? Will it ever be possible for all people to read at Stage 5, or even 4? Don't these advanced stages depend primarily on language and cognition? Again, it seems to me that we will not know until we try. Much data shows that language and mental ability are highly correlated with reading ability, particularly at the higher stages. And there is general agreement that the limits of literacy are set by cognition and language. Yet some evidence also shows that training in and growth of literacy affects linguistic and cognitive development.

It would seem, therefore, to be worthwhile to try—to try to bring as many people as possible to the highest levels of literacy. This is particularly needed in a post-industrial age when fewer people are engaged in manufacturing and more in making and distributing knowledge. Indeed, an age that is devoted to high-speed computers and word processors cannot afford to settle for less.

REALITY OF THE READING STAGES: EVIDENCE FROM PSYCHOLOGY, LINGUISTICS, AND THE NEUROSCIENCES

THIS APPENDIX CONTAINS summaries of the research relevant to the proposed stages from psychology, linguistics, and the neurosciences. The psychological research is discussed under visual perception and other psychological processes, eye movements, and eye-voice span. The linguistic research is grouped under phonology, syntax, and semantic development, along with the relationship of reading and listening comprehension. The last section presents research on neurological factors.

The evidence from psychology related to the reading stages is not meant to be exhaustive. We relied most heavily on the classic and more recent accepted works, such as those of Buswell (1922) on eye movements, those of E. Gibson and her associates (1960, 1962, 1972) on perception, and those of H. Levin (1979) on eye-voice span. To assure that we had not overlooked the most essential studies, we searched through such widely accepted works on the psychology of reading as Vernon (1970 and 1977) and Gibson and Levin (1975).

PSYCHOLOGICAL PROCESSES

As evidence for the proposed reading stages, we turn first to the research on basic perceptual processes. At what age, for example, can children perceive that given words and letters are the same or different? At what age can children use visual information not directly in focus? A review of available research on these and other aspects of visual perception indicates a steady growth with age and school grade. Table 2-2, A-1, summarizes these processes indicating their development with age, grade, and reading stage.

In Table A-1, we note that the ability to discriminate letter-like forms is available to most children as early as Stage 0 and is generally fully accomplished by Stage 1 (Gibson, Gibson, Pick, and Osser, 1962). The rate of matching letters visually develops somewhat more slowly, beginning at Stage 1. Rate of matching letters increases by Stage 2 and continues to increase through Stage 3 (to Grade 4). By Stages 4 and 5 letter matching is done at a very fast rate (Doehring, 1976).

To what extent does the development of the visual ability to discriminate letter features depend upon normal development with its normal interactions with visual stimuli, including pictures? And to what extent does it depend on training? Some of the researchers seem to place first importance on growth (Gibson and Levin, 1975); others, on the child's experience, particularly with print (Vernon, 1971).

Table A-1 UNDERLYING PROCESSES FOR READING AS THEY RELATE TO THE READING STAGES

STAGE	PROCESSING OF GRAPHOLOGICAL FEATURES OF LETTERS	PERIPHERAL PROCESSING OF VISUAL INFORMATION	SELECTIVE ATTENTION	USE OF ORTHOGRAPHIC AND PHONOLOGICAL RULE SYSTEMS	RATE OF AUDITORY VISUAL MATCHING	USE OF SEMANTIC AND SYNTACTIC CONSTRAINTS IN WORD SEQUENCES	RATE OF EXTRACTING MEANING FROM WORDS AND PICTURES	RATE OF VISUAL WORD SEARCH (SCANNING)
Stage 0 Children up to Age 6 Grades K to 1.5	Increasing specificity in discrimination of letter-like forms (Gibson, et al., 1962). Children know what to look for in scanning figures, numbers, single and double letters by grade 1.5 (Doehring, 1976).	Cannot simultaneously process foveal and peripheral visual information (Gibson & Olum, 1960; Hochberg, 1970; Sticht, 1974)	No specific ages or grades were given but					
Stage 1 Grades 1.5 to 2.5	Increasing specificity in discrimination of letter-like forms (Gibson, et al. 1962). Letter matching faster than word matching (Doehring, 1976).	Cannot simultaneously process foveal and peripheral visual information (See Stage 0)	the findings are reported in developmental terms by Sticht (1974): 1. Processing of preattentive information that guides the focus of attention and permits the child to search displays more efficiently and effectively improves with age (Neisser, 1967)	Familiar 3-letter words and syllables matched in familiar words* faster than consonant strings (Doehring, 1976; Gibson, et al., 1963) Scanning rate for letters in syllables and words improves rapidly till grade 2.5 (Doehring, 1976)	Comparatively slow rate even in familiar words* (Biemiller, 1977–78).	From grade 1.5 on, words in sentences are read faster than random words (Doehring, 1976).		

179

Table A-1 UNDERLYING PROCESSES FOR READING AS THEY RELATE TO THE READING STAGES (cont.)

STAGE	PROCESSING OF GRAPHOLOGICAL FEATURES OF LETTERS	PERIPHERAL PROCESSING OF VISUAL INFORMATION	SELECTIVE ATTENTION	USE OF ORTHOGRAPHIC AND PHONOLOGICAL RULE SYSTEMS	RATE OF AUDITORY VISUAL MATCHING	USE OF SEMANTIC AND SYNTACTIC CONSTRAINTS IN WORD SEQUENCES	RATE OF EXTRACTING MEANING FROM WORDS AND PICTURES	RATE OF VISUAL WORD SEARCH (SCANNING)
Stage 2 Grades 2.5 to Beginning Grade 4	Letter matching faster than word matching till grade 3 (Doehring, 1976). Rate of visual matching increases till grade 6 (Doehring, 1976).	Developing simultaneous processing of foveal and peripheral visual information (See Stage 0)	2. Attention becomes less captive and more exploratory (E.J. Gibson, 1969) 3. Exploratory attention becomes more systematic and less random (E.J. Gibson, 1969)	Random words read as fast as letters after grade 2.5 (Doehring, 1976). By end of grade 2 children have a visual sense of what makes up a real word. (Golinkoff, 1974).	Rate for familiar words increases rapidly to grade 2.5 and rate for syllables increases rapidly to grade 3 (Doehring, 1976).	From grade 2.5 on, words in sentences are read faster than single letters (Doehring, 1976). From grade 3 on, words in sentences are read faster than words in 7th order approximation to discourse (Doehring, 1976).	2nd graders are faster at matching pairs of pictures than pairs of words (Gibson. et al., 1972). Rate in picture-word matching increases from grade 2 to 4 (Gibson, et al., 1972).	Search rate is slower in grade 2 than grades 4, 6 and adults (Leslie and Calfee, 1971).

Table A-1 UNDERLYING PROCESSES FOR READING AS THEY RELATE TO THE READING STAGES (cont.)

STAGE	PROCESSING OF GRAPHOLOGICAL FEATURES OF LETTERS	PERIPHERAL PROCESSING OF VISUAL INFORMATION	SELECTIVE ATTENTION	USE OF ORTHOGRAPHIC AND PHONOLOGICAL RULE SYSTEMS	RATE OF AUDITORY VISUAL MATCHING	USE OF SEMANTIC AND SYNTACTIC CONSTRAINTS IN WORD SEQUENCES	RATE OF EXTRACTING MEANING FROM WORDS AND PICTURES	RATE OF VISUAL WORD SEARCH (SCANNING)
Stage 3 Grades 4 to 8	Word matching is the same or faster than letter matching (Doehring, 1976). Rate of visual matching increases till grade 6 (Doehring, 1976).	Should be able to process foveal and peripheral visual information (See Stage 0)	4. Attention becomes more selective and exclusive (E.J. Gibson, 1969)	Scanning rate for letters in syllables and words continues to improve slowly until grades 5 or 6 (Doehring, 1976). CVC and CVCC words matched visually as fast as letters by grade 5 and syllables as fast as words and letters by grade 6 (Doehring, 1976).	Rate for syllables continues to improve, but slowly, till grade 7 (Doehring, 1976). Between grades 3 and 6 able readers are faster than less able readers (Biemiller, 1977–78).	Established		Search rate steadily increases through grades 4 and 6 to adults (Leslie and Calfee, 1971).

181

Table A-1 UNDERLYING PROCESSES FOR READING AS THEY RELATE TO THE READING STAGES (cont.)

STAGE	PROCESSING OF GRAPHOLOGICAL FEATURES OF LETTERS	PERIPHERAL PROCESSING OF VISUAL INFORMATION	SELECTIVE ATTENTION	USE OF ORTHOGRAPHIC AND PHONOLOGICAL RULE SYSTEMS	RATE OF AUDITORY VISUAL MATCHING	USE OF SEMANTIC AND SYNTACTIC CONSTRAINTS IN WORD SEQUENCES	RATE OF EXTRACTING MEANING FROM WORDS AND PICTURES	RATE OF VISUAL WORD SEARCH (SCANNING)
Stage 4 Grades 9 to 12	Word matching is faster than letter matching (Doehring, 1976).	Able to simultaneously process foveal and peripheral visual information (See Stage 0)		Established	Word matching is faster than syllable matching till grade 10 (Doehring, 1976).	Established		Search rate steadily increases (Leslie and Calfee, 1971).
Stage 5 College Level and Adult	Established	Able to simultaneously process foveal and peripheral visual information (See Stage 0)		Established	Established	Established	Adults are faster at matching word pairs than matching picture pairs (Gibson et al. 1972).	Established

*Biemiller (1977–78) used random letter matching as a general index of rate. He suggests that there appears to be an underlying verbal ability to identify print items quickly irrespective of context and orthographic information which improves between grade 2 and adult reading.

182

The ability to process and use visual information not directly in focus but from the periphery of vision (Gibson and Olum, 1960; Hochberg, 1970; Sticht et al., 1974) occurs first during Stage 2 and appears to be fully established by the middle of Stage 3. Because reading first becomes fluent during Stage 2, it would appear that some processing by peripheral vision is needed for fluency to develop.

Attentional processes appear to develop during Stage 1 and Stage 2 and to become more effective during Stage 3 and later. LaBerge and Samuels (1974) also suggest that in reading it is necessary to coordinate shifts in attention to the many component processes which make up reading. Therefore, if any one of the processes—decoding, for example—requires too much attention, it may exceed the attentional capacity of the reader and may result in poor reading.

The ability to use knowledge of spelling patterns and of phonological rules seems to begin in Stage 1 and is fully established by the end of Stage 2, but it continues to become more efficient during the first part of Stage 3 (Gibson, Osser, and Pick, 1963; Doehring, 1976; Biemiller, 1977–1978). It appears that some knowledge of phonological rules functions for Stage 1. But it seems that only when the phonological and orthographic rule systems are fully functional and efficient does reading at Stage 3 and above occur.

Studies of the use of semantic, syntactic, and decoding constraints show that by the time the child is at the beginning of Stage 2, he is able to integrate decoding with the use of contextual clues (Clay, 1966; Biemiller, 1970). This ability seems to improve during Stage 2 [Doehring (1976) found differences up to Grade 3].

PSYCHOLOGICAL CHANGES IN THE READER BY READING STAGES[1] (see Table A-1)

Stage 0, prereading, includes research findings for children up to age 6. These studies appear to show an increasing specificity in discriminating letter-like forms with age. In processing visual features of letters and numbers, children of this age ap-

---

[1]The results are for "average" children at these ages or grades. Many children develop faster or slower on these processes, so characteristics at any level should not be interpreted as representing all children.

pear to know what to look for when they scan figures, numbers, and single and double letters. However, they cannot simultaneously process visual information from both the fovea (sharpest point of vision) and the periphery of vision.

There is no experimental evidence that most children of this age are able to make use of the spelling and sound rules, that is, to learn phonics. Nor is there experimental evidence that they can integrate decoding with semantic and/or syntactic constraints. In other words, they cannot yet read in the sense of Stage 1 reading. However, in her study of oral reading errors of young beginning readers, Clay (1967) found that they do try to guess at a word when pretending to "read" a familiar book, using semantic and syntactic constraints. A case study by Bissex (1980) of the reading and writing development of her son from age 5 to age 10 confirms this.

Stage 1 includes the research evidence on children from Grade 1 to Grade 2.5. We note particularly those studies that found changes in processing skills and abilities as compared to the preceding and following stages. The research on perceptual processes indicates an increasing specificity during Stage 1 in the discrimination of letter-like forms. Letter matching is faster than it was in Stage 0.

At Stage 1, readers do not yet simultaneously process foveal and peripheral visual information. Nor do they make full use of spelling- and sound-rule systems, although these are beginning to develop. At Stage 1, children seem to be able to match familiar three-letter words and syllables faster than strings of consonants, indicating that they are beginning to "interiorize" the alphabetic principle. Also, they match letters faster than words, and they do so until Grade 2.5 (the beginning of Stage 2).

During Stage 1 and particularly after Grade 1.5, most children read words faster when they are in the context of a sentence than when they are isolated.[2] But they continue to read single letters faster than they read words in sentences until Grade 2 or 2.5 (beginning Stage 2).

There is evidence, therefore, that Stage 1 readers are be-

[2]There is evidence that children with severe reading disabilities persist for a longer time to read words better in isolation than in context (Shankweiler and Liberman, 1972).

ginning to use semantic and syntactic constraints in word sequences, but they are still attending more to letters than to
words. Their rate of auditory-visual matching is slow, even for
familiar words (compared to more advanced readers).

Stage 2 includes research findings from Grades 2.5
through Grade 3 (until beginning of Grade 4). *Stage 3* covers
studies from Grades 4 to 8. Stage 2 seems to bring a strong
change in processing as compared with Stage 1. The research
evidence, however, seems less definite with regard to the division between Stages 2 and 3.

During Stage 2, letter matching continues to be faster than
word matching. During the beginning of Stage 3, rate of word
and letter matching is the same. After Grade 6, the end of the
first phase of Stage 3, words are matched faster than
letters. The rate of overall visual matching, whether letters or
words, continues to increase through Grade 6.

Somewhere within Stages 2 and 3, the reader develops the
ability to simultaneously process foveal and peripheral visual
information. Also, during these two stages, there seems to be a
continued increase in the ability to use spelling- and sound-rule
systems, as seen in the more proficient recognition of words.

The visual matching of CVC[3] and CVCC[4] words becomes as
fast as visual matching of letters by Grade 5, and visual matching of syllables becomes as fast as matching of words and letters by Grade 6. This suggests that although the spelling- and
sounding-rule systems are established by Stage 2, their fuller
use, particularly the spelling system, continues to be refined
until about Grade 6 (the end of the first phase of Stage 3).

Readers at Stage 2 and 3 make use of semantic and syntactic constraints. Words in sentences are read faster than single
letters from Grade 2.5 on and are read faster than words in seventh order approximation to discourse.[5] From Grade 3 on, the

---

[3]CVC = consonant, vowel, consonant words like *hat, pet, her.*
[4]CVCC = consonant, vowel, consonant words like *cost, camp, post.*
[5]Used by Doehring (1976), these are sets of words (with combined totals of 34 syllables
per set) presented in a scrambled sentence form, wherein each 7-word sequence is
meaningfully related but the sequences do not fit together as a plausible semantic and
syntactic whole. Doehring's example: "Spill over the edge and fall when the first tiny
snowflakes of rope and pick it up but something made when she hit the glass in his
school and he."

rate of all kinds of auditory and visual matching increases. Although word latency drops rapidly until Grade 2.5, and syllable latency drops rapidly to Grade 3, syllable latency continues to drop, but slowly, until Grade 7.

One area where there is a definite difference between Stage 2 and Stage 3 is in the rate of extracting meaning from words and pictures. The evidence shows that 2nd graders match pairs of pictures faster than pairs of words, whereas adults are faster at matching pairs of words. For both children (Grades 2, 4, and 6) and adults, the slowest task is matching pictures to words. However, the latency in this task shows the greatest decrease from 2nd to 4th grades (Stage 2 to Stage 3).

Within both Stages 2 and 3, visual scanning of print continues to increase steadily (through the 2nd, 4th, and 6th grades to the adult level). Many of the studies on visual scanning appear to show changes at Stage 3 (beginning of Grade 4, beginning of Grade 6, at Grade 6, or Grade 7).

Stage 4 readers can match words faster than letters. They are able to process foveal and peripheral visual information simultaneously. There is full use of spelling- and sound-rule systems and of semantic and syntactic constraints in word sequences. Interestingly, though, word matching continues to be faster than syllable matching until Grade 10. Somewhere between Stage 3 (Grade 6) and Stage 4, reading matching word pairs becomes faster than matching picture pairs. Until this time, picture matching is faster than word matching.

Stage 5 is not covered by the existing research on basic psychological processing.

Eye movements have been studied from the beginning of scientific research on reading. Through an analysis of fixations (the time during which the eyes fixate on print), regressions (backward eye movements), and recognition spans (the amount of print seen during a fixation), the nature of the reading process has been studied.

We analyzed 22 eye-movement studies from ages 3 to college and adults, published from 1917 to the present. (These include the classic studies of Buswell, 1920–1922; Taylor, 1937, 1957; Ballantine, 1951). Table A-2, presents these findings as well as findings regarding other psychological processes as they relate to the reading stages.

Table A-2

EYE MOVEMENTS, EYE-VOICE SPAN AND OTHER PSYCHOLOGICAL
PROCESSES AS THEY RELATE TO THE STAGE

STAGE	CHANGES IN EYE MOVEMENT PATTERNS				RATE OF READING	EYE-VOICE SPAN	PERIPHERAL GUIDANCE AND SCANNING
	FIXATIONS PER GIVEN UNIT OF READING	REGRESSIONS PER GIVEN UNIT OF READING	DURATION OF FIXATIONS (PER SECOND)	AVERAGE SPAN OF RECOGNITION (IN WORDS)			
Stage 0 Children up to age 6 Grades K to 1.5	4-year-olds do not select information areas for fixation in pictures or print, make many fixations per unit.	3-year-olds do not adequately cover the picture display. Kindergarteners spend less time on target letters; however, they do fixate on the presumed feature contrast.	Kindergarteners require more fixation time than 1st or 3rd graders.				A developmental change occurs from age 3 to 6 in awareness of what to look for when scanning pictures (Mackworth and Bruner, 1970; Vurpillot, 1968; Zinchenko, 1963). Kindergarteners are less efficient in locating information and differentiating distinctive features of print (Nodine & Evans, 1969; Nodine & Lang, 1971; Nodine & Stuerle, 1973; Nodine & Simmons, 1973).
Stage 1 Grades 1.5 to 2.5	Rapid growth in the reduction of fixations. For print, 1st graders require fewer fixations than kindergarteners.	Drops sharply.	Sharp drop. 1st graders require less fixation time than kindergarteners.	Rises sharply. Rapid increase in tachistoscopic span from grade 1 to grade 3.	Increases.	Increases with age (Buswell, 1920, Levin and Turner 1968). Young readers (grade 2) read word by word (Levin and Cohn, 1968).	By 3rd grade, scanning is more efficient. Fixations are qualitatively attuned to the informative features of the letters (see Stage 0).

187

Table A-2

EYE MOVEMENTS, EYE-VOICE SPAN AND OTHER PSYCHOLOGICAL
PROCESSES AS THEY RELATE TO THE STAGE (*cont.*)

STAGE	CHANGES IN EYE MOVEMENT PATTERNS				RATE OF READING	EYE VOICE SPAN	PERIPHERAL GUIDANCE AND SCANNING
	FIXATIONS PER GIVEN UNIT OF READING	REGRESSIONS PER GIVEN UNIT OF READING	DURATION OF FIXATIONS (PER SECOND)	AVERAGE SPAN OF RECOGNITION (IN WORDS)			
Stage 2 Grade 2.5 to Beginning grade 4	Number of fixations drops sharply to grade 4. For print 3rd graders require fewer fixations than 1st graders.	Sharp drop continues to grade 4 or 5.	Sharp drop continues to grade 4 and then levels off.	Continues to rise sharply until grades 4 or 5. Tachistoscopic span increase apparent until grade 5.	50% increase has occurred by grade 5.5. Most rapid increase is from grade 3 to grade 4 (some say to grade 5).	Rapid increase (Levin, 1980). Generally fully developed by grade 4 or 5 (Buswell, 1920).	Continues to become more efficient.
Stage 3 Grades 4 to 8	Decreases slowly. Most gains achieved by grade 5.	Continues to decrease but more slowly. However, Buswell found a slight rise at grade 7.	Levels off.	Continues to rise, but more slowly.	75% increase has occurred by grade 8.	Continues to increase with age, but more slowly (Levin and Turner, 1968; Levin, 1980).	X's written in white spaces between the words in a passage produce greater decrement in 5th and 6th graders than for younger children (grades 1 & 2). Spaces have become important cues (Hochberg, 1970).

Eye movement patterns more efficient for grade 7 than for grade 5

Table A-2

EYE MOVEMENTS, EYE-VOICE SPAN AND OTHER PSYCHOLOGICAL
PROCESSES AS THEY RELATE TO THE STAGE (cont.)

STAGE	CHANGES IN EYE MOVEMENT PATTERNS				RATE OF READING[2]	EYE-VOICE SPAN	PERIPHERAL GUIDANCE AND SCANNING
	FIXATIONS PER GIVEN UNIT OF READING[1]	REGRESSIONS PER GIVEN UNIT OF READING[2]	DURATION OF FIXATIONS (PER SECOND)[3]	AVERAGE SPAN OF RECOGNITION (IN WORDS)[4]			
Stage 4 Grades 8 to 12	General agreement that there is a slight decrease until college. But Buswell found a 2nd drop from high school sophomore to senior.	Continues to slightly decrease.	General agreement that this levels off.	Slow continued increase through college.	90% increase has occurred by grade 13.	Older readers (11th graders) have longer EVS's than younger readers and their reading is more flexible (Levin and Cohn, 1968).	Efficient.
Stage 5 College level and adult	Few fixations per given unit.	Few regressions per given unit.	Short duration of fixation time.	Widest span of recognition.		Long EVS's, flexible reading	Efficient.

[1]Taken from the following studies: Ballantine, 1951; Buswell, 1922; Gilbert, 1953; Gray, 1917; Mackworth and Bruner, 1970; Morse, 1951; Nodine and Evans, 1969; Nodine and Lang, 1971; Nodine and Simmons, 1973; Nodine and Stuerle, 1973; Schmidt, 1917; E. Taylor, 1937, 1957; S. Taylor, Frankenpohl, and Pettee, 1960; Vurpillot, 1968; Walker, 1938; Zinchenko, et al. 1963.

[2]Taken from the following studies: Ballantine, 1951; Buswell, 1922; Gilbert, 1953; Gray, 1917; Levin and Cohn, 1968; Mackworth and Bruner, 1970; Morse, 1951; Nodine and Evans, 1969; Nodine and Lang, 1971; Nodine and Simmons, 1973; Nodine and Stuerle, 1973; Schmidt, 1917; E. Taylor, 1937, 1957; S. Taylor, Frankenpohl, and Pettee, 1960; Vurpillot, 1968; Zinchenko et al. 1963.

[3]Taken from the following studies: Buswell, 1922; Gilbert, 1953; Gray, 1917; Levin and Cohn, 1968; Morse, 1951; Nodine and Stuerle, 1973; Rode, 1974; Schmidt, 1917; E. Taylor, 1937, 1957; S. Taylor, Frankenpohl and Pettee, 1960; Walker, 1938.

[4]Taken from the following studies: Buswell, 1922; Hoffman, 1927; E. Taylor, 1937, 1957; S. Taylor, Frankenpohl, and Pettee, 1960.

[5]Taken from the following studies: Ballantine, 1951; Buswell, 1920, 1922; Morse, 1951; Schmidt, 1917; E. Taylor, 1937, 1957; S. Taylor, Frankenpohl, and Pettee, 1960.

The eye-movement studies found essentially the same trends—whether conducted in the 1920s, when eye-movement photography was more crude, or in the late 1970s or early 1980s, with improved technology. All found greater growth during the earlier years when compared to the later years. The first four grades of school were characterized by the greatest growth, followed by a slower rate of growth through the upper elementary grades, high school, and college.

Figures 1 and 2 from Gelatt's (1978) review of eye-movement studies vividly illustrate the course of development—fast rate of growth in the early years and a slowing of the rate in later years. Thus, Figure A-1 shows the span of recognition [the number of words read in a single fixation increase from about a half a word per fixation at the end of Grade 1 (Stage 1) to about one word for a fixation between Grades 4 and 5]. Figure A-2 shows an equally rapid decrease in the fixation time between the 4th and 5th grades. The improvement from 5th grade on levels off, but it is still evident.

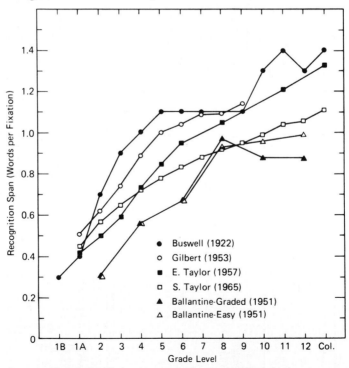

Figure 1. The relationship between recognition span and grade level. From Gelatt (1978)

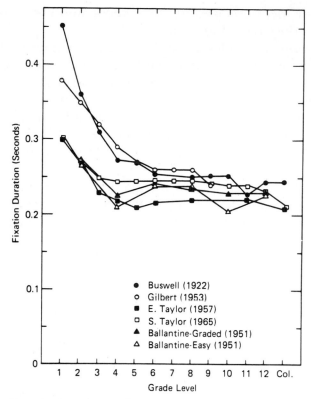

Figure 2. The relationship between fixation duration and grade level.
From Gelatt (1978).

Here is a review of eye-movement research in terms of our proposed reading stages.

At Stage 0 (up to age 6), eye movements are less guided by the target picture or letter than they are at later stages. Four-year-olds do not seem to fixate well on information areas. Kindergarten children make more fixations per unit than 1st graders, who make more fixations than 2nd graders. Children in kindergarten also require more fixation time than 1st graders.

At Stage 1 (Grades 1–2.5), eye movements change rapidly—the sharpest increase occurs at Stage 1 (from the middle of Grade 1 to the middle of Grade 2) and at Stage 2 (beginning of Grade 3). During Stage 1 the greatest improvement occurs in number of fixations (they decrease markedly), in the duration of fixations (they take less time), and in the number of regressions (they decrease greatly). The recognition span also increases, as does rate of reading.

The *Stage 2* (Grades 2.5 and 3) child continues to undergo a rapid change in eye movements. Although the rate of improvement seems to be somewhat slower than during Stage 1, the eye movements continue to improve rapidly. The number of fixations continues to decline rapidly (until Grades 4 and 5). Fixation time continues to decline substantially to Grade 4 or 5. The number of regressions also continues to decrease at a fast pace.

Both the average span of recognition and the rate of reading increase at an even and rapid pace to Grades 4 or 5 (Stage 3), by which time the span of recognition has doubled as compared with Grade 1 (Stage 1). By Grade 5, most readers have reached half of their full speed. Thereafter, the rate of increase slows down considerably.

Stage 3 (Grades 4–8) is characterized by a slowing down of the eye-movement changes. The number of fixations and regressions continues to decrease during Stage 3, although more slowly than in the preceeding stages. However, the fixation time seems to remain the same.

The span of recognition and rate of reading continue to increase, but more slowly than before. Buswell (1922) found that the span of recognition reached a plateau during this period. By Grade 4 or 5, the span of recognition has doubled as compared to Grade 1.

Stages 4 and 5 include high school and college. From Grade 9 to college, fixations continue to decrease slowly, with some evidence that fixations change from high-school sophomores to high-school seniors (Buswell, 1922). The number of regressions also continues to decrease slowly, although some investigators found them to level off (Ballantine, 1951).

The duration of fixations seems to remain constant during Stage 4, dropping again at the end of high school. Recognition span continues to increase slowly and evenly during Stage 4. Rate of reading also continues to increase, but more slowly than previously, with 90 percent of full maturity reached at Grade 12, as compared with 75 percent reached at Grade 8 and 50 percent at Grade 5.

EYE-VOICE SPAN

For eye-voice span research, I have relied heavily on Harry Levin's (1979) comprehensive review.

Research findings on eye-voice span (EVS), that is the distance of the eye ahead of the voice in reading aloud, are similar to those on eye movements. EVS also has a long history in the scientific study of reading. Similar to eye-movement research, there is great consistency in the findings of eye-voice-span research. Generally they show an increase in the eye-voice span with age and grade placement—the more advanced the age and school grade, the longer the eye-voice span.

Referring to the Buswell (1920) study of the development of EVS from Grade 2 to adult level, Levin (1980) concluded:

> . . . the development of the EVS, though irregular, is definitely upward. At the college level the age changes of the EVS are not so evident as at the lower levels. The sharpest rise on the developmental curve of the EVS occurs during the second, third, and fourth grades. There is some gain for high school readers (15.2 letter spaces) compared to the average for the fifth, sixth, and seventh grades (14.9 letter spaces). The fourth grade seems to be critical (p. 49.)

The Buswell findings have been confirmed by Anderson and Dearborn (1952), Levin and Turner (1968), Levin and Cohn (1968), Levin (1980), and Tinker (1965). In all, the evidence is considerable that readers increase their eye-voice span as they grow more advanced in their reading abilities.

The developmental progression of the EVS by grade level, eye movements, and visual perception tend to parallel those of the reading stages. The sharpest rise in the developmental curve of the EVS, according to Levin, occurs during the 2nd, 3rd, and 4th grades—the years classified as the latter part of Stage 1, Stage 2, and the very beginning of Stage 3. The peak of the EVS growth, placed at Grade 4 by the research evidence, comes at the beginning of Stage 3, when reading is sufficiently skillful and fluent to permit "reading for the new" as a tool for learning. The slower rate of growth of the EVS in Grades 5, 6, and 7 may well reflect the longer period of time needed to master the more varied tasks of Stage 3—the broader and more difficult vocabulary, the more abstract concepts, the more unfamiliar ideas, and the more complex syntax. High-school readers (stage 4) also have a longer EVS, reflecting their ability to read more complex materials for more sophisticated purposes. And even at the college level, although the EVS increase is relatively small, there is still a change, reflecting, perhaps, the ability to deal with the still greater complexity of the reading task.

The size of the EVS is also related to the readability of the text. The more difficult the text, the shorter the EVS. The easier the text, the longer the EVS. This also parallels the increasing readability levels of the materials that can be read by those at increasingly higher reading stages. The EVS is also related to the reading ability of the reader. At each grade level, the better the reader, the longer the EVS.

The course of development of the EVS is similar to that of eye movements. For both, the major growth occurs during Stages 1 and 2 (Grades 1, 2, and 3), with a peak at about Grade 4 or 5 (Stage 3), then a slower increase at higher ages and grades. For both, the more rapid gains are made during the early stages of reading, when the major learning task is "the medium"—i.e., the basic decoding and word-recognition skills needed to bring the reading skill close to the reader's speaking and listening skills. The rate of growth beyond Grade 4 (Stage 3 and beyond) is slower probably because these stages deal more with growth in language and cognition. The rate of growth in the upper elementary grades (Stage 3) is slower than for the primary grades, but it is relatively faster than in high school and college (Stages 4 and 5) where the growth needed in language and cognition is still greater than that needed by preceding stages.

LINGUISTIC RESEARCH AND THE READING STAGES

Considerable research exists on language development but less on language development in relation to reading. We confine ourselves, here, to the studies that relate to reading development. Linguistic research is further divided into the three common areas of language study—phonology (the sound system), syntax (the grammatical aspects of language), and semantics (the meaning aspects).

• **Phonology** Phonology is considered critical in learning to read an alphabetic language by psycholinguists and reading specialists, particularly at the beginning stages. A brief review of the research on children's knowledge of the sound system highlights the changes by grade and age.

The ability to isolate phonemes (the separate sounds in words) grows from ages 6 to 8 (Liberman and Shankweiler, 1979). Phonemic segmentation, or the ability to identify a familiar word when a sound is omitted from the beginning, middle, or end, also increases steadily from the mental ages of 5–9 (Bruce, 1964). At a mental age of 7, 30 percent of the words were correct, and at a mental age of 8, 60 percent were correct. Those with mental ages of 7 and 8 who had received phonic teaching performed better than those who had not.

The ability to synthesize sounds to form words (sound blending) also increases with age. Among a group of 5–8-year-olds, the ability to combine a consonant and a vowel sound into a syllabic unit increased with age, but the youngest children in the group could not do the task of synthesis (Leroy-Boussion, 1963; Roberts, 1979). Children aged 7–12 can blend separate sounds into words, improving steadily with age (Chall, Roswell, and Blumenthal, 1963; Connors, Kramer, and Guerra, 1969).

Both phonemic segmentation and sound-blending ability increase with age and grade, particularly during the primary school years. Both are further correlated with beginning reading (Stages 1 and 2) achievement, especially with accuracy of oral reading, word recognition, and phonics (Chall, Roswell, and Blumenthal, 1963; Chall and Feldmann, 1966; Connors, Kramer, and Guerra, 1969).

The studies of phonology tend, overall, to show a progression with age (and also with training). The question crucial for instruction is not only the correlational one—the older, the more ability—but what is the minimal level needed for use in learning phonics?

The studies on this question are not very satisfactory in that too few children of 6–7, when most of phonics is taught, are tested, and for too many who are tested the tests are too difficult and too far removed from the actual teaching and learning of phonics. Some investigators concluded from experiments that a mental age of 7 or 8 is minimal. However, other studies and practice indicate that most 1st graders can learn phonics (see Chall, 1967, for a review of this evidence). In spite of the fact that most children are now learning phonics as preschoolers from *Sesame Street* and *The Electric Company* and in the reading programs published since the late 1960s (Popp, 1975), and in spite of the early writing and spelling reported by linguists such as Carol Chomsky (1976, 1979) and Charles Read (1971), there are still reports that these children perform poorly on phonological tests. These differences in research findings and evidence from practice will become of even greater importance as more linguists come to study metalinguistic awareness—the child's awareness of the abstractions of language. The positive relation between metalinguistic awareness and reading and language development currently being reported raises an old question—what are the minimal requisites of metalinguistic awareness for learning at the various stages? For example, how much and what kind of metalinguistic awareness is needed for reading at Stage 1? Shankweiler and Liberman (1972), for example, found that for preschool, kindergarten, and Grade 1 children, segmenting phonemes is much harder than segmenting syllables, although the ability to do both improves developmentally. From this they concluded that explicit phoneme segmentation ability is needed in order to read an alphabetic script. A similar position was taken by Gleitman and Rozin (1973) who developed a syllabic beginning reading program based on this principle (Rozin and Gleitman, 1977) to be used as a way of introducing the more difficult phoneme blending. Their experiment found no significant gains as compared to phoneme blending among poor readers, but there were indications that the use of syllables might have effected improved learning of phonics.

To what extent segmentation and blending stem from neurophysiological development or from training is still not known (Chall et al., 1963), although an interactional hypothesis seems most likely among children with reading disability.

Some researchers propose training of these abilities (Elkonin, 1973; Liberman and Shankweiler, 1979; Rosner, 1971, 1974; Wallach and Wallach, 1976, 1977) in order to enhance early reading development.

The development of phonology and the learning of metalinguistic awareness have many similarities with regard to reading development. Generally, they show a rapid growth from the preschool years to age 8. Thus, in terms of the proposed reading stages, the growth in phonology seems to precede that of the development of the reading process in Stage 1 and 2—knowledge, skill, and insight into the alphabetic code and the sound system and growing use of it in the reading of words, sentences, and stories in Stage 2.

With the exception of those children who have severe reading and language disabilities, most phonological studies stop at Grade 3 or 4 (Stage 3). When phonic abilities are measured beyond Grade 4, the students studied are usually "poor readers" functioning on a lower reading level than expected.

The Development of Syntax   Children's sentences increase in length and complexity with increasing age—from an average of four words at 3 years to five and a half words at 5 years. At age 5, the sentences include prepositions and conjunctions and a fair number of inflections (Templin, 1957). Compound sentences begin to occur at ages 6 to 7, but structurally incomplete sentences are numerous even at 9½ years (Loban, 1963; McCarthy, 1960; Strickland, 1962).

The child's understanding of syntax increases rapidly from ages 3–5, as found in their ability to apply nonsense syllables having functions of nouns and verbs to pictures indicating actions, objects, and substances (Brown, 1973). Children between 5 and 6 were able to use plurals, possessives, and other inflections using pictures of objects labelled with nonsense syllables (the Wug Test). Even the younger children showed considerable proficiency in the task, though the older children were more correct. Neither were as proficient as adults. The commonest inflections, s for plurals and possessives, were known before the less common ones (Berko and Brown, 1960).

Simple transformations in the spontaneous speech of children ages 3–4 and 6–7—negatives, passives, past tense, and interrogatives—were used correctly. More complex transformations were used correctly by the older children.

The acquisition of syntax at ages 5–10 (kindergarten to Grade 4) proceeds along similar paths, occurring earlier for the older and later for the younger children (Chomsky, 1969). Children of 6–12 and adults tested on their facility with certain transformations—active and passive, affirmative and negative—varied with age in the number of errors. The older children made fewer errors and were faster. But the order of difficulty of the transformations was much the same at all ages (Slobin, 1966).

Relationships have also been reported between metalinguistic awareness, book exposure, and reading achievement. Chomsky (1972) found among 5- to 10-year-old children a significant positive relationship between extent of syntactic awareness, extent of exposure to reading (being read to or reading on their own), and reading achievement. She further found that the more challenging in readability the books read to and by children, the more advanced the level of the children's syntactic development and reading achievement.

It would appear that syntactic development, like phonemic development, is related to reading development. It seems to act both as a prior condition for reading development and also as a consequence of reading instruction. With regard to the reading-stage scheme I have proposed, it is important to note that while phonemic development has an important impact on early reading—during Stages 1 and 2 when insight into "sounding the letters" is crucial—the impact of syntactic development may come at somewhat higher stages when the reading matter becomes more complex. Further evidence of the relation between syntax and reading development comes from studies by Vogel (1974), Wiig and Semel (1976), and Roit (1977) who found difficulties with syntax among children diagnosed as learning disabled. Also relevant is the research in readability which has, in most studies, found syntactic factors to be highly related to reading comprehension, second only to those of vocabulary (see Evidence from Education in Chapter 4, pages 65–76).

• **Semantic Development**   Research on vocabulary and its relation to reading goes back to the early 1900s, when investigators tried to estimate the extent of vocabulary knowledge of children and adults at various ages and grades (Lorge and Chall, 1963). There has been a general lull until the past few years in the study of vocabulary, no doubt related to the Chomskian revolution in linguistics which stressed the study of syntax. We can see some glimmers of a new interest in vocabulary (Becker, 1978; Anderson and Freebody, 1978), but it has far to go to match the earlier intensity of interest.

A consistent finding from the vocabulary research is the high relationship between vocabulary knowledge, cognitive development, and reading achievement.

Factor analytic studies of reading comprehension by Davis (1968) and R. L. Thorndike (1974) concluded that if there were one factor outside of a general reading factor, it would be word meaning. The correlations between word meaning and reading comprehension are high, almost as high as between two comprehension or two word meaning tests. The correlations are higher at higher reading levels.

The strong correlation of vocabulary and reading comprehension is found also in readability research. Most studies on readability have found that some measure of vocabulary difficulty (whether measured by word frequency, familiarity, abstract/concrete, or by word length in syllables, letters, etc.) is the most important predictor of comprehension difficulty, or readability (Lorge, 1939, 1944; Chall, 1958; Klare, 1963, 1974–1975). Syntactic factors are usually second in importance in predicting comprehension difficulty.

Vocabulary knowledge is also highly related to tests of verbal intelligence [Stanford-Binet and Wechsler Intelligence Scale for Children (WISC)]. On the WISC and the WAIS (Wechsler Adult Intelligence Scale), the vocabulary subtest has the highest correlation with the total verbal test score. Wechsler, in fact, has suggested that if only one test can be given, it should be the vocabulary subtest.

The research on the development of vocabulary with age is considerable and only limited aspects of the findings can be reported here.

1. Vocabulary increases with age and keeps increasing, even when other abilities cease to develop after maturity. Because vocabulary continues to grow with age and experience, it has been used as a criterion of stability for estimating growth or decline in cognitive abilities.

2. There seem to be periods of greater and lesser growth, with the greatest rate of growth during the preschool years.

3. During the school years, estimates of vocabulary size vary considerably. Some are ten times as large as others[6] (Lorge and Chall, 1961). But when the rate of growth is examined, irrespective of exact amount, the greatest increases are in Grades 1, 2, and 3 (Stages 1 and 2). During Stage 3 (Grades 4–8) the rate of increase slows somewhat.

4. Vocabulary also changes qualitatively with age, going from the fairly concrete to the more abstract.

In a review of the literature on vocabulary development, Feifel and Lorge (1950) concluded "that growth with age occurs not only in vocabulary range but in the character of the word definitions as well, and the quality and completeness of word definitions change considerably from the lower to the higher grades" (p. 3). The younger children among the 6–14-year-olds tested more often employed use, description, illustration, demonstration, and repetitive types of definitions. The older gave significantly more synonym and explanation types of responses. Similar to Piaget's findings on changes in conceptual levels, they found that "to the child 8 or younger, an 'orange' is 'what you eat' or 'it's round.' Only as he grows older does he see it as a 'citrus fruit' or 'a fruit' which grows in California or Florida" (p. 16). Younger children perceive words as "concrete" ideas and emphasize their isolated or particular aspects, whereas older children stress the abstract or "class" features of the word meanings. These vocabulary findings generally parallel the qualitative changes in the reading stages. Thus, the "concrete" definitions of the 6–8-year-olds

[6]In an analysis of these studies, Lorge and Chall (1961) concluded that the large differences can be explained by different methods used to sample the universe of words. The more recent estimates are based on sampling from unabridged dictionaries.

are generally adequate for the reading tasks needed in Grades 1, 2, and 3 (Stages 1 and 2).

Beginning with Stage 3, when most children begin to use reading to learn the new, a more extensive and qualitatively more abstract vocabulary is needed. That is when most children seem to make the qualitative leap to abstractions.

Figure 3 from Feifel and Lorge illustrates the sharp rise in defining through synonyms from ages 9–13 (Stage 3). Such ability shows a considerable advancement over the earlier emphasis (in Stages 1 and 2) on the particular or isolated aspects of a word.

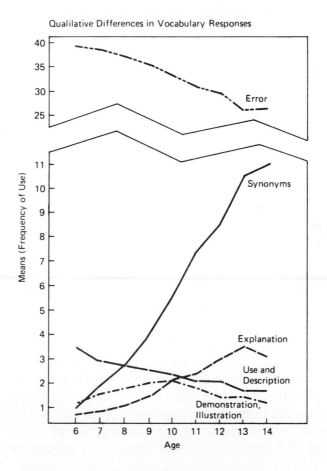

Figure 3. Mean frequency of use of five qualitative categories by age. From Feifel and Lorge (1950).

Similar changes in vocabulary development were found by Werner and Kaplan (1952) for children of ages 9–13. They noted an abrupt shift in children's performance on their language tests between the ages of 10 and 11, which they interpreted as a "qualitative reorganization of language behavior" (p. 98). At that time, they noted a noticeable decrease in primitive forms of definition and an observable increase in the use of abstract words.

It would appear, then, that the research of Werner and Kaplan, as well as that of Lorge and Feifel, supports a fundamental change in vocabulary knowledge which takes place around Grade 5 or 6—from a concrete to a more abstract knowledge. This is the time I have characterized as Stage 3, the beginning of "reading for the new" which requires and gives further practice in dealing with less familiar, less concrete, and more abstract ideas and processes.

THE RELATIONSHIP OF READING AND LISTENING COMPREHENSION

Research on the relation between reading and listening was reviewed comprehensively in 1974 by Sticht and his associates for Grades 1 to college and adult levels. He concluded that "the relationship between auding (listening comprehension) and reading grows as grade level increases up to the fourth grade, and remains fairly constant thereafter at around .58 to .60" (p. 89). [See Figure 4, Sticht, p. 90, based on Loban's (1963) longitudinal study.]

The review also revealed that up to Grade 4, listening comprehension is more efficient than reading comprehension. From Grade 5 to 7 or 8, listening is still ahead, but it begins to level off, and reading becomes equal to listening. During the high school years, reading and listening are mostly equal. It is only at the college and adult levels that reading moves ahead of listening in efficiency (see Figure 5). These research findings fit the data on the rate of development of oral and reading vocabulary, with oral vocabularies considerably ahead of reading vocabularies through most of the elementary grades (see Chapter 5).

Correlation between auding and reading test performance for various studies, as a function of school grade level.

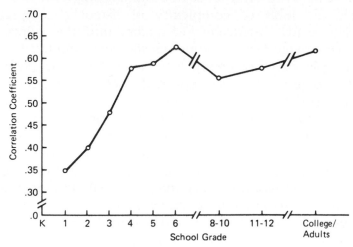

Figure 4. From Sticht et al. (1974) based on Loban (1964).

Comparison of auding and reading performance at five schooling levels.

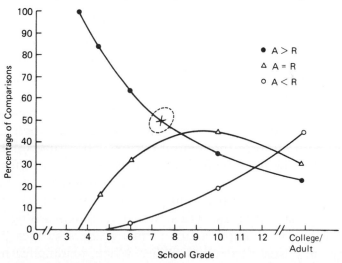

Figure 5. From Sticht et al. (1974)

The findings on the relative effectiveness of listening and reading are also related to the proposed stage-development scheme. It, more than the other background research evidence, stresses the slow development of reading maturity.

According to the Sticht data, it takes all of the elementary school years to reach a level of reading comprehension that matches the level of complexity of listening comprehension. The relative inefficiency of reading until the college and adult levels (Stage 5) raises some questions. Could this be why most people make relatively little use of reading (Marston, 1982)? And could this also explain the relative preference for TV as compared to reading as a medium for entertainment and instruction (Chall and Gregory, in preparation)? If reading is to be a medium by choice, it would seem that readers need to reach an advanced level, at least that of Stage 4 or 5, earlier than they now do. Our analyses of the realistic reading demands for most work, professional, personal, and civic needs (see Chapter 9) would indicate that a high level of reading is indeed required—a level that would permit the reading and understanding of a sophisticated newspaper like *The New York Times,* a weekly newsmagazine like *Newsweek,* and governmental forms like the Internal Revenue Service Income Tax Instructions.

NEUROLOGICAL DEVELOPMENT

Some studies have been concerned with reading development in relation to neurological development, particularly with regard to children with reading disability. Paul Satz, a neurologist, and his associates (Satz, Friel, and Rudegair, 1976; Satz, Rardon, and Ross, 1971; Taylor, Satz, and Friel, 1979) have hypothesized that children with reading/learning disabilities have a delay in maturation of the central cortex. This causes delays in their reading development, such delays being of a different quality at different ages. At ages 7–8, Satz proposes, delay is mainly in sensory-perceptual abilities; at 9–12, the delays are in cognitive-linguistic abilities. Thus, when reading/learning disability children are compared to normal readers at ages 7–8, they vary on visual-perceptual skills. When reading/learning disability children are compared with normal readers at ages 11–12, they are poorer in language/cognitive skills.

The Satz hypothesis tends to fit the proposed reading stages in that poor readers who are delayed in the early grades (at Stage 1) tend to have difficulty with the tasks of Stage 1—decoding, word recognition, and other factors related to mastery of the printed medium and its rules. A delay or difficulty with reading at ages 9–12 (Grades 4–7), which usually means reading of more abstract, general content that uses less common and abstract concepts, could mean difficulty with language and cognition as Satz hypothesizes.

An earlier research review (Chall, 1967) found that early reading (Grades 1–3) is more highly associated with visual, auditory, and visual-perceptual and sequencing skills. At higher grades, it was more highly related to language and cognitive abilities (verbal intelligence). Beginning with Grade 4 (Stage 3), the correlations of reading achievement with linguistic-cognitive abilities increase while those with perceptual factors decrease.

Birch and Belmont (1965) came to similar conclusions from studies of auditory-visual integration among normal and retarded readers ages 5–11. The correlation of auditory-visual integration with reading for both groups was greatest at Grade 1 and lower for Grade 2. After Grade 2, there was no longer a significant relationship between reading achievement and auditory-visual integration. Correlations between IQ and reading increased with age. They concluded from their finding that "perceptual" factors were most important for initial acquisition of reading skills but that factors more closely associated with IQ were more important in its elaboration. Blank, Bridger, and DeFiaiercies (1966) challenged the developmental view of Birch and Belmont, proposing instead that language and language deficits explain the earlier as well as the later stages of reading. A similar position is held by Vellutino (1979).

A somewhat different concept comes from the work of Mattis, French, and Rapin (1975), who found three patterns among 53 dyslexics examined: a language disorder group, an articulating and graphic dyscoordination group, and a visuo-perceptual disorders group.

This conception is not based on development, i.e., that different groups of disability are more prevalent at different ages. Rather, these groups of disability may be related to difficulties in particular parts of the cerebral hemisphere not necessarily related to age.

It is fitting to cite here M. D. Vernon's (1977) review of the research on reading difficulties in which she lists four main deficiencies which can occur along the successive phases of reading:

1. Deficiencies in the capacity to analyze complex, sequential visual and/or auditory-linguistic structures, which prevent the coding of the linguistic structures and their organization in short- and long-term memory.

2. Difficulty in linking visual and auditory-linguistic structures.

3. Inability to establish regularities in variable grapheme-phoneme correspondences. A basic maturational lag or disability in the development of interhemispheric integration might also operate here.

4. Despite an ability to recognize words, an inability to group them into meaningful phrases. This may be caused in part by the inability to automatize grapheme-phoneme correspondences.

Although Vernon notes that some of these may overlap and that some may not altogether prevent reading but may retard it, it is interesting that the listing proceeds from the perceptual to the meaning aspects of reading and language.

Further evidence on the possible relationship with neurological and reading development comes from the prediction studies of de Hirsch et al. (1966), Jansky and de Hirsch (1972), and more recently Popp (1980). They found high-risk children differed from those who made normal reading progress in visual/auditory perception and in cognitive/linguistic skills. The most immature children among the high risks tended to be most deficient in the perceptual.

AN HISTORICAL PERSPECTIVE ON READING STAGES

W<small>E PRESENT HERE</small> highlights of the reading-stage schemes of William S. Gray, Arthur I. Gates, David Russell, and Francis Ilg and Louise Ames first published between 1925 and 1956. The scheme of Rozin and Gleitman, published in 1977, is summarized briefly at the end of this appendix.

THE READING STAGES OF WILLIAM S. GRAY (1925 AND 1937)

The view that children pass through various stages from beginning to mature reading first received attention from William S. Gray in the 1925 *NSSE Yearbook, Report of the National Committee on Reading.* Gray, chairman of the committee, stated, "A careful study of the progress of children in reading shows that they pass through different stages of development in acquiring mature habits" (p. 21). He believed that reading instruction should be planned with these stages in mind so that appropriate training could be provided at each stage. According to Gray, the reading program should be organized around "five important periods or divisions" (p. 24):

1. Period of preparation for reading.

2. The initial period of reading instruction.

3. The period of rapid progress in fundamental attitudes, habits, and skills.

4. The period of wide reading to extend and enrich experience and to cultivate important reading habits and tastes.

5. The period of refinement of specific reading attitudes, habits, and tastes.

In the 1937 *NSSE Yearbook, The Teaching of Reading,* Gray again discussed "five important stages of development in reading" (p. 76). He stated that in order for reading instruction to follow an orderly sequence ". . . a clear recognition of the broad divisions into which a reading program may be divided" (p. 71) is required. Gray then described the five stages in essentially the same terms he used in the 1925 yearbook. The 1937 version, however, made some changes in terminology, using "stages" instead of the earlier "period," for example, and it provided further elaboration and detail. Tables B-1 to B-5 summarize the developmental stages proposed by Gray in the 1937 yearbook, specifying the duration of each stage, the goals, and expected levels of achievement.

It is interesting to compare this account of reading readiness with Gray's earlier one in 1925. It was not until the 1930s that the first elaborate discussions appeared of factors affecting readiness for reading instruction and the term "reading readiness" was launched (Harrison, 1936; Gates and Bond, 1936). In the 1937 yearbook, Gray referred to the then newly published readiness studies and summarized their findings, stating that the following factors were generally agreed upon as influencing the readiness of a child for reading: physical, intellectual, emotional, and social maturity.

Gray also took the following positions on the question of readiness in the 1937 account: (1) Readiness could and should be developed through appropriate training for those who need it; (2) if a child was not ready to learn to read a particular kind of material by a particular method, it did not mean that he was not ready to learn to read another type of material by a different method. He cautioned against using a mental age of 6½ as a criterion of readiness, as recommended by Morphett and Washburne (1931). For Gray the questions were "Ready to read what?" and "Ready to read how?" (p. 85).

Table B-1

GRAY'S READING STAGES: STAGE 1, READING READINESS

DURATION	GOALS	ACHIEVEMENT EXPECTED
Preschool years, K, sometimes early Grade 1	1. To provide the experience and training that will develop readiness for beginning readers 2. To remediate physical and emotional deficiencies	Seven "essential prerequisites to reading" (p. 81): 1. Wide experience, to help pupils interpret what they read 2. "Facility in the use of ideas" (p. 83), i.e., the ability to use past experience and information in conversation, in approaching and solving relatively simple problems, and in thinking clearly about what has been read 3. "Reasonable command of simple English sentences" (p. 83) 4. A large speaking vocabulary 5. Accurate pronunciation 6. Skill in visual and auditory discrimination (observing likenesses and differences in word forms and in the sounds of words) 7. A strong desire to learn to read

SOURCE: *NSSE Yearbook,* 1937.

Gray's 1937 account of reading readiness contained one further addition to that of 1925. In 1937 Gray added a seventh factor to readiness achievement—auditory and visual discrimination.[1]

Table B-2 summarizes the facts of Gray's (1937) Stage 2, Initial guidance in learning to read: Grade One. The goals are presented for the overall initial reading period and for the levels of school materials commonly used—preprimer, primer, and first reader.

[1] It is significant to note that this factor, and more specifically the knowledge of letter names which has been the highest predictor of reading in Grade 1, is given least weight by Gray. His emphasis here, as for beginning reading (Chall, 1967), was on the cognitive and linguistic aspects of reading.

Table B-2

GRAY'S READING STAGES: STAGE 2, INITIAL GUIDANCE IN LEARNING TO READ

DURATION	OVERALL GOALS	ADDITIONAL GOALS	ACHIEVEMENT LEVELS AT END OF STAGE 2
Grade 1	1. To develop an interest in reading 2. To develop "a thoughtful reading attitude" (p. 76) 3. To "learn to engage in continuous, meaningful reading" from simple materials (p. 76) 4. To begin to read simple materials with interest and absorption 5. To begin to read independently		1. Reads simple material with interest and absorption 2. Has the desire to read independently 3. Is able to read silently with limited or no lip movements 4. Asks about and discusses intelligently the content of what has been read 5. Reads progressively longer units for pleasure or for a specific purpose 6. Can read orally in thought units rather than word by word 7. Uses a variety of techniques for attacking unknown words 8. Understands the significance of various punctuation marks 9. Understands the order of paging and can find what he needs 10. Scores 2.0 or higher on a standardized silent reading test
The preprimer period		1. To acquire a small sight vocabulary 2. To learn to recognize and interpret simple sentences in silent and oral reading 3. To learn to read and follow directions 4. To develop good habits in reading from left to right 5. To develop good habits in caring for and using books	

210

Table B-2
GRAY'S READING STAGES: STAGE 2, INITIAL GUIDANCE IN LEARNING TO READ (cont.)

DURATION	OVERALL GOALS	ADDITIONAL GOALS	ACHIEVEMENT LEVELS AT END OF STAGE 2
The primer period		1. To learn to anticipate the meanings of words and to use context in recognizing new words	
		2. To continue to acquire a sight vocabulary	
		3. To learn to recognize new words with the help of simple kinds of analyses, e.g., noticing distinguishing features of words, comparing and contrasting words for similarities and differences, observing frequently occurring elements of words	
		4. To be able to discuss and ask questions about what has been read and to make deductions	
		5. To continue to develop proper left-to-right eye movements	

211

Table B-2

GRAY'S READING STAGES: STAGE 2, INITIAL GUIDANCE IN LEARNING TO READ (cont.)

DURATION	OVERALL GOALS	ADDITIONAL GOALS	ACHIEVEMENT LEVELS AT END OF STAGE 2
The first reader period		1. To become familiar with various kinds of reading material—stories, informational, study-type 2. To begin to read for different purposes e.g., to enjoy a story, to answer questions 3. To become accustomed to thinking while reading and to interpret material intelligently 4. To develop greater independence in recognizing unknown words, a wider span of recognition, and more rapid recognition 5. To develop greater fluency in oral and silent reading	

SOURCE: *NSSE Yearbook*, 1937.

212

It should be noted that Table B-2 (Gray's Stage 2) reflects a particular view as to how reading should be taught—that it should be introduced to the child from the start as a "thought-getting process" (p. 89). (The readiness prerequisites in Table B-1 indicate the same.) Meaning and comprehension were paramount. Accordingly, the child was to be taught a sight vocabulary, to read simple, connected text based on these words, and was to be encouraged to discuss the material read.

From Grade 1 on, comprehension was to be stressed. Pre-primer, primer, and first-reader goals are all concerned with comprehension and interpretation of the material which is to be read silently as well as orally, beginning with the first reader. From the start, the reader is encouraged to ask questions about and interpret the material he reads.

How are readers at the end of Gray's Stage 2 (Grade 1) described? What are their achievements? They can, at the end of Gray's Stage 1 (Grade 1), read simple material with interest and with some independence,[2] and are "able to read silently with limited or no lip movements." They are to read in thought units rather than word by word and to be able to discuss and interpret what they have read in an intelligent manner. New words are to be recognized by using context and by simple kinds of word analysis such as noticing commonly occurring elements of words (syllables, phonograms, letters, etc.) and comparing words to note similarities and differences. Gray seems to mention these techniques of word analysis in passing, and refers the reader at one point to a later chapter by Paul McKee (1937) in the same NSSE yearbook where word recognition is discussed in some detail. It is interesting to note that the 1925 *NSSE Yearbook* chapter on word analysis seems very cautious about phonic analysis and warns about the negative aspects of "phonetic training" (p. 89).

Table B-3 summarizes the goals and achievements of Gray's Stage 3 (Grades 2 and 3)—the stage of "unusually rapid development" (p. 100) as found in such skills as (a) accuracy and independence of word recognition, (b) rate and span of recognition, (c) speed of silent reading, (d) fluency of oral read-

[2]In the 1925 yearbook Gray also points out that pupils in Stage 2 who read many books progress more rapidly than those who do only a small amount of reading. (He makes a similar statement concerning Stage 3.)

ing, (e) comprehension and interpretation, and (f) ability to read for different purposes.[3]

Table B-3

GRAY'S READING STAGES: STAGE 3, RAPID PROGRESS
IN FUNDAMENTAL READING ATTITUDES AND HABITS

DURATION	SPECIFIC AIMS	LEVELS OF ACHIEVEMENT
Grades 2 and 3	1. To provide varied reading experiences from "the world's greatest stories for children" (p. 101) and from a variety of informational materials 2. To stimulate an interest in reading and to continue to develop the habit of reading independently 3. To promote rapid growth in comprehension and "intelligent interpretation" (p. 101) when reading for a variety of purposes, e.g., to find the answers to questions, to find the main idea, to draw conclusions, etc. 4. To develop speed of silent reading, including rapid growth in span and rate of recognition and corresponding decline in number and duration of fixations per line 5. To develop fluent oral reading 6. To stimulate independence and accuracy in word recognition by enlarging the sight vocabulary and by providing training in attacking unfamiliar words 7. To continue to train to use books skillfully	1. Have acquired the habit of independent reading 2. Read with "ease, understanding, and pleasure" (p. 76) informational and story materials that are usually assigned at the beginning of grade 4 3. Obtain a score of 4.0 or higher on a standardized silent reading test 4. Comprehend material in the content areas 5. Read silently more rapidly than orally 6. Read appropriate material at sight 7. Exhibit greater skill in the use of context clues together with visual and phonic clues in attacking unknown words 8. Exhibit greater skill in adjusting reading to different purposes

SOURCE: *NSSE Yearbook,* 1937.

In the 1925 version Gray also pointed out that the unusually rapid progress during Grades 2 and 3 in accuracy and rate of word recognition, in span of recognition, eye-voice span,

[3]Gray includes this skill in his discussion but omits it in his summaries (p. 76).

and rhythmical progress of perception along the lines of print leads to progress in the accuracy and speed of oral and silent reading and that these grow more rapidly in Grades 2 and 3 than at any other time. He noted, for example, that by the end of grade 3, good readers have attained four-fifths of the average reading ability of college students as measured by the Gray Oral Reading Paragraphs. Gray based these statements on his own research (1917) and that of Buswell (1922).

Gray also points out that by the beginning of the 4th grade, pupils are expected to be able to comprehend material from various content fields. He believed that introducing pupils to various kinds of informational material (health, science, travel, children's newspapers, etc.) in Grades 2 and 3 would enable them to acquire experience beyond their immediate surroundings and beyond the world of "pictures, conversation, and story telling" (p. 99). Exposure to informational material would also help prepare the pupil for later study activities. In the 1925 yearbook Gray stated, "One reason why so many pupils fail in content subjects in the fourth grade is because they have not been trained to interpret simple, factual material effectively" (p. 52).

Gray's Stage 3 again illustrates his emphasis on comprehension and interpretation. Comprehension was to be stimulated by focusing attention on new meanings for known words, new concepts, sequence of ideas, major thought divisions, significance of facts, and so on. In addition, pupils were to be trained to read for specific purposes, i.e., to answer questions, to find the main idea, to draw conclusions, and to interpret the simple material they read (1918).

The emphasis on silent reading is even stronger at this stage, with a specific aim of "speed of silent reading" and an achievement level specification of silent reading more rapid than oral reading. Independence in word recognition was to be achieved by visual and "phonetic analysis" of short words and syllabication of polysyllabic words (p. 104). Generally, it receives minor attention in the total set of goals and achievement for Grades 2 and 3. As noted earlier for Gray's Stage 2, word recognition in Stage 3 receives little elaboration. Instead, Gray refers the reader to a detailed account by McKee in a later chapter. McKee's cautious tone against "certain types of inten-

GRAY'S READING STAGES: STAGE 4 , THE EXTENSION
OF EXPERIENCE AND THE INCREASE
IN READING EFFICIENCY

DURATION	MAJOR AIMS	LEVELS OF ACHIEVEMENT

Grades 4–6	1. To broaden and enrich the experiences of pupils by exposure to various content fields
	2. To extend reading interests and tastes and to create a desire to read "the better forms of literature" (p. 112)
	3. To develop greater "power and efficiency" (p. 110) in the various phases of reading
	  a. Accuracy and independence in the recognition of increasingly difficult words
	  b. Increase in meaning vocabulary
	  c. Accurate and thorough comprehension while reading for a variety of purposes such as to find the main idea, to support an opinion, to draw conclusions, to verify, etc.
	  d. Depth of interpretation, i.e., comparing and evaluating ideas and information, understanding implications, etc.
	  e. Speed of silent reading
	  f. Quality of oral reading
	4. To develop competence in study activities such as locating information (index, table of contents, maps, tables, graphs, encyclopedias, etc.); choosing and evaluating material (judging validity, relevant from irrelevant, etc.); organizing material (seeing relationships, being able to summarize, etc.); solving problems; remembering what is read; and so on
		1. Is able to pronounce unfamiliar words or locate them quickly in a dictionary
		2. Has achieved relative maturity in rate and span of recognitions, in the "rhythmical progress of perceptions along the lines" (p. 119), in eye-voice span, and in rate of silent reading for pleasure
		3. Has a greatly enlarged meaning vocabulary and is able to use the dictionary to find the meanings of words
		4. Comprehension and interpretation is such that a score of 7.0 or better is obtained on a silent reading test
		5. Is able to work independently in a variety of study situations
		6. Has acquired skill in the use of the dictionary, encyclopedia, and other sources

SOURCE: *NSSE Yearbook,* 1937.

sive and formal phonetic practices" (p. 293) is not as strong as it was in the 1925 yearbook. Here McKee (1937) merely states that such practices are to be avoided. What is recommended is a continued comparing and contrasting of like and unlike words (*blue, black, blow; can, cup, cat; big, hit*), noticing the most distinguishing word parts, phonograms, and commonly occurring elements within words.

Gray's Stage 4, covering Grades 4–6, is summarized in Table B-4. Gray also presents three commonly held views of this reading stage, the first two of which he rejected. (1) The essential skills have been mastered in the primary grades, and therefore no further formal instruction is necessary beyond Grade 3. Pupils continue to advance by engaging in a wide variety of reading activities. (2) Reading skills beyond the primary grades will best be enhanced by reading in the various content areas and by independent reading. (3) Full maturity is not reached at the end of the primary grades and therefore some basic reading instruction should supplement the reading in other parts of the curriculum. Many of the uses of reading are shared by reading instruction and reading in the content areas and can best be developed during a period set aside especially for such a purpose.

Gray further points out that his Stage 4 has a "unique educational and social significance" (p. 110) in that this is the level necessary for the reading of adult material of average difficulty. Although Stage 4 (Grades 4–6) is viewed as preparation for adult reading, it is interesting to note that Gray placed greater emphasis at this stage than in the previous ones on "accuracy and independence in the recognition of increasingly difficult words." Indeed, this is the first of his stages in which word recognition is given first priority in the "levels of achievement" as "is able to pronounce unfamiliar words or locate them quickly in a dictionary" (Table B-4).

Gray's Stage 5, which he placed at junior, senior high and junior college, "is largely a reflective and interpretive" stage (p. 123). The goals are presented in Table B-5. As the title of this stage indicates, it is a time for refinement of reading attitudes, habits, and tastes introduced earlier, with stress on reading of varied materials, on advanced study skills, and on developing meaning vocabulary, comprehension, and interpretation.

GRAY'S READING STAGES: STAGE 5, THE REFINEMENT
OF READING ATTITUDES, HABITS, AND TASTES

DURATION	OVERALL AIMS	SPECIFIC AIMS
Junior high, senior high, junior college	1. To broaden still further the experiences of pupils by wide exposure to books, newspapers, and periodicals 2. To refine reading interests and tastes, with particular attention to the development of an interest in current events 3. To develop still further comprehension and interpretation skills 4. To develop advanced skills in study activities	
For junior high		1. To broaden the meaning vocabulary of students 2. To extend still further comprehension and interpretation by examining the significance of material read, evaluating ideas presented, discussing the relevance and validity of information presented, recognizing the author's purpose 3. To develop an understanding of the procedures for reading different kinds of material for different purposes 4. To improve performance in study activities requiring reading, e.g., finding relationships, applying principles or facts to new situations, generalizing, etc. 5. To teach pupils to vary their rate of reading in relation to purpose and materials
For senior high		1. To help develop particular "modes of thought and interpretation" (p. 125) that are necessary in particular fields, e.g., history, science, "argumentation"

Table B-5
GRAY'S READING STAGES: STAGE 5, THE REFINEMENT
OF READING ATTITUDES, HABITS, AND TASTES (cont.)

DURATION	OVERALL AIMS	SPECIFIC AIMS
For senior high (cont.)		2. To improve efficiency in study activities requiring reading, e.g., interpretation of graphs, tables; use of card catalogue, reference books; summarizing
For junior college		1. To extend skills of "intelligent interpretation and critical study" (p. 126) of various kinds of writing by giving attention to the nature of historical and scientific writings, logic, scientific method, inductive and deductive thinking, underlying assumptions, errors in logic, inferences, etc. 2. To continue to provide guidance in reading and study activities that are assigned in the various content areas, e.g., the purpose of the reading and the most effective reading and study procedures to be used should be stated; new concepts, specialized vocabulary, and new principles should be explained; supplementary reading should be given

SOURCE: *NSSE Yearbook,* 1937.

Gray also suggests a sixth stage but does not elaborate: "The chief purpose of the guidance at that advanced stage would be to promote a high level of efficiency in critical reading and library research among students pursuing specialized and professional programs" (p. 120).

A review of Gray's reading stages reveals certain characteristics. Although he presented fairly detailed descriptions of goals and achievements for each stage, the distinctions between them are not always clear. Rather there is a certain degree of sameness to the stages. An examination of Tables B-1 to B-4 reveals this overlap. The same goals appear at each stage, although at the higher levels they are more fully developed. The aims for the most part concern what Gray calls the various "phases" of reading, namely, word recognition, oral reading, silent reading, comprehension, and interpretation. For example, we find the following with respect to word recognition:

Stage 2 (First Reader)	"To develop increased independence in the recognition of new words" (p. 96). (Table B-2, First Reader, 4.)
Stage 3 (Grades 2 and 3)	"To promote continuous development in accuracy and independence in word recognition" (p. 101). (Table B-3, 6.)
Stage 4 (Grades 4–6)	". . . greater accuracy and independence in word recognition" (p. 108).
	"Accuracy and independence in pronouncing increasingly difficult words" (p. 113). (Table B-4, 3).

The only distinction with regard to word recognition and analysis between Stages 2, 3, and 4 seems to be the reference to the increasing difficulty of the words in Stage 4. Indeed, from the above and from the tables, it would appear that word recognition received a greater emphasis at Stage 4 (Grades 4–6) than at Stage 1 (Grade 1) and Stage 2 (Grades 2 and 3). Nor can one find in Gray's description of goals and achievements at the various stages that the ability to recognize words independently reaches a point of mastery at a particular stage. Instead, similar references to it start at Stage 2 (Grade 1, First Reader) and continue through Stage 4 (Grades 4–6). It is only at Stage 5 (junior high, senior high, and junior college) where no mention is made of the need for accuracy in independent word recognition and analysis.

There is a similar lack of distinction between the stages with regard to oral reading. The following are special references to oral reading in Gray's Stages 2, 3, and 4:

Stage 2 (First Reader)	"To increase fluency in both oral and silent reading" (p. 96). (Table B-2, First Reader, 5.)

Stage 3 (Grades 2 and 3)   "To provide for the development of desirable standards and habits involved in good oral reading" (p. 101). (Table B-3, 5.)

Stage 4 (Grades 4–6)   "To promote the development of increased power and efficiency in . . . quality of oral reading" (p.110). (Table B-4, 3.)

In a sense, the lack of distinctiveness among Gray's reading stages should not come as a surprise in light of his view of reading as a thought-getting process from the very beginning. It was Gray, perhaps more than any other reading scholar, who called for "reading for meaning" from the very beginning (Chall, 1967). His reading stages emphasized comprehension and meaning as early as his Stage 2 (Grade 1). Yet in spite of the central role given to comprehension at all the reading stages, and in spite of the sameness of the goals for the different stages, Gray was definite that there were differences between beginning and mature reading. He noted that content reading should start at Stage 4 (Grades 4–6) and that Stage 5 (junior and senior high, junior college) is characterized by achievement in meaning vocabularies, interpretation, and wide reading in a variety of books and media. Overall, it is probably the characteristics described in the labels for the stages that came to be associated with the particular reading stage rather than the detailed overlapping aims presented for each stage.

For example, in their second edition of *Effective Teaching of Reading,* Harris and Sipay (1971) refer to Gray's reading stages saying, "The reading program has been considered for more than thirty years to have five main stages or periods" (pp. 20–21): development of reading readiness; beginning reading; period of rapid skills development; period of wide reading; and refinement of reading. Similarly, Harris, in the 1970 edition of his widely read textbook *How to Increase Reading Ability,* refers to Gray's stages and states: "Although many years have passed, this classification is still useful" (p. 60).

It is also important to note Gray's statement that the reading stages were based on the research available at the time—primarily his own and that of Buswell. He wisely cautioned that since these studies were based on instruction of the past, conclusions from them should be regarded as tentative and open to revision.

The following research results were cited by Gray as evidence for emphasizing given aspects of reading at particular stages or grade levels:

1. The ability to interpret simple material accurately increases rapidly in the primary grades and may reach a high level of peformance by the end of the 3rd grade (Gray, 1918).

2. The ability to interpret material of increasing difficulty and to read for different purposes continues to improve through college (Gray, 1917).

3. Speed of silent reading increases rapidly during grades 1–4 and continues to increase, although less rapidly through grade 8 (Gray, 1917).

4. Speed and accuracy of oral reading increases rapidly in the primary grades and continues to increase, although less rapidly, during the upper grades. By the end of the 3rd grade, students have acquired four-fifths of the ability of college students (Gray, 1917).

5. Rate and span of recognition and the "rhythmical progress of perceptions" improve very rapidly in the first four grades but only slowly and somewhat irregularly in the higher grades. There is usually very little increase in span of recognition after the 4th grade. Rate of recognition continues to improve during the 5th and 6th grades. There is some progress in the rhythmical progression of perceptions as late as the 9th grade. (Buswell, 1922).

Finally, one must note that Gray tied his stages to reading materials published for the particular grades and to scores on standardized achievement tests. For example, he notes that at the end of Stage 3 (Grades 2 and 3) pupils should be able to score 4.0 on a silent reading test. Similarly, at the end of Stage 4 (Grades 4–6) pupils should be able to obtain a score of 7.0. According to Gray, "In this Yearbook the minimal standards set up are those that enable pupils to engage with reasonable efficiency in the reading activities required in the various curricular fields of the grades in question" (p. 74). Thus, in essence, Gray tied his reading stages to the increasing complexity of the standardized achievement tests and to the difficulties of the curriculum materials then used in reading and in the content subjects at the various grade levels.

THE READING STAGES OF ARTHUR GATES (1947)

Arthur I. Gates, in the 1947 edition of his *The Improvement of Reading,* devoted a chapter to a discussion of stages in reading development entitled "A Brief Sketch of the Nature and Development of Reading Abilities." He believed that the concept of reading stages would contribute to an understanding of the nature of reading. Gates pointed out that different authors might present slightly different stages and that the stages selected by each would depend on the particular author's purpose. He referred generally at the end of his chapter to Gray's discussion of stages in the 1937 *NSSE Yearbook.*

Gates viewed the importance and purpose of reading stages as follows:

> The stages to be presented shortly are selected for the purpose of illustrating some of the more important techniques and limitations shown by the typical pupil as he progresses through the elementary school. Study of these stages will point out the nature of the different kinds of abilities and techniques that tend to be adopted at particular times and the importance of advancing from one form of technique to more advanced types as experience makes this possible (p. 23).

Gates described eight stages:[4]

1. The prereading period
2. The reading readiness program period
3. The beginning reading period
4. The initial independent reading period
5. The advanced primary reading period
6. The transition period from primary to intermediate reading
7. The intermediate reading period
8. The mature reading period

The prereading and reading readiness program periods precede actual reading instruction. These together are very similar to Gray's reading readiness stage. Table B-6 summarizes the main features of these two prereading periods.

[4]It is interesting to note that in the naming of the eight stages, he returned to the earlier term, *period,* used in Gray's first delineation of stages in 1925.

GATES'S READING PERIODS (1947): PERIODS 1 AND 2,
PREREADING AND READING READINESS PROGRAM

PERIOD	DURATION	REQUIREMENTS FOR LEARNING TO READ	PURPOSE
Prereading	Birth to development of reading readiness in 1st grade	1. Ability to understand and speak English and to pronounce words correctly 2. Ability to discriminate the sounds of words and to note recurring parts of syllables 3. Ability to pay attention when someone is speaking 4. Ability to remember what has been said 5. Wide vocabulary 6. Story sense—ability to listen to and analyze a story 7. Ability to interpret pictures 8. Ability to discriminate colors 9. Ability to handle books and follow a line of print 10. Familiarity with words from signs, stories, newspapers, etc. 11. Interest in reading 12. Favorable emotional adjustment to school and classroom	
Reading readiness program	Early 1st grade (a few weeks to several months)		"To develop all those forms of information, skill, and interest" (p. 26) which are essential for learning to read as described for the prereading period

The next three stages proposed by Gates can be viewed as a "primary reading stage," with three subdivisions: the "beginning reading period," the "initial independent reading period," and the "advanced primary reading period." These correspond approximately to Gray's Stage 2, "initial guidance in learning to read," and our Stages 1 and 2.

Table B-7
GATES'S READING PERIODS (1947): PERIOD 3,
BEGINNING READING PERIOD

PERIOD/ DURATION	SPECIFIC CAPABILITIES AND LIMITATIONS DURING PERIOD	GENERAL ACHIEVEMENTS AT END OF PERIOD
First 3 months of Grade 1	1. Will recognize some words quickly, others not as fast, still others more slowly; therefore reading of a sentence will be uneven, with some words needing more attention than others	1. Knows how "to progress along a line of print" (p. 29)
	2. Reads word by word: must look at each word, sometimes more than once	2. Can read sentences, phrases, and familiar words in isolation
	3. Understands the meaning of a sentence less easily by reading than if same sentence spoken to pupil (since some attention goes to mechanics of recognition), although will understand a sentence after reading it	3. Has developed skill in deriving meaning of unknown words from context
	4. Speed of reading will be slower than rate of speaking	4. Is able to learn new words more quickly
	5. Only recognizes words that have been taught to pupil; incapable of working out pronunciation of a new word in isolation; reading must therefore be limited mainly to words known	5. Has begun to note certain features of words and relate these features to other words which contain them
	6. Can use context to derive meaning of unfamiliar word	

Gates provides considerable detail on the reading behaviors characteristic of these primary grade years. Gates, as Gray, was, of course, writing from a specific viewpoint as to how reading was taught at the time and how it should be taught. Some of the characteristics Gates attributes to readers, therefore, may be a function not only of a "natural course of development" but also of how the reader was taught.

Table B-8

GATES'S READING PERIODS (1947): PERIOD 4,
INITIAL INDEPENDENT READING PERIOD

PERIOD/ DURATION	SPECIFIC CAPABILITIES AND LIMITATIONS DURING PERIOD	GENERAL ACHIEVEMENTS AT END OF PERIOD
2 to 3 months (from 3rd to 5th or 6th month of Grade 1)	1. Reads word by word; usually cannot recognize a phrase at one glance	1. Has acquired a large sight vocabulary
	2. Can recognize some words very rapidly; is changing "from a careful study of each individual word to recognition by the slightest glance" (p. 31); errors in word recognition may concomitantly increase	2. Has greater skill in using context to recognize words
	3. Speed for first reading will be slow; cannot read as rapidly as speaks	3. Has greater skill in using visual and "phonetic elements" to figure out the pronunciation of unfamiliar words
	4. After a silent reading, can read a passage at normal speaking rate	4. Has greater skill in organizing and making use of the thought of the material read
	5. Uses elementary techniques for working out the pronunciation of unknown words, i.e., using letter-sound relationships (helpful with monosyllabic words) or noticing particular syllables and phonograms (helpful with polysyllabic words as well)	

Gates states that in the "beginning reading period" (the first 3 months of Grade 1) the pupil begins to recognize words and to read sentences. However, he can do fluent reading only with material composed mainly of familiar words. If there are too many unknown words, there will be interference with fluent reading and comprehension, and the reader will not be able to give attention primarily to the thought of the passage.[5]

In the "independent reading period" (4–6 months of Grade 1) the pupil gradually learns "to work out the recognition and pronunciation of words in simple material" (p. 30) and achieves "reasonable mastery of the process of reading simple, connected material with appropriate eye movements and full understanding" (p. 30). He uses elementary techniques to work out the pronunciation of unfamiliar words.

In the "advanced primary reading period" (second half of Grade 1), the child can read material which has a larger number of unknown words and therefore can begin to read easy supplementary material. However, he "is still functioning in what may be called the 'primary' kind of reading" (p. 32).

Table B-9
GATES'S READING PERIODS (1947): PERIOD 5, ADVANCED
PRIMARY READING PERIOD

PERIOD/ DURATION	SPECIFIC CAPABILITIES AND LIMITATIONS DURING PERIOD
2nd half of 1st grade; a few months of 2nd grade	1. Still exhibits considerable inner speech; seems to be translating the written word into the spoken word to derive meaning
	2. Cannot get meaning as quickly by reading a sentence as by hearing the same sentence spoken
	3. Still reads word by word
	4. Can read easy supplementary material; can handle more unfamiliar words
	5. Will still make errors in word recognition and may not get the full thought of a passage
	6. After reading a passage silently, can read same passage orally both confidently and accurately

[5]Gates assumes here, as did Gray, that the first steps in reading are to recognize whole words and to get the thought of a selection. As noted earlier, this characteristic appears to depend on how the child is taught to read. When both Gray and Gates wrote, in 1937 and 1947, most children in the U.S. learned to read by a meaning-emphasis approach, which taught whole word recognition considerably before teaching letters and sounds, i.e., phonics.

How do the stages of Gates and Gray view readers at the end of Grade 1? There are many similarities. Both view the beginner as acquiring first a sight vocabulary and then reading simple, connected material usually word by word. Gradually the reader begins to develop some skill in pronouncing unknown words by "guessing" from context and by noticing similar letters, syllables, and phonograms.

Pupils differ on word recognition and fluency. A typical reader in Gates's "advanced primary period" (end of Grade 1 to a few months of Grade 2) is still reading word by word and making errors in word recognition that may prevent getting the full thought of a passage. It is during Gates's "transition period from primary to intermediate reading" (2nd–3rd grades) that readers move from primary methods of word attack to more advanced techniques and proceed to reading by thought units. Gray's scheme, however, has typical pupils at the end of Grade 1 "read orally in thought units, rather than word by word" (see Table B-2). An additional difference can be seen in the fact that Gray also includes as specific aims for Stage 2 (Grade 1) the reading of different kinds of material (story, informational, study) for different purposes and for interpreting intelligently. Gates does not present these as goals for his periods covering Grades 1 and early Grade 2.

Of critical importance in Gates's scheme is his 6th period—the transition from primary to intermediate reading. This period begins a few months into the 2nd grade and continues until the last quarter of the 3rd grade, when the typical child "will begin to shift from a primary type of reading to a higher level of reading ability which we shall call 'intermediate reading' " (p. 33). "During this period marked changes in many respects are going on under the surface even though the curve of growth in rate of reading and in other respects may show a continuous, unbroken advance. This is the period in which the pupil must replace many primary or beginning reading techniques with more advanced and more subtle types of abilities" (p. 33).

With regard to word recognition, the pupil begins to replace primary methods with more advanced techniques. In the 1st grade, the reader could get along by knowing and making use of letter-sound associations for single letters or simple phonograms. This technique is useful with monosyllabic words which occur to a great extent in early reading materi- al. However, as a pupil continues in the 2nd grade, he or she begins to meet a greater number of long, polysyllabic words. According to Gates, such words cannot be attacked solely by a letter-sound approach. The child must "be able to perceive instantly as units component words and syllables" (p. 33). He or she must begin to "acquire some skill in discovering and combining syllables. For many children this represents a very distinct shift or transition in methods" (p. 33). According to Gates, this shift from primary methods of word attack to more advanced techniques is necessary if the pupil is to make the transition from primary to intermediate reading.

A second important change takes place during the "transi- tion" period. "During this stage a transition to a higher level of perception becomes possible. The pupil will begin to recog- nize certain phrases or word combinations at one glance quite as readily and as quickly as he previously recognized each of the single words in the thought unit" (p. 34). This refined per- ception enables him or her to read with greater smoothness and speed, to make fewer fixations, and to organize the mate- rial better. He or she is about to acquire the "eye-voice span" or the "eye recognition" span (p. 34). In short, according to Gates, at the end of the transition period, the reader will have advanced from "word-by-word reading to reading by thought units" or "from the stage of 'reading by talking' to the stage of 'reading by thinking' " (p. 34). Table B-10 summarizes the major features of the "transition period."

Table B-10

GATES'S READING PERIODS (1947): PERIOD 6, TRANSITION PERIOD FROM PRIMARY TO INTERMEDIATE READING

DURATION	CHARACTERISTICS
A few months into 2nd grade until last quarter of 3rd grade	1. Makes the transition from primary methods of word attack to more advanced techniques, i.e., must begin to respond to syllables rather than to rely completely on a single-letter approach 2. Refines his perception, i.e., can respond to reduced cues in recognizing words; the result is greater speed, fewer fixations, better organization of material, eye-voice span—all of which enable student to read by thought units rather than word by word

Thus Gates attributes to the transition period a major advance of movement from word-by-word reading to reading by thought units. This is possible, he noted, because of pupils' more refined perception and their use of more advanced word recognition techniques. Gates thus went a step beyond Gray by explaining how reading by thought units develops. He also placed this achievement at a higher grade than Gray.

Table B-11
GATES'S READING PERIODS (1947): PERIOD 7,
INTERMEDIATE READING PERIOD

DURATION	CHARACTERISTICS

Latter part of Grade 3 and 4–6	1. Greater "differentiation and versatility," i.e., the ability to read in different ways for different purposes
	2. Greater speed as a result of
	   a. Improved techniques of word and phrase recognition
	   b. Larger reading vocabulary
	   c. Ability to read for different purposes in different ways, i.e., the differentiation and versatility noted above

The "intermediate reading period" (Grades 4–6, see Table B-11) is characterized as follows by Gates: "Word recognition in reasonably familiar material has now become so effective that the pupil can and does give his mind more fully to the thought. He understands and remembers better what he has read. He has reached a stage in which he can do more than merely comprehend the thought during reading. He can evaluate, even reflect upon it somewhat, during the process" (p. 34). To Gates this meant that the pupil can effectively use various comprehension techniques such as reading rapidly to select certain information or to note the organization; reading to find details; reading slowly to "study"; skimming, etc. Gates points out that these special comprehension skills do not develop exclusively in the "intermediate stage." They begin to develop long before in the primary grades. However, at that time they are rudimentary. In Grades 4–6 where there is wide reading and study, they are perfected considerably. To Gates "differentiation and versatility," learning to read in different ways for different purposes, are the chief objectives of the "intermediate stage."

Gates's "intermediate stage" corresponds timewise to Stage 4 (Grades 4–6) of Gray, and there is a good deal of similarity between the two. Gray, however, emphasized the "differentiated" comprehension skills in the earlier stages to a greater extent than did Gates. Gates points out, as noted, that these skills do begin to develop earlier but that they are rudimentary. Gray, on the other hand, mentions them as goals for the earlier stages—for Grade 1 (Stage 2) and for Grades 2 and 3 (Stage 3). (See Tables B-2 and B-3.)

What enables the child to "evaluate" and "reflect upon" his reading at this point? According to Gates, this phenomenon is partly due to the fact that word recognition is so smooth and easy that the reader can give more attention to the thought (with less to the mechanics of reading). Gates also adds, "He understands and remembers better . . ." (p. 34). Was Gates saying that by the "intermediate stage" the pupil has reached a level of intellectual development that allows him to "evaluate, even reflect"?

Reading development continues beyond Grade 6 to mature reading. During this period skills are refined and perfected, and the reader becomes still more versatile in adapting his reading techniques to the task at hand. "As he becomes more proficient, the pupil can give more of his attention to thinking about, evaluating, comparing, organizing, or otherwise using the content during the actual process of reading" (p. 39). Gates does not elaborate as much as Gray does concerning this period. Table B-12 presents its main characteristics.

Table B-12
GATES'S READING PERIODS (1947): PERIOD 8,
MATURE READING

DURATION	CHARACTERISTICS
Beyond grade 6	1. "Gradual improvement in efficiency" (p. 38)
	2. Improved skill in figuring out the pronunciation of unfamiliar words
	3. Improved skill in recognizing words on the basis of reduced cues
	4. Improved phrasing and organization of material
	5. Greater speed
	6. Increased flexibility
	7. Refinement of the various reading comprehension skills

DAVID RUSSELL'S READING STAGES (1949 AND 1961)

In the 1949 *NSSE Yearbook,* the concept of developmental stages in reading was again discussed—this time by David Russell. Russell took a somewhat different point of view from Gray and Gates, being concerned more with the implications of child development data for the teaching of reading. He presented some of the characteristics of children at various ages and their possible implications for reading (Table B-13). It should be noted here that the child development characteristics listed for Grades 1–3 are largely cognitive, i.e., style of thinking, "thinking evolving from use of concrete experiences to somewhat more abstract symbols," "some understanding of cause and effect relationships," etc.

Table B-13

RUSSELL'S READING STAGES: THE RELATIONSHIP OF
CHILD DEVELOPMENT DATA TO READING

AGE GROUP	CHARACTERISTICS	POSSIBLE IMPLICATIONS FOR READING
6–8 (Grades 1–3)	1. "Interested in here and now of immediate environment" (p. 13)	1. Reading material should be centered mainly around objects or events in the immediate environment; by the 3rd grade reading should be used to broaden experiences
	2. Thinking is somewhat but not completely egocentric	2. Discussions should relate to home, farm, or community rather than "generalizations about society" (p. 13)
	3. "Thinking is evolving from use of concrete experiences to somewhat more abstract symbols" (p. 13)	3. Animal stories and stories (both imaginary and realistic) about boys and girls are enjoyed
	4. Find it easier to note differences than similarities	
	5. Beginning to show some understanding of cause-effect relationships	
	6. Draw conclusions after partial examination of data	

Table B-13
RUSSELL'S READING STAGES: THE RELATIONSHIP OF
CHILD DEVELOPMENT DATA TO READING (cont.)

AGE GROUP	CHARACTERISTICS	POSSIBLE IMPLICATIONS FOR READING
9–11 (Grades 4–6)	1. "Depth of comprehension of concepts increases" (p. 14) 2. Sense of time and space improves, and children begin to be able to differentiate historical periods 3. Rapid growth in vocabulary 4. Interests begin to extend beyond the immediate environment 5. Ability to note similarities and differences and cause-effect relationships improves	1. Beginning reading skills have been acquired; efficiency in reading and the use of reading for specific purposes should be emphasized 2. Vocabulary and concept development should be encouraged by exposure to a wide variety of concrete experiences and by providing numerous opportunities to use language in reading and writing
12–14 (Grades 7–9)	1. Exhibit more mature habits in study activities, solving problems, and "creative reading situations" (p. 15) 2. Language abilities continue to grow; differentiation of manner of expression into formal and informal becomes more distinct 3. Exhibit greater ability to memorize and organize	1. Able to organize what they read 2. Increased ability to generalize 3. Can read material concerning abstract social concepts (such as justice) or material pertaining to international affairs

SOURCE: *NSSE Yearbook,* 1949.

Before presenting his reading stages, Russell refers to the ones of Gates in *The Improvement of Reading* (1947) and McCullough, Strang, and Traxler in *Problems in the Improvement of Reading* (1945). Interestingly, he does not refer to Gray's earlier presentations of reading stages in the 1925 and 1937 *NSSE Yearbooks*.

Russell's stages (see Table B-14) tend to be more similar to those of Gates than to Gray, except that he has six as compared to Gates's eight. He includes, as did Gates, a transition stage between primary and intermediate reading and emphasizes the critical role which this period plays in reading development. Russell points out, as did Gray, that during the "intermediate stage" (Grades 4–6) popular adult reading material comes within the range of pupil comprehension.

Table B-14
RUSSELL'S READING STAGES

STAGE	DURATION	CHARACTERISTICS
Prereading	Birth to sometime in Grade 1	
Beginning-reading	Grade 1	1. Acquires a sight vocabulary 2. Reads connected material composed of the studied words 3. Reads word by word 4. Begins to use word form, "phonetic," and context clues 5. Begins to read "in a variety of thoughtful ways" (p. 20) 6. Cannot work out the pronunciation of words not yet studied
Initial Stage of Independent Reading	Grade 2	1. Has greater ability to work out the pronunciation of unfamiliar words; word analysis and word recognition techniques develop very rapidly 2. Has greater skill in using context to derive meaning 3. "Craves to read all sorts of material" (p. 20); much reading material should be provided

Table B-14
RUSSELL'S READING STAGES (cont.)

STAGE	DURATION	CHARACTERISTICS
Initial Stage of Independent Reading (cont.)	Grade 2	4. "Thorough comprehension" and "intelligent use of ideas after reading" (p. 20) are ranked among the major objectives
Transition	Grade 3 and early Grade 4	1. Must make a transition from primary type of reading to reading of a more mature form a. Speed at beginning of period may be slower than speaking rate but will equal or surpass it at end of period b. Reads word by word at the beginning of period but must begin to read by thought units c. Must begin to apply more advanced methods of word recognition than the use of single letters, phonograms, and vague whole-word impressions
Intermediate or Low Maturity	Grades 4–6	1. Achieves steady but slow growth in all phases of reading 2. Speed of reading begins to exceed that of speaking 3. Uses more advanced techniques of word recognition, e.g., syllabication 4. Recognizes two or more words at one fixation 5. "Comprehension of more accurate, advanced, and subtle forms emerges" (p. 21)

Table B-14
RUSSELL'S READING STAGES (cont.)

STAGE	DURATION	CHARACTERISTICS
Intermediate Grades 4–6 or Low Maturity (cont.)		6. "Popular" adult reading material can be understood; "the world of the printed word is thus opened up" (p. 21) 7. Can use skills such as skimming, reading to outline or summarize, to select or compare, in a flexible manner
Advanced Grade 7+		1. Skills are perfected and diversified; reading in a variety of ways for different purposes 2. Able to "select, judge, compare, or criticize while reading" (p. 22)

SOURCE: *NSSE Yearbook,* 1949.

In the 1961 *NSSE Yearbook,* in contrast to those of 1925, 1937, and 1949, Russell gave only perfunctory treatment to the concept of reading stages. After referring to the 1937 and 1949 yearbooks and listing the reading stages presented in that of 1949, Russell states,

> Research and teachers' experience indicate that school children normally go through a sequence of stages in their development of reading abilities. . . . The committee for the present yearbook believes that such descriptions are still valid but wishes to point out that, at best, they are general descriptions giving rough approximations of a child's reading status (p. 229).

The notion of reading stages gave way in the 1961 yearbook to a discussion of reading skills to be taught at the primary, intermediate, junior high, and senior high levels (and sometimes college as well).

In summary, there is a good deal of similarity among the developmental reading schemes of Gray, Gates, and Russell. All have a prereading, a beginning reading, an intermediate, and an advanced reading stage. The specific characteristics of these periods also tend to be similar, but some differences exist, particularly between Gray and Gates's schemes.

All three authors assumed that beginning reading was taught by the introduction of a sight vocabulary, the reading of connected material using this vocabulary, and the gradual addition of word-analysis techniques. This view of how reading should be and, in fact, was taught at that time influenced their descriptions of the beginning reading stage. For example, each of the authors stated that there would be a period when only words specifically taught could be recognized by the child. He or she would be unable to work out the pronunciation of words that had not yet been presented. Gates characterized the reader during the first three months of 1st grade instruction (beginning reading period) in this manner (see Table B-7). Russell depicted the beginner as having very little skill in attacking unstudied words for the entire first year: "cannot work out the pronunciation of words not yet studied." It was not until Russell's initial stage of independent reading in Grade 2 that the child was characterized as being able to work out new words' on his own: "Has greater ability to work out the pronunciation of unfamiliar words; word analysis and word recognition techniques develop very rapidly" (see Table B-14). This dependence on a particular view of reading means that at least some characteristics described may not be features of readers in general but rather are a function of how the child has been taught to read. Gray seemed to put even less emphasis on the development of word recognition and analysis in Grades 1–3, and the greatest seemed to be placed in Grades 4–6.

There is even greater agreement concerning the features which characterize readers at the intermediate stage: the reader can find the main idea, locate information, summarize, outline, etc. (the so-called reading comprehension skills). We can ask here whether these skills represent what the reader does or can do at this stage or whether they are the particular skills that have been taught. Each of the authors does refer, in a limited way, to the intellectual functioning of children during this stage. Gray enumerates depth of interpretation (comparing and evaluating ideas, understanding implications) as one of the aspects of reading to be stimulated at the intermediate stage.

Gates stresses "differentiation and versatility," i.e., the ability to read in different ways for different purposes. Russell refers to "comprehension of more accurate, advanced, and subtle forms." However, in all three descriptions the intellectual functioning of the child seems to receive less attention than the specific reading comprehension skills, although Russell's list of child development characteristics with implications for reading are primarily aspects of intellectual functioning (see Table B-13). It should be noted that Gray and Russell both refer to the fact that at the conclusion of this stage popular adult reading material comes within the comprehension level of students.[6]

The advanced reading stage, placed at beginning Grade 7 and beyond by all three authors, is described by them as a time for refinement and perfection of skills previously developed during the intermediate stage. Gates and Russell do not provide many details; only Gray elaborates. Gray also specifies that the advanced stage includes junior high, senior high, and junior college, and he stresses the "interpretive and critical study" of various kinds of writing—scientific, historical, and logical, requiring inductive and deductive thinking, and reading and study of activities in the various content areas, including new concepts, specialized vocabulary, and the like. It should be noted that Gray also suggested, although he did not elaborate, a more advanced stage, Stage 6, to promote "a high level of efficiency in critical reading and library research among students pursuing specialized and professional programs" (p. 120).

Beyond these basic similarities, certain differences among the three authors should be noted. One relates to the period between the beginning reading and intermediate stages. Both Gates and Russell include a transition stage at this particular point, and emphasize that the reader must change from a pri-

[6]If we assume at the end of the intermediate stage the average student is able to read at a 7.0 level on a standardized test, this would make available only limited aspects of adult reading material since most newspapers have a readability level of at least 8th grade and the national and international news is written on a higher level, about 11th–12th grade. Indeed, the most widely read newsmagazines (*Time, Newsweek*) are estimated to be on a 10th grade level.

mary type of reading to a more advanced form. Gray does not refer to such a transition. According to Russell, the transition period extends from Grade 3 to Grade $4^{1}/_{4}$; for Gates, from Grade 2 to Grade $3^{3}/_{4}$. Gray's stage of rapid progress in attitudes and habits (Grades 2 and 3) corresponds in time to this transition period.

A second difference pertains to the change from word-by-word reading to reading by thought units. For Gates, the change occurs during the transition period (Grades 2 and 3). According to Russell the change also takes place during the transition stage, but for Russell this stage corresponds to Grades 3–4. For Gray the change occurs at the end of Stage 1 (Grade 1), initial guidance in reading. Gates is the only one who attempts to explain how this phenomenon occurs. He notes that the development of two abilities enables readers to increase their span of recognition which leads to advances in reading by thought units: (1) the ability to use more advanced methods of word attack, focusing on syllables rather than single letters, and (2) the ability to perceive phrases instantly by responding to "reduced cues" within words.

Overall, Gates and also Russell showed a greater concern for the changes in the psychological characteristics of the reading stages, while Gray seemed more concerned with the instructional goals and procedures suggested by the stages.

THE ILG AND AMES READING GRADIENT

In 1950, a year following that of Russell's reading stage scheme in the 1949 *NSSE Yearbook,* Frances L. Ilg and Louise Bates Ames (1950) of the Yale University School of Medicine published their Reading Gradient—developmental trends in reading behavior among children 15 months to 10 years.

> The child's ability to read does not develop suddenly at or about the time of school entrance. The roots of reading ability lie far back in the preschool years, at least as far back as 15 months when the child is able to pat identified pictures in a picture book. From then on, reading ability develops by slow stages through the time when the child can name objects printed in a book, recognize salient printed capitals, recognize salient printed words in a familiar book, until the time when he can read sentences, recognizing unfamiliar words accurately and rapidly (p. 291).

Even more strongly than Gray, Gates, and Russell, they assert the hierarchical nature of the development: "These and other stages follow each other in lawful, inevitable order."

The reading gradient was obtained as follows. Up to age 5 naturalistic observations were made in the home and in the nursery school of the children's responses to pictures and to books as they were being read to and as they "read" to themselves. Observations were supplemented by parents' reports. Children of 5–10 were given tests of reading readiness and the Gray Oral.

> Responses of subjects to the above-described reading situations were analyzed to determine the components of a "reading gradient" which would present a step by step outline of the path which the child follows in his reactions to pictures and printed words from earliest reactions of some selective response to pictures on through fluent reading of sentences and paragraphs, and which would demonstrate the continuity of this development.
>
> Particular attention was paid to the errors which occurred during the child's reading performance, on the assumption that many so-called errors might well be relatively benign and characteristic responses of certain age levels, and might indeed have definite developmental import, as giving real clues to the rate of the child's progress through the reading gradient (p. 292).[7]

Their findings, in a developmental frame of reference, are presented below:

Reading Gradient
15 months
Pats identified pictures in book.
18 months
Points to identified pictures in book.
24 months
Names objects pictured in book.
36–42 months
May identify some capital letters, in alphabet book or on blocks.

Some select letters by form: i.e., the round letters (O, C, D, G), or the vertical and horizontal ones (T, I); some by association, *M* for Mummy, *D* for Daddy, *J* for Johnny, etc.

May know alphabet through songs or poems. Enjoys this but does not necessarily learn the letters.

Wants to look at pictures in book when being read to.

[7]It is interesting to note how this benign view of errors predates the Goodmans' "miscue" analysis (1977) which is also based on the assumption that errors reveal process.

48 months

May recognize salient capital letters.

Spontaneous demand to print a few salient capital letters.

May identify a letter without naming: "That's in my name."

5 years

Knows all or at least many capital letters.

Likes to spell c-a-t, d-o-g, m-u-m-m-y, n-o, y-e-s, own name, names of siblings.

Asks, "What does c-a-t spell?"

Picks out familiar words on signs, or on a page, or "hot" and "cold" on faucets.

Can underline certain letters on request.

May use wooden letters, spelling names of self or siblings.

Likes to identify repetitious phrases or words in familiar books such as exclamations or sounds that animals make.

May recognize own first name.

May recognize several or all numbers on the clock.

5¹/₂ years

Most know the entire alphabet.

Can recognize letters or even some single words on a page in a familiar book. Often first or last word in a line. May thus read vertically down a page. Looks right at the written words (instead of at pictures) as read to. Sound words or proper names most easily recognized.

Likes to be read to; pretends to read; likes to spell; likes to print; interested in new and large words and their meaning.

Memory so excellent and accurate that they may sound as if they are actually reading when they are not.

Errors: Substitutions of plural form in reading single words most frequent, chiefly single letter substitutions: want = went, cat = can; or giving word of same general appearance, caught = could. Or reversal of single letter, b = p, or whole word, saw = was.

Omissions and repetitions also occur.

6 years

Interest in small as well as capital letters.

Finds words as they relate to a picture or story. Matches words.

Picks out single words or combinations of words. *About one-third can actually read sentences.*

Learns mechanics of reading: holding book, turning page, etc.

Becomes able to recognize words out of their familiar setting.

Gets clues from length of word, beginning sound or letter.

Likes to read nursery books. May now read, though earlier memorized.

Some like to pick out letters on a typewriter and have mother spell words for them. May supply beginning letter but need help with the rest.

Still likes to be read to.

Errors: Substitutions of visual form most frequent in reading single words. Mostly single letter substitutions as *some* for *same, even* for *ever;* or general appearance, as *scratchily* for *scarcely.*

In reading sentences, having to be told words is the outstanding error (90 percent of the cases from 1 to 7 words each). (Gray Reading Test).

Reversals of single letter or of word, very strong as *saw* = *was.*

Repetitions and substitutions of meaning also occur conspicuously, as *palace* = *castle, go* = *come, I* = *you.*

Words are occasionally added to give balance, as a *king and queen.*

Often repeats a word previously used a sentence or two above.

Apt to add the word "little" wherever it will fit.

7 years

Nearly all can now read sentences.

Can recognize familiar words accurately and rapidly.

Many can master new words through the context.

Many can read accurately, rapidly and comprehensively.

Likes to know how far to read. Otherwise likely to go on and on. Can use a marker. Likes to be told words he cannot get.

Can read orally to a group.

The range in score (Gray Reading Test) for this group is from Grade 0 to Grade 5.4, average = 2.5.

Also marked individual differences in reading rate.

Very good readers may become "chain readers" at this age—go from one book to the next without stopping. May have four or five books each open to their "place" at the same time.

Errors: Substitutions of visual form, single letter (100 percent of cases) the most common error; or giving word of same general appearance.

Reversals of word, substitution of meaning, repetitions, some additions, having to be told, omissions, also occur.

Reads mechanically and continuously, overlapping sentences and paragraphs without pausing. Doesn't like to be stopped in reading, therefore welcomes adult's supplying words he hesitates over.

Often attacks word from last letter instead of first letter. Has trouble with vowels, easily confused; *i* is most common substitution.

Apt to omit word "little" whenever it occurs.

8 years

All can read sentences and paragraphs.

Masters new words through context, division into syllables, initial consonants, prefixes and suffixes. Now sees word in a flash as a total whole including beginning, end and middle. Less trouble with vowels.

Mechanics and reading for meaning now in better balance.

Begins to be able to stop and discuss what he is reading.

Can read rapidly without losing the thought.

Can read orally to a group in an easy, effective manner. Enjoys reading in a group and taking turns.

Beginning of ability to use dictionary.

Uses table of contents and index.

Book usually held easily on lap with some little shifting of head distance. Seldom needs to point to maintain place. May point or bring head closer for a new and difficult word.

The range in score for this group is Grade 0 to 6.4, average = 3.3.

Errors: Substitution of visual form most common (100 per cent of cases). Either substitution of a single letter; a short word which looks much the same; or a long word, using some of the given letters and guessing. Substitutions of meaning increase greatly, nearly equalling those of visual form.

Repetitions, omissions and additions (though more omissions than additions), and having to be told, also occur conspicuously, though child is more likely to guess at a word than to wait to be told.

9 years

All read sentences and paragraphs. Many, especially boys, become "great" readers.

Reading now more related to various subjects.

Knows how and when to skim for thought, and when to read thoroughly.

Knows how and when to read for pleasure or recreation and when for information.

May do better in silent reading but need to be checked in oral reading. Many prefer silent reading but when reading for facts and information may retain better when read orally.

Can use dictionary to find simple words, and in order to get definitions and pronunciations.

Can use index, glossary and table of contents.

Marked individual differences continue. Girls read better than boys. Girls in this group average a score of 5.9; boys of 4.0.

Errors: Substitutions of meaning now predominate; *room = house, his mother = she.* Also substitution of visual form, omission of words or letters, repetitions and some additions (pp. 293–296).

The errors also fell into a developmental progression, with a steady decrease of "having to be told the words," the most prevalent at age 6, decreasing to about half at age 9. From age 7, the chief errors in reading sentences were substitutions. The most common until age 8 were visual substitutions, when visual and meaning substitutions were about equal. Beginning at age 9, meaning substitutions became more common than visual substitutions.

They also found marked individual and sex differences among children of the same chronological age. Table B-15 (Table I from Ilg and Ames) presents the average rate of oral reading on the Gray Oral (paragraphs 1 and 5) by boys and girls at ages 6–9. It indicates steady decrease of rate by age, with girls superior to boys at each age.

Table B-15
MEAN ORAL READING RATE BY AGE AND SEX

| | PARAGRAPH 1 | | PARAGRAPH 5 | |
	MALE	FEMALE	MALE	FEMALE
6 years	47″	26″	—	—
7 years	36″	20″	55″	43″
8 years	31″	21″	44″	36″
9 years	21″	12″	45″	19″

The grade equivalent scores for ages 7, 8, and 9 by sex are reported in Table B-16 (Table II from Ilg and Ames).

Table B-16
GROUP AVERAGES AND SEX DIFFERENCES IN
READING SCORE

	7 YEARS	8 YEARS	9 YEARS
Average score			
Male	2.9	3.4	4.0
Female	3.2	4.6	5.9
Range in score			
Male	1.6–3.7	1.9–6.1	1.4–8.0
Female	1.6–5.4	3.2–6.4	4.7–7.6

SOURCE: Ilg and Ames (p. 302).
AUTHOR'S NOTE: It is important to note also that the lowest achieving boys remain at a first grade level at 7, 8, and 9. The lowest achieving girls rise to a 3.2 and 4.7 at ages 8 and 9.

Ilg and Ames's major concern was with readiness for reading. They believed the reading behavior gradient would be helpful in determining whether a child is or is not ready for formal reading instruction by comparing the child's "reading development" to that found typical for others of the same age. "Any given child is ready to read when he has reached a certain definite stage on a reading gradient, and not before, regardless of his chronological age or school placement'' (p. 308). They state this even more strongly:

> It is probably that reading readiness tests which merely test specific functions and not the whole response to the reading situation are only partially satisfactory in detecting actual readiness for reading unless used in conjunction with such a gradient. . . . That is, to determine whether a child is or is not "ready" for reading, we must consider not his chronological age, but rather what stage in a reading gradient he has attained (p. 308).

Their work on the development of reading from age 10–16 was published later (1956) and is presented in Table B-17. In addition to the reading characteristics by succeeding ages, the characteristic changes in emotions, interests, TV and radio use, and school life interests are also included.

The table is of interest in terms of what it notes and does not note about reading development. Essentially the changes noted are those in the uses of reading, the time spent reading, and the quality of what is read. The changes in reading skill noted in such detail in the reading gradient to age 9 are no longer noted or seem to have been "tested" for ages 10–16. The gradient for 10–16-year-olds is richer, however, in showing how the uses of reading are related to other aspects of human growth and development.

The Ilg and Ames reading gradient, although based on probably the largest collection of data on young children's reading, seems to have received little attention in the reading literature. It was not mentioned in the methods textbooks published in the 1970s or in the earlier editions of these texts. (See Appendix C.) Ames was a child psychologist, Ilg an M.D. listed as an educator in Who's Who, and their article was not published in a reading or an educational journal. Their work was significant in many ways: the large body of data collected, the analysis of errors as a way to study natural development which predated by about two decades the miscue and error analyses of Weber, Biemiller, and Kenneth and Yetta Goodman. Perhaps they were overlooked in the 1950s because they emphasized the study of the specifics of reading development while the reading field seemed to be concerned with emotional and physical development as they influenced reading.

Table B-17
DEVELOPMENT OF READING AND OTHER ACTIVITIES FOR AGES 10–16

AGE	EMOTIONS	GROWING SELF	ACTIVITIES INTERESTS (INDOOR)	READING	RADIO, TV	SCHOOL LIFE
10	Direct, matter-of-fact	Evaluate self in terms of abilities	Collections	Up to 5 books a week; many read as much as watch TV; avid comics, few magazines, animals, adventures, mysteries	Declining	School OK; social important; concrete learning, facts, like to know what things are *called* —not how work
11	Sensitive, proud with parents, polite with other adults, competitive	Search for self; highly critical	Big collections	0–8 books a week; quality, like it if is good; 2/3 read comics, look through magazines; animals, biography, information, classics	Less systematic, less intensive, mostly after dinner	Uneven performance, short attention span; interest in grades
12	Expansion, outgoing; school main source of worry; humor more adult	Search for self through peer approval; less egocentric	Collections; some pen pals; creative art, music, etc.	0–10 books a week; some decline; some adult books coming in	Some have regular programs	Strong feelings about either love or hate; girls more interested in boys than vice versa; arrange, classify, generalize (boys—astronomy, science);

Table B-17

DEVELOPMENT OF READING AND OTHER ACTIVITIES FOR AGES 10–16 *(cont.)*

AGE	EMOTIONS	GROWING SELF	ACTIVITIES INTERESTS (INDOOR)	READING	RADIO, TV	SCHOOL LIFE
12	Expansion, outgoing; school main source of worry; humor more adult (cont.)					think too much home-work, but more independent about doing it
13	Quiet, self-contained; pride in accomplishment	Search for self within self; inner life important; respects "brains"; more say want to go to college	Narrowing interests; reading strong; want to be alone; fewer collections, more hobbies	Still increase in reading; re-reading plot, action; some adult, but avoid emotional passages	Real drop in radio, TV; may be background for reading or studying	Need to be independent; better organized, more sense of responsibility; may like "hard" subjects; broadened outlook on world affairs; boys, science; girls, language
14	Experience: out-going; adult humor; punning; competitive	Other-directed concern with "normal"; wants to seem grown-up	More social "time-killing"	Variable, 0–15 books a week; good library use; adult books, preferred authors	Only occasional; some have favorite programs	Many dislike school, like extracurricular activities; enjoy evaluating subjects and teachers; like subjects with psychological bent

Table B-17
DEVELOPMENT OF READING AND OTHER ACTIVITIES FOR AGES 10–16 (cont.)

AGE	EMOTIONS	GROWING SELF	ACTIVITIES INTERESTS (INDOOR)	READING	RADIO, TV	SCHOOL LIFE
15	More self-confident; more aware of problems	Self in relation to ideas, ideals; analyze thoughts (own and others); more objective re self	Parties, dancing, dating; some reading, TV	Some read exhaustively, some collect books; boys, sexy books; all adult novels, classics, adventures, sports, historians, mystery; almost no comics; some magazines.	Still declining; radio as background	Wide range of attitudes toward subjects like what affects own life (e.g., biology); girls, English, social studies; boys, math, science
16	Positive; can analyze own emotions; interested in self-control; good sense of humor	Better sense of self; "have to work out for myself"	Dating, parties, church, clubs; reading, records; girls, talking with friends; boys, radios, cars	Less than at 15; don't have time; don't read for pleasure; no comics; some only magazines, newspapers	Still decreasing; only while doing something else	Some like all subjects; some difficulty with skills (first mention of this)

SOURCE: A. Gesell, F. Ilg, and L. Ames. *Youth: The Years from Ten to Fifteen.* New York: Harper & Row, 1956.

Many of the findings of Ilg and Ames continue to be of interest today.

1. The sex differences in reading development. The levels and rates of reading found suggest that for beginning reading to age 9 the differences may be neurophysiological, and not only social and environmental.

2. The changes by age in the quantity and quality of errors suggest that the reading task shifts from concern with word recognition to concern with word meanings and comprehension. This would fit our proposed stage development scheme.

3. The use of oral reading errors as a window on the reading process. They were not the first to employ this technique, citing others who used error analyses before them (e.g., Davidson, 1931; Wilson and Fleming, 1938). Nevertheless they were pioneers in analyzing the errors for the purpose of studying reading development.

4. Their reading gradient contains changes not only in reading behaviors but in the uses of reading. Thus we find in their gradient for age 8, "Can use dictionary to find simple words and in order to get definitions and pronunciations."

The Ilg and Ames gradient bears considerable resemblance to the reading stage schemes of the past (Gray, Gates, Russell) and to the proposed stage scheme. All of the reading stage schemes agree that by age 9, our proposed Stage 3, reading begins to be used as a tool for information, study, and recreation.

THE READING STAGES
OF ROZIN AND GLEITMAN (1977)

The work of Rozin and Gleitman (1977) covers the very earliest years, culminating in the introduction to the alphabet. Their stages are based on the history of the development of written languages, proceeding from representation by pictures through several stages to the most sophisticated and abstract alphabetic representation.

Figure 6 from Rozin and Gleitman (their Figure 2, p. 112) presents the five stages of representation and the curriculum activities by which they might be taught.

Conceptual Outline of the Syllabary Curriculum

	Semasiography	Logography	Phoneticization	Syllabary	Introduction to the Alphabet
Description	Reading for meaning through pictures	Mapping between spoken words and visual symbols	Focusing on sound rather than meaning by developing awareness of sound segmentation	Constructing and segmenting meaningful words and sentences in terms of syllables	Segmenting and blending initial consonant sounds
Activities	Interpretation of pictures	Reading material of the form: 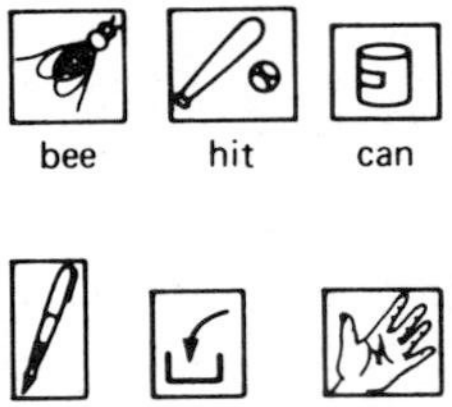 bee hit can pen in hand	"Speaking slowly" game Nonsense noise game 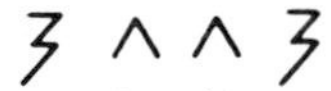 goo la la goo Rebus homonyms 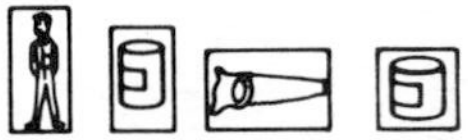 man can saw can Concrete blends 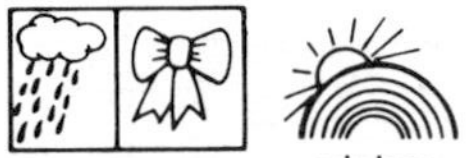 rainbow	Basic blends of meaningful syllables 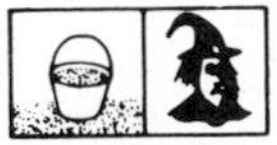 sand witch sandwich Addition of meaningless syllables (e.g., terminal y, er, ing) long er Partial fading of segmentation cues 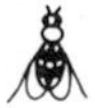 be-ing	Blends using initial consonant sounds: s-ing s-and

Figure 6. From Rozin and Gleitman (1977).

According to Rozin and Gleitman, "the developing child seems to traverse, in his conscious discovery of properties of his own speech, the road travelled in historical time by those who designed successful writing systems" (p. 111)—ontogeny recapitulates phylogeny.

They recommend a "historically oriented curriculum" (see chart) which would consist of the following sequence:

1. Teach the child that meaning can be represented visually.
2. Give each word its own logographic representation.
3. Teach phoneticization notions (i.e., segmentation).
4. Teach syllabic reading.
5. Teach phonemes.

CURRENT VIEWS
ON READING STAGES:
AN ANALYSIS
OF READING
METHODS TEXTBOOKS

W<small>HAT ROLE HAVE</small> the reading development schemes played in contemporary reading instruction? An answer to such a seemingly simple question is not easy to come by. While one can note trends in methods and materials of teaching reading, it is more difficult to be accurate with regard to the theoretical bases of these practices. This is further complicated by the variations in practices in different schools and communities at any one time.

I thought that perhaps a study of the most popular textbooks used to prepare teachers on methods of teaching reading would give some insight into whether these developmental models were still considered significant. I assumed further that the extent of mention of *reading stages, reading development,* or other relevant categories would be a kind of index of their importance. Toward this end, we selected 25 textbooks on

252

methods of teaching reading published during the 1970s. These are widely used for undergraduate and graduate preparation in the teaching of reading. Most covered general classroom methods of teaching reading. A few were concerned also with reading difficulties and remediation. The list of textbooks analyzed is found at the end of this section on pages 263–264.

The steps taken in the analysis included: (1) A list of categories under which the concept of reading development or stages of development were searched. These came from a preliminary search of the textbooks and from categories used in the relevant reading research. The following categories were used: *reading development, developmental reading, development, growth, reading growth, reading stages,* and *stages of reading development.* In addition, the analysts were instructed to follow up any other category that might lead to a discussion of reading stages or development. (2) The index of each textbook was searched for these categories. (3) The information was entered on a schedule. And (4) the schedules were analyzed for the extent of treatment of reading development, the relation of the treatment to time of publication, and the like.

THE RESULTS

Overall, for the 25 methods textbooks, few entries were found in the indexes for any of the reading or stage development categories. The largest number of entries were found under *development,* but in most of the textbooks this referred to the social, intellectual, and emotional development of children in relation to their reading development, especially during the preparatory or reading readiness period. Thus, the term "development" in most of these reading methods textbooks referred more often to children's psychological development than to their reading development.

Nearly half of the reading methods textbooks contained listings under *reading development* and *developmental reading.* Only three of the textbooks, however, discussed these in the sense of stages of reading development. Seven referred to developmental reading as reading instruction for pupils who progress normally, as distinguished from those needing corrective or remedial reading. The term was also used to refer to basic reading instruction, as distinguished from functional, applied, or recreational reading instruction.

The categories *growth* or *reading growth* were found in only two of the textbooks and were used mainly for discussing the influence of physical, mental, and emotional growth on reading. In none of the textbooks did an entry under "growth" refer to reading growth or reading development.

When reading growth was discussed under such terms as *reading development, reading growth,* and *reading stages,* it generally referred to the scope and sequence of reading skills to be taught or to the necessity of individualizing instruction, since individuals develop at different rates.

Two of the textbooks that give considerable treatment to *reading development* (Harris and Sipay, 1975; Kennedy, 1974) discuss it as a phenomenon undergoing development and change from its beginnings to its increasingly more advanced forms. In most other textbooks that discuss reading development (e.g., Tinker and McCullough, 1975) it is treated in terms of the changes in the skills that need to be learned as the student advances. Generally, these 25 widely used textbooks give little attention to changes in the learner and in what he or she can do, as reading develops.

Why was so little attention paid to reading development in the methods textbooks of the 1970s? We attempted to answer this question by comparing the "younger" with the "older" textbooks. We classified as "younger" textbooks those copyrighted originally in the 1970s. Those textbooks in their second, third, or later editions in the 1970s were classified as "older."

Nearly half of the textbooks fell into the "older" category (10 out of the 25). Most of these books were in their second or third editions, and one was in its sixth. Were there differences in the treatment of reading development by date of publication of the text? Our analyses indicated that there were. More of the "older" textbooks—6 out of 10—contained references to *growth, reading stages, developmental reading,* and the like.

The "younger" textbooks had few references to reading development. Of the 15 "younger" textbooks (those whose first editions were published in the 1970s), only two had listings and discussions of one or more of these reading development categories—*growth, development,* or *reading stages.*

That "age" of original publication was a factor in whether reading development was or was not discussed can be seen further from the fact that among the "older" textbooks where the treatment of reading development was more prevalent, those whose original publication dates were earliest had the strongest emphasis on reading development.

The following excerpt is from the textbook with the oldest original publication date (Harris, 1940). In its sixth edition, Harris and Sipay (1975) refer to Gray's 1925 stages of reading as "a classification that remains useful." The authors proceed to note that "although each stage of reading instruction has distinct features, certain problems and issues are present at all levels and stages" (p. 79).

In the second edition of their shorter text, *Effective Teaching of Reading* (1971), Harris and Sipay also refer to the Gray reading stages, but these are treated in much less detail under the broad topic of developmental reading (designed basically to learn how to read) as distinguished from recreational reading (for pleasure) and functional reading (for learning subject matter like science and social studies).

Another "older" text, Bond and Tinker's *Reading Difficulties: Their Diagnosis and Correction* in its 3rd edition (1973), also discussed developmental stages of reading and proposed that in spite of individual differences, "normal growth in reading tends to be fairly continuous and developmental in nature. At each stage, the abilities essential for success at the succeeding level were acquired. When this progress is continued without serious interruptions, the child eventually becomes a fairly mature reader" (p. 23).

They soon add a note of caution, however: "Although a discussion of growth in reading may refer to steps or stages of development, this is done for convenience of exposition. There are no discrete steps of development involved. . . . Growth is more or less continuous throughout the successive school grades" (p. 23).

For convenience of exposition, they present a description of normal reading growth under the following rubrics reminiscent of Gray's and Gates's reading stages (although neither is mentioned): the prereading period, progress in reading readiness, introduction to reading, progress in primary grades, progress in intermediate grades, progress in the basic reading abilities, and progress in the special reading abilities.

Tinker and McCullough's *Teaching Elementary Reading,* another "older" text (4th edition, 1975), also makes reference to "many successive stages of development" (p. 8), but they do not describe these successive stages. Instead they define reading in terms of skills that characterize reading at all levels of growth—from reading as a perceptual act to reading as a thinking process—and as Gray's four components of the reading act: (1) word perception; (2) comprehension of the ideas represented by the words; (3) reaction to these ideas; and (4) assimilation or integration of the ideas with previous knowledge or experience" (p. 8).

Spache and Spache, in *Reading in the Elementary School* (4th edition, 1977), discuss reading stages by citing William D. Sheldon in a section on reading as skill development. They note:

> William D. Sheldon describes the reading process in terms of stages, somewhat as follows. The first stage is a transitional period which begins with listening and concept building, and proceeds through picture reading. Stage two is characterized by experience charts, picture story reading, and the gradual introduction to reading of words in pre-primers. The third stage promotes wide development of sight vocabulary, supported by training in auditory discrimination. A fourth stage introduces more careful discrimination by initial consonants, word endings, and the other phonic and structural details, as sight vocabulary continues to grow. The fifth stage in the primary period is, in Sheldon's words, a plateau during which the fundamental vocabulary is strengthened. The sixth stage introduces the intermediate-grade child to reading tasks in the content fields, to technical vocabularies and technical concepts. A seventh stage develops flexibility in reading—the adjustment of rate and degree of comprehension to varying purposes. The maturing reader also begins to show the rudiments of critical reading involving judgmental, comparative, and inferential thinking, as well as creative ability to use reading as a tool for solving personal and group problems. Here, again, we have a view of the reading process as it evolves through various skills and stages (p. 5).

Spache and Spache seem, however, to be skeptical of reading stages, as Bond and Tinker were. They question stages even when used to refer to the sequence of reading skills to be taught:

> "The enumeration of stages and skills gives the impression that these are built upon each other or occur in some sort of sequence. However, such an overview is not realistic. Except for a few technical details which we introduce at certain stages in the process, *practically all the skills enumerated are being taught to the child almost simultaneously*" (p. 5, emphasis mine).

Heilman's *Principles and Practice of Teaching Reading* (2nd edition, 1977), the youngest of the "older" textbooks, also devotes considerable space to reading development and reading stages. But there also seems to be ambivalence towards them.

Heilman expresses doubts about the usefulness of viewing reading within a developmental framework because of the great individual variations in learning. Yet he notes that there may be some value in it. Although "reading is a developmental process," Heilman notes that this concept deserves more respect and attention than it has received. "Reading ability is a developmental process" means that the very complicated process of learning to read is not mastered at any particular time, such as age 10 or age 12. Nor can it be assumed that the ultimate ability to read critically is achieved at any particular point on the educational continuum.

> Thus, an adequate reader at grade three may be considerably less efficient at grade four and be in serious trouble by grade six. The statement implies recognition that the nature of human learning and the nature of the reading task precludes the possibility of mastering the reading process by a given chronological age or a designated number of years of formal schooling . . . (p. 515).

Heilman then devotes considerable attention to the increasing complexities that "must be mastered as children move upward through the grades," the growing length and abstractness of words and the developmental nature of word attack skills "at least up to the point where they are utilized automatically," for example (p. 516).

A final illustration consists of six sentences each taken from a basal reader at successive grade levels. This material, Heilman notes, reflects the need for growth on the part of the reader in regard to sight words, sentence patterns, profiting from punctuation, using proper intonation, and drawing inferences, as well as other skills:

Grade 1   "I will run and bring some water."
Grade 2   "I know where the field mouse lives down by the brook."
Grade 3   "The next night, when his father got home, Bob said,
          'I read that book about the other Bob.' "
Grade 4   "Sir," said the duck, who was trying to recover his while hopping around on one foot—not an easy thing to do, "Sir, I am minding my own business and I suggest you do the same."
Grade 5   The missile range was known as Station One, and when the men talked over the radio from there they would say, "This is Station One," or just, "This is One."
Grade 6   "We can be sure that the Trojans, on hearing this, will not risk bringing her wrath down upon themselves by destroying our offering."

(David H. Russell et al., *The Ginn Readers.* Boston: Ginn and Co., 1961, pp. 516–517.)

As a group, then, the "older" reading methods textbooks, those whose first editions were published before 1970, devoted considerable attention to reading development and reading stages. The earlier the first publication date of the textbook, the more attention paid to reading development. Generally, however, one senses a growing caution, over time, about the value of stages. Yet, most seem to see the value of a developmental framework for reading, particularly with regard to sequencing the skills to be taught and learned. But, even on this point, there is some questioning, since some authors felt that most reading skills are learned simultaneously.

There is also some concern expressed in these "older" textbooks that reading development stages might not be helpful for individual students whose courses of development may not fit the time sequence proposed for a particular stage. But in spite of these cautions, most of the authors of these pre-1970 methods texts paid *some* attention to reading development, considerably more than the authors of the "younger" texts.

Indeed, the "younger" textbooks, as a whole, devoted little attention to reading development, growth, reading stages, and the like. Only 2 of the 15 "younger" textbooks made any reference to our various reading development categories. The first, Kennedy's *Methods in Teaching Developmental Reading* (1st edition, 1974), notes that with regard to the content of developmental reading programs, there is

> disagreement on the sequential order in which specific skills should be introduced and taught, but it is agreed that developmental programs should provide experiences that enhance learning in all curriculum areas. And yet, the trend is away from listing specific skills and stages of progress in developmental reading (p. 26).

He refers to publications of a few years back which gave

> practical, detailed information on the content and developmental stages to be considered in program organization. These writers prepare a hierarchy of skills beginning with prereading abilities and continuing with increasingly more difficult skills and competencies through the primary, intermediate and upper grades (p. 26).

Kennedy then refers to Gates's (1947) reading periods as making one of the earliest and most succinct statements on reading stages.

Ruddell's *Reading-Language Instruction and Innovative Practices* (first edition, 1974), refers to stages of reading development only with regard to decoding.

> You should be cognizant of developmental stages in the decoding process. Singer's research, for example, supports the idea that as the reader becomes more mature in his ability to decode the printed page, he tends to reorganize and shift strategies to use more efficient decoding units, which results in more proficient decoding performance. As we previously mentioned, this reorganization may directly relate to the child's cognitive development as Piaget has posited in his theory of intellectual growth (pp. 295–296).

And in a later section, affective as well as cognitive development are considered by Ruddell with regard to progress in decoding.

> The act of decoding requires that the child perceive, match, sort, and reorganize language units. As we discussed earlier . . . cognitive strategies must be developed to process symbols and conceptualize experience. The child must be effective in drawing decoding inferences from sentence context and in shifting to new decoding sets when one decoding approach fails. To do this his cognitive development must be at a level that enables him to use reversible operations and to reorganize decoding units in ways that lead to independent word analysis (p. 296).

It is interesting to note that Ruddell makes no reference to the reading stages of Gray, Gates, or Russell. His main concern seems to be with relating the cognitive stages of Piaget to readiness for beginning reading and more specifically to decoding. No mention is made of the developmental nature of later reading.

It would seem from our analysis of the 25 reading methods textbooks published in the 1970s that a concern for developmental concepts of reading is generally related to the age of the first publication of a textbook. The older the original publication date, the more mention and discussion of reading development. Those textbooks that discussed developmental concepts of reading at some length tended to be the second, third, or later editions of textbooks originally published before 1970—some as early as the 1930s, 1940s, and 1950s. But even these tended to express caution about the use of the concept.

The "younger" textbooks, that is those whose first editions were published in the 1970s, tended to pay less attention to reading development. When it was discussed, it was followed by the cautions that not all children can read at the same stage level at the same time and that it may encourage holding up a child by teaching a skill to mastery longer than may be needed before proceeding with another.

Whether the caution was expressed by the authors of the "older" or the "younger" textbooks, most had to do with the progress of the individual. They were concerned lest use of developmental stages encourage "lockstepping" or holding children back.

What brought about the change in attitudes toward reading development concepts from a favorable one in the 1930s and 1940s to at best a cautious one in the 1970s, particularly among those who published their first textbook in the 1970s? Why did the teachers of teachers during the 1930s and 1940s think a mapping of the changes in reading by periods or stages would help teachers? Why did they tend to see primarily its dangers in the 1970s?

I think several factors may have been at work. First, and probably the strongest, is the "absorption" of at least some of the aspects of the reading stages by the instructional programs and the standardized reading tests—both acknowledged to be most influential in setting standards of American reading instruction. It should be noted that the authors of three of the four reading stage schemes were also authors of very widely used basal series.

It may well be that the highly detailed "scope and sequence" charts for Grades 1 to 6 (or 8) available with each reading series took the place of the stages or reading development schemes originally formulated by their authors. To answer the criticism of "lockstepping" the children into artificial hierarchies, basals seem to have changed from grade level designations to reading levels of 1 to 17, which can, of course, be translated into traditional grades if one knows the code.

The sequencing and grading also became more universal through standardized reading tests. So although teachers would find it difficult to characterize a Reading Grade Equivalent of 2, 3, 4, or 5, they were informed by the scores on norm-referenced tests that some 4th graders were reading on level, others on the 3rd or 2nd, and still others on the 5th.

The desire to make the scores more meaningful for instruction was instrumental in the development of criterion-referenced tests which tested children on skills considered of importance for given levels of reading achievement.

The concern for individual differences in reading has produced research on the broader developmental factors as they relate to reading achievement. The 1930s studied intellectual growth and its effect on reading; the 1940s and 1950s, the emotional and social factors; the 1960s and 1970s, the perceptual and neurophysiological factors; the late 1970s and early 1980s, linguistic and cognitive factors.

In short, the research on reading development, particularly since the 1950s, has been concerned primarily with the factors that influence reading development, not primarily with development and growth in reading itself.

While most reading educators seemed to move away from the concept of reading development by about 1950, the term took on other meanings. One new meaning was the distinction between developmental reading from basic and remedial reading, and later from recreational reading. Developmental reading thus began to refer to regular reading instruction (for those who make normal progress) as compared with remedial reading (for those with severe reading problems), particularly at the secondary level. All of these were distinguished from recreational reading, which refers to reading for pleasure—not work or study.

It seems somewhat strange that reading instruction for those with special needs would be separated from that for those progressing normally. Indeed, one can make a good case for remedial reading being more developmental than developmental reading because remedial reading more than any other is geared to the student's level of reading development.

Thus, the concept of reading development shifted around the 1950s from the way reading develops to a study of the way the child develops in relation to his or her reading. When the concept was used in reading, it referred mostly to the scope and sequence of the reading skills to be taught as found in basal readers. But they tend to omit the broad characterizations and psychological explanations of the hierarchies and the transitions.

TEACHER-TRAINING TEXTBOOKS
USED IN THE ANALYSIS

Aukerman, Robert C. *Approaches to Beginning Reading.* New York: Wiley, 1971.

Aukerman, Robert C. *Reading in the Secondary School Classroom.* New York: McGraw-Hill, 1972.

Bannatyne, Alexander. *Language, Reading and Learning Disabilities.* Springfield, Ill.: Charles C Thomas, 1971.

Bond, Guy L., and Tinker, Miles A. *Reading Difficulties: Their Diagnosis and Correction.* Englewood Cliffs, N.J.: Prentice-Hall, 1973.

Burmeister, Lou E. *Reading Strategies for Middle and Secondary School Teachers* (2nd ed.). Reading, Mass.: Addison-Wesley, 1978.

Bush, Clifford L., and Huebner, Mildred H. *Strategies for Reading in the Elementary School.* New York: Macmillan, 1970.

Dechant, Emerald V. *Improving the Teaching of Reading* (2nd ed.). Englewood Cliffs, N.J.: Prentice-Hall, 1982.

Durkin, Dolores. *Teaching Them to Read* (2nd ed.). Boston: Allyn and Bacon, 1974.

Fry, Edward. *Elementary Reading Instruction.* New York: McGraw-Hill, 1977.

Hafner, Lawrence E. *Developmental Reading in Middle and Secondary Schools: Foundations, Strategies, and Skills for Teaching.* New York: Macmillan, 1977.

Harris, Albert J., and Sipay, Edward R. *How To Increase Reading Ability* (6th ed.). New York: McKay, 1975.

Harris, Albert J., and Sipay, Edward R. *Effective Teaching of Reading* (2nd ed.). New York: McKay, 1971.

Heilman, Arthur W. *Principles and Practices of Teaching Reading* (4th ed.). Columbus, Ohio: Merrill, 1977.

Hittleman, Daniel R. *Developmental Reading: A Psycholinguistic Perspective.* Chicago: Rand McNally, 1978.

Kennedy, Eddie C. *Methods in Teaching Developmental Reading.* Itasca, Ill.: F.E. Peacock Publishers, Inc., 1974.

Kennedy, Eddie C. *Classroom Approaches to Remedial Reading.* Itasca, Ill.: F.E. Peacock Publishers, Inc., 1973.

May, Frank B. *To Help Children Read.* Columbus, Ohio: Merrill, 1973.

Olson, Joanne P., and Dillner, Martha H. *Learning to Teach Reading in the Elementary School.* New York: Macmillan, 1976.

Ruddell, Robert B. *Reading-Language Instruction: Innovative Practices.* Englewood Cliffs, N.J.: Prentice-Hall, 1974.

Schnepf, Virginia, and Meyer, Odessa. *Improving Your Reading Program.* New York: Macmillan, 1971.

Smith, Richard J., and Johnson, Dale D. *Teaching Children to Read.* Reading, Mass.: Addison-Wesley, 1976.

Spache, George D., and Spache, E.B. *Reading in the Elementary School* (4th ed.). Boston: Allyn and Bacon, 1977.

Tinker, Miles A., and McCullough, Constance M. *Teaching Elementary Reading* (4th ed.). Englewood Cliffs, N.J.: Prentice-Hall, 1975.

Thomas, Ellen Lamar, and Robinson, H. Alan. *Improving Reading in Every Class* (abridged, 2nd ed.). Boston: Allyn and Bacon, 1977.

Wallen, Carl J. *Competency in Teaching Reading.* Chicago: Science Research, 1972.

BIBLIOGRAPHY

Almy, M. Commentary in J. Stallings, *Implementation and child effects of teaching practices in follow-through classrooms.* Monographs of the Society for Research in Child Development, Serial No. 163, Vol. *40,* No.7–8, 1975.

Ambert, A. "Language disorders in Spanish-speaking children: A language intervention program. Unpublished Ed.D. thesis, Harvard Graduate School of Education, November, 1980.

Altschuler, J.M. Intra-word and inter-word developmental differences in the oral reading of good and poor readers, special qualifying paper, Harvard Graduate School of Education, 1979.

Anderson, I.H. & Dearborn, W.F. *The psychology of teaching reading.* New York: Ronald Press, 1952.

Anderson, R.C. & Freebody, P. Vocabulary Knowledge, in J. T. Guthrie (ed.), *Comprehension and learning: Research reviews,* Newark, Del.: I.R.A., 1981.

Atkinson, R.C. Teaching children to read using a computer, *American Psychologist,* 1974, *29,* 169–178.

Atkinson, R.C., Fletcher, J.D., Chetin, H.C. & Stauffer, C.M. *Instruction in initial reading under computer control: The Stanford project* (Tech. Rep. 158). Stanford: Stanford University, Institute for Mathematical Studies in the Social Sciences, 1970.

Auerbach, I.T. "Analysis of Standardized Reading Comprehension Tests." Dissertation, Harvard Graduate School of Education, 1971.

Ballantine, F.A. Age changes in measures of eye movements in silent reading. In Morse, W.C., Ballantine, F.A., & Dixon, W.R. *Studies in the psychology of reading,* New York: Greenwood Press, 1951; reprinted 1968.

Balmuth, M. *The roots of phonics.* New York: McGraw-Hill, 1982.

Baratz, J.C. & Shuy, R. (eds.) *Teaching Black children to read.* Washington, D.C.: Center for Applied Linguistics, 1969.

Barr, R.C. The effect of instruction on pupil reading strategies. *Reading Research Quarterly,* 1974, *10,* 555–582.

Beck, I.L. & McCaslin, E.S. An analysis of dimensions that affect the development of code-breaking ability in eight beginning reading programs. Pittsburgh: University of Pittsburgh, Learning Research and Development Center, 1977.

Becker, W. Teaching reading and language to the disadvantaged. *Harvard Educational Review,* 1978, *47,* 518–543.

Bennett, N. with Jordan, J., Long, G., & Wade, B. *Teaching styles and pupil progress.* Cambridge, Mass.: Harvard University Press, 1976.

Bettelheim, B. and Zelan, K. *On learning to read: A child's fascination with meaning.* New York: Knopf, 1981.

Biemiller, A. The development of the use of graphic and contextual information as children learn to read. *Reading Research Quarterly,* 1970, 6, 75–96.

Biemiller, A. Relationships between oral reading rates for letters, words, and simple text in the development of reading achievement. *Reading Research Quarterly,* 1977–8, *13,* 223–253.

Birch, Herbert G. & Belmont, L. Auditory-visual integration in normal and retarded readers. *American Journal of Orthopsychiatry, 34,* October, 1964, 852–861.

Bissex, G. *Gnys at wrk.* Cambridge, Mass.: Harvard University Press, 1980.

Blank, M. & Bridger, W.H. Deficiencies in verbal labeling in retarded readers. *American Journal of Orthopsychiatry,* 1966, *36,* 840–847.

Bloom, B.S. *Stability and change in human characteristics.* New York: Wiley, 1964.

Bloom, B.S. *Human characteristics and school learning.* N.Y.: McGraw-Hill, 1976.

Bloom, B.S. *All our children learning.* New York: McGraw-Hill, 1981.

Bond, G.L. & Dykstra, R. The cooperative research program in first-grade reading instruction. *Reading Research Quarterly,* 1967, *2,* 1–142.

Bond, G.L. & Tinker, M.A. *Reading difficulties: Their diagnosis and correction.* Englewood Cliffs, N.J.: Prentice-Hall, 1973.

Bonger, H. *The history and principles of vocabulary control.* Holland: Wocopi-Woerden, 1947.

Brown, R. *A first language.* Cambridge, Mass.: Harvard University Press, 1973.

Bruce, D.J. Analysis of word sounds by young children. *British Journal of Educational Psychology,* 1964, *34,* 158–169.

Bruner, J.S. *Beyond the information given,* edited by Jeremy M. Anglin. New York: Norton and Co., 1973.

Buswell, G.T., *An experimental study of the eye-voice span in reading.* Chicago: University of Chicago Press, 1920.

Buswell, G.T. *Fundamental reading habits: A study of their development.* Chicago: Supplementary Educational Monographs, No. 21. University of Chicago, June, 1922.

Calfee, R.D. & Drum, P.A. Learning to read: Theory, research, and practice. *Curriculum Inquiry,* 1978, *8,* 183–249.

Carroll, J.B. Developmental parameters of reading comprehension. In J.T. Guthrie (ed.), *Cognition, curriculum, and comprehension.* Newark, Del.: I.R.A., 1977.

Carroll, J.B. & Chall, J.S. *Toward a literate society.* New York: McGraw-Hill, 1975.

Cazden, C.B. Play with language and metalinguistic awareness: One dimension of language experience. *Urban Review,* 1974, *2,* 28–39.

Chall, J.S. The influence of previous knowledge on reading ability. *Educational Research Bulletin,* 1947, *26,* 225–230.

Chall, J.S. How reading and other aids to learning may be coordinated to promote growth in and through reading in grades 4 to 6. In W.S. Gray (ed.), *Keeping reading programs abreast of the times,* Supplementary Educational Monographs, No. 72. Chicago: University of Chicago Press, 1950.

Chall, J.S. Readability: *An appraisal of research and application.* Columbus: Ohio University Press, 1958.

Chall, J.S. *Learning to read: The great debate.* New York: McGraw-Hill, 1967.

Chall, J.S. Research in linguistics and reading instruction: Implications for further research and practice. *Reading and realism,* J. Allen Figurel (ed.), Vol. *13,* Part I, Proceedings of the thirteenth annual convention, International Reading Association, Newark, Delaware, 1969, 560–571.

Chall, J.S. *Reading 1967–1977: A decade of change and promise.* Bloomington, Indiana: Phi Delta Kappa Foundation, 1977.

Chall, J.S. *Technical manual: The Roswell-Chall diagnostic test of word analysis skills* (Rev. and extended edition), San Diego: Essay Press, 1978a.

Chall, J.S. A decade of research on reading and learning disabilities, in S.J. Samuels (ed.) *What research has to say about reading instruction.* Newark, Del.: I.R.A., 1978b.

Chall, J.S. The great debate: Ten years later, with a modest proposal for reading stages, in Resnick and Weaver (eds.), *Theory and practice of early reading.* Hillsdale, N.J.: Erlbaum Associates, 1979a.

Chall, J.S. Dialogue: Reading research—for whom? *Curriculum Inquiry,* 1979b, *9,* 37–43.

Chall, J.S. *Learning to read: The great debate,* second edition, with a new introduction. New York: McGraw-Hill, 1982.

Chall, J.S., Bissex, G., Conard, S.S., & Harris-Sharples, S. *Readability assessment scales for literature, science, and social studies.* New York: McGraw-Hill, 1982.

Chall, J.S., Conard, S.S., & Harris-Sharples, S. *An analysis of textbooks in relation to declining S.A.T. scores.* New York: College Entrance Examination Board, 1977.

Chall, J.S. & Feldmann, S. First grade reading: An analysis of the interactions of professed methods, teacher implementation, and child background. *The Reading Teacher,* 1966, *19,* 569–75.

Chall, J.S., Freeman, A., & Levy, B. Minimum competency testing of reading: An analysis of eight tests designed for Grade 11, paper presented at the Conference on the Courts and Content Validity in Minimum Competency Testing, Boston College, October 13, 1981.

Chall, J.S. & Mirsky, A. (eds.) *Education and the brain,* the 77th yearbook of the National Society for the Study of Education, Part II. Chicago: NSSE, 1978.

Chall, J.S., Roswell, F., & Blumenthal, S. Auditory blending. *The Reading Teacher,* November, 1963, 113–118.

Chall, J.S. & Stahl, S.A. Reading, in H. Mitzel (ed.) *Encyclopedia of Educational Research,* 5th ed. Washington, D.C.: American Educational Research Association, in press.

Chomsky, C. *The acquisition of syntax in children from 5 to 10,* Cambridge, Ma.: M.I.T. Press, 1969.

Chomsky, C. Stages in language development and reading exposure, *Harvard Educational Review, 42,* 1, February, 1972.

Chomsky, C. Invented spelling in the open classroom, in W. vonRaffler-Engel (ed.) *Child Language–1975.* Milford, Conn.: International Linguistics Association, 1976.

Chomsky, C. When you still can't read in third grade: After decoding, what? in S.J. Samuels (ed.), *What research has to say about reading instruction.* Newark, Del.: I.R.A., 1978.

Chomsky, C. Approaching reading through invented spelling, in L.B. Resnick and P.A. Weaver (eds), *Theory and practice of early reading,* Vol. 2. Hillsdale, N.J.: Erlbaum, 1979.

Clark, M.M. *Young fluent readers: What can they teach us?* London: Heinemann Educational Books, 1976.

Clay, M.M. The reading behavior of five-year old children: A research report. *New Zealand Journal of Educational Studies,* 1966, *2,* 11–31.

Clay, M. *Sand—Concepts about print.* Auckland, New Zealand: Heinemann Educational Books, 1972.

Clay, M. *What did I write?* Auckland, N.Z.: Heinemann Educational Books, 1975.

Coleman, J.S. et al. *Equality of educational opportunity.* Washington, D.C.: U.S. Government Printing Office, 1966.

Conard, S.S. *The difficulty of textbooks for the elementary grades: A survey of educators' and publishers' preferences.* Unpublished Ed.D. thesis, Harvard Graduate School of Education, 1981.

Connors, C.K., Kramer, K. and Guerra, F. Auditory synthesis and dichotic listening in children with learning disabilities. *Journal of Special Education,* 1969, *3,* 163–170.

Cross, P. *Adults as learners.* San Francisco: Jossey-Bass, 1981.

Dahl, P.R. A mastery based experimental program for teaching high-speed word recognition skills. *Reading Research Quarterly,* 1975–76, *11,* 205–211.

Dale, E. *Can you give the public what it wants?* New York: Cowles Educational Corp., 1967.

Dale, E. & Chall, J.S. A formula for predicting readability. *Educational Research Bulletin,* 1948a, *27,* 11–20.

Dale, E. & Chall, J.S. A formula for predicting readability. *Educational Research Bulletin,* 1948b, *28,* 37–54.

Dale, E. & Chall, J.S. Developing readable materials. *Fifty-fifth Yearbook of the National Society for the Study of Education,* part 2, 1956, *55,* 218–250.

Dave, R.H. *The identification and measurement of environmental process variables that are related to educational achievement.* Unpublished Ph.D. dissertation, University of Chicago, 1963.

Davis, F.S. Research in comprehension in reading. *Reading Research Quarterly,* 1968, *3,* 499–545.

Denckla, M.B. The neurological basis of reading disability, in Florence G. Roswell and Gladys Natchez (eds.), *Reading disability: A human approach to learning.* New York: Basic Books, Inc., 1977.

de Hirsch, K., Jansky, J., & Langford, W.S. *Predicting reading failure.* New York: Harper and Row, 1966.

Doehring, D. *Acquisition of rapid reading responses.* Monograph of the Society for Child Development, Vol. *41,* No. 2, 1976.

Downing, J. & Thackray, D. *Reading readiness,* 2nd ed. London: Hodder and Stoughton, 1975.

Durkin, D. The achievement of pre-school readers: Two longitudinal studies. *Reading Research Quarterly,* 1966, *1,* 5–36.

Durkin, D. A six-year study of children who learned to read in school at the age of four. *Reading Research Quarterly,* 1974, *10,* 9–6.

Durkin, D. What classroom observations reveal about reading instruction. *Reading Research Quarterly,* 1979, *14,* 481–533.

Durrell, D.D. and Catterson, J.H. *Manual of directions: Durrell Analysis of Reading Difficulty,* revised edition. New York: Psychological Corporation, 1980.

Dwyer, C.A. Sex differences in reading: An evaluation and a critique of current theories. *Review of Educational Research,* 1973, *43,* 455–467.

Edmonds, R. Effective schools for the urban poor. *Educational Leadership,* 1977, *37,* 15–24.

Elkind, D. Cognitive development and reading, in Singer, H. and Ruddell, R. *Theoretical models and processes of reading,* 2nd ed. Newark, Del.: I.R.A., 1976.

Elkonin, D.B. U.S.S.R., in Downing, J. (ed.), *Comparative reading.* New York: Macmillan, 1973.

Englemann, S. & Bruner, E.C. *DISTAR reading.* Chicago: Science Research Associates, 1969.

EPIE Institute, *EPIE Educational Product Report, Selecting and Evaluating Beginning Reading Materials,* Vol. VII, No. 62/63, New York: EPIE Institute, 1974.

Epstein, H.T. Growth spurts during brain development: Implications for educational policy and practice, in Chall, J.S. and Mirsky, A.F. (eds.), *Education and the brain,* 77th yearbook of the National Society for the Study of Education, Part II. Chicago: NSSE, 1978.

Erickson, E.H. *Childhood and society* (2nd ed.). New York: Norton, 1964.

Ervin, J. *Your child can read and you can help,* Garden City, N.Y.: Doubleday, 1979.

Evanechko, P., Ollila, L., Downing, J., and Braun, C. An investigation of the reading readiness domain, *Research in the Teaching of English.* 1973, 7, 61–78.

Feifel, H. & Lorge, I. Qualitative differences in the vocabulary responses of children. *Journal of Educational Psychology,* 1950, *41,* 1–18.

Feitelson, D. Israel. In J. Downing (ed.), *Comparative reading.* New York: Macmillan, 1973.

Feldman, C. Reply to *On meddling* by L. Thomas. Unpublished manuscript, Harvard University, 1976.

Flanagan, J.C. Changes in school levels of achievement: Project talent ten and fifteen year retests. Paper presented at the symposium of Division D and National Council on Measurement in Education, during the 1976 meeting of the American Educational Research Association, San Francisco, April 22, 1976.

Flesch, R.F. *Why Johnny still can't read.* New York: Harper and Row, 1981.

Fowler, W. A developmental learning strategy for early reading in a laboratory nursery school. *Interchange,* 1971, *2,* 106–125.

Freire, P. Cultural action for freedom. *Harvard Educational Review,* 1970, *40,* 205–225.

Gagne, Robert M. Diagnostic Test Requirements for Reading in the Elementary Grades. Tallahassee, Fla.: Office of Dissemination/Diffusion, Department of Education, 1978.

Galaburda, A.M. & Kemper, T.L. Cytoarchitectonic abnormalities in developmental dyslexia: A case study. *Annals of Neurology,* 1979, *6,* 94–100.

Gardner, H. *Artful scribbles.* New York: Basic Books, 1980.

Gates, A.I. The necessary mental age for beginning reading. *Elementary School Journal,* 1937, *37,* 497–508.

Gates, A.I. *The improvement of reading.* New York: Macmillan Co., 1947.

Gates, A.I. Sex differences in reading ability. *Elementary School Journal,* 1961, *51,* 431–434.

Gates, A.I. & Bond, G.L. Reading readiness: A study of factors determining success and failure in beginning reading. *Teachers College Record* (1936), *37,* 679–685.

Gates, A.I. & Russell, D. Workbooks, vocabulary control, phonics, and other factors in beginning reading. *Elementary School Journal,* 1939, *39,* 27–35.

Gelatt, R. Word recognition and the development of the recognition span. Qualifying paper, Harvard Graduate School of Education, Harvard University, Cambridge, Mass., 1978.

Gesell, A.L., Ilg, F.L., & Ames, L.B. *Youth: The years from ten to sixteen.* New York: Harper, 1956.

Gibson, C.M. & Richards, I.A. *Language through pictures series.* New York: Washington Square Press, Pocket Books, 1963.

Gibson, E.J. *Principles of perceptual learning and development.* Englewood Cliffs, N.J.: Prentice-Hall, 1969.

Gibson, E.J., Barron, R.W. & Garber, E.E. The developmental convergence of meaning for words and pictures, in Appendix to Final Report, Project No. 90046, Grant No. OEG-2-9-420446-1070 (010), Cornell University and U.S. Office of Education, 1972.

Gibson, E.J., Gibson, J.J., Pick, A.D., & Osser, H. A developmental study of the discrimination of letter-like forms. *Journal of Comparative and Physiological Psychology,* 1962, *55,* 897–906.

Gibson, E.J. & Levin, H. *The psychology of reading.* Cambridge, Mass.: M.I.T. Press, 1975.

Gibson, E.J. & Olum, V. Experimental methods of studying perception in children, in Mussen (ed.), *Handbook of research methods in child development.* New York: Wiley, 1960.

Gibson, E.J., Osser, H. & Pick, A. A study in the development of grapheme-phoneme correspondences. *Journal of Verbal Learning and Verbal Behavior,* 1963, *2,* 142–146.

Gibson, E.J., Pick, A., Osser, H., & Hammond, M. The role of grapheme-phoneme correspondences in the perception of words. *American Journal of Psychology,* 1962, *75,* 554–570.

Gilbert, L. *Function of motor efficiency of the eyes and its relation to reading.* University of California Publications in Education, 1953, *11* (3), 159–232.

Gleitman, L. & Rozin, P. Teaching reading by use of a syllabary. *Reading Research Quarterly,* 1973, *8,* 447–483.

Gollinkoff, R.M. A comparison of reading comprehension processes in good and poor comprehenders. *Reading Research Quarterly,* 1975–76, *11,* 623–659.

Goodman, K.S. The psycholinguistic nature of the reading process. In K.S. Goodman (ed.), *The psycholinguistic nature of the reading process.* Detroit: Wayne State University Press, 1968.

Goodman, K.S. & Goodman, Y. Learning about psycholinguistic processes by analyzing oral reading. *Harvard Educational Review,* 1977, *43,* 317–33.

Goodman, K.S. and Goodman, Y. Learning to read is natural. In L.B. Resnick and P.A. Weaver (Eds.) *Theory and practice of early reading,* vol. 1. Hillsdale, N.J.: Lawrence Erlbaum Associates, 1979.

Gough, P.B. & Hillinger, M.L. Learning to read: An unnatural act. *Bulletin of the Orton Society,* 1980, *30,* 179–196.

Gray, C.T. *Types of reading ability as exhibited through tests and laboratory experiments.* Supplementary Educational Monographs, No. 5. Chicago: University of Chicago Press, 1917.

Gray, W.S. *Studies of elementary school reading through standardized tests.* Supplementary Educational Monographs, Vol. 1, No. 1. Chicago: University of Chicago, 1917.

Gray, W.S. The use of tests in improving instruction. *Elementary School Journal,* 1918.

Gray, W.S. *24th Yearbook of the NSSE, Part I—Report of the National Committee on Reading.* Bloomington, Ill.: Public School Publishing Co., 1925.

Gray, W.S. *36th Yearbook of the NSSE, Part I—The Teaching of Reading: A Second Report.* Bloomington, Ill.: Public School Publishing Co., 1937.

Gray, W.S. How well do adults read? In N.B. Henry (ed.), *Adult reading,* 55th Yearbook of the National Society for the Study of Education, Part II. Chicago: NSSE, 1956.

Guthrie, J.T., Martuza, V., & Seifert, M. Impacts of instructional time in reading. In Resnick, L.B. and Weaver, P.A., *Theory and practice of early reading,* Vol. 3. Hillsdale, N.J.: Erlbaum, 1979.

Hall, S.L. *Black dialect and reading.* Unpublished Ed.D. thesis, Harvard Graduate School of Education, 1980.

Hammill, D.D. & Larsen, S.C. The relationship of selected auditory perceptual skills and reading ability. *Journal of Learning Disabilities,* 1974, *7,* 429–435.

Harris, A.J. *How to increase reading ability,* 5th edition. New York: David McKay, 1970.

Harris, A.J. & Sipay, E.R. *Effective teaching of reading,* 2nd edition. New York: David McKay, 1971.

Harris, A.J. & Sipay, E.R. *How to increase reading ability,* 6th edition. New York: David McKay, 1975.

Havighurst, R.J. *Developmental tasks and education,* 3rd edition. New York: David McKay and Co., 1972.

Heilman, A.W. *Principles and practices of teaching reading,* 4th edition. Columbus, Ohio: Charles E. Merrill, 1977.

Hochberg, J. Components of literacy: Speculations and exploratory research. In Levin, H. and Williams, J. (Eds.), *Basic studies in reading.* New York: Basic Books, 1970.

Hoffmann, J. Experimentall-psychologische. Untersuchungen Uber Leseleitungen von Schulkindern, *Archiv für die gesamte Psychologie,* 1927, *58,* 190–191.

Hornik, R.C. Television access and the slowing of cognitive growth. *American Educational Research Journal,* 1978, *15,* 1–15.

Huck, C.S. *Taking inventory of children's literary background.* Glenview, Ill.: Scott-Foresman, 1966.

Hunt, J. McV. *Intelligence and experience.* New York: Ronald Press, 1961.

Hunter, C. St.J. & Harman, D. *Adult illiteracy in the United States.* New York: McGraw-Hill, 1979.

Hyman, H.H., Wright, C.R., and Reed, S.S. *The enduring effects of education.* Chicago: The University of Chicago Press, 1975.

Ilg, F.L. & Ames, L.B. Developmental trends in reading behavior. *Journal of Genetic Psychology,* 1930, 76, 261–312.

Ilg, F.L. & Ames, L.B. *School readiness.* New York: Harper and Row, 1970.

Inhelder, B. & Piaget, J. *The growth of logical thinking from childhood to adolescence.* New York: Basic Books, 1958.

Jansky, J. & de Hirsch, K. *Preventing reading failure.* New York: Harper and Row, 1972.

Jencks, C. et al. *Inequality.* New York: Basic Books, 1972.

Karger, G.W. *The performance of lower class black and lower class white children on the Wepman Auditory Discrimination Test: The effects of dialect and training, and the relationship to reading achievement.* Unpublished Ed.D. thesis, Harvard Graduate School of Education, 1973.

Kean, M.H. et al. *What works in reading? Summary and results of a joint school district/Federal Reserve Bank empirical study in Philadelphia.* Philadelphia School District, Pa., Office of Research and Evaluation, May, 1979 (ERIC Document No. ED 176 216).

Kennedy, E.C. *Methods in teaching developmental reading.* Itasca, Ill.: F.E. Peacock Publishers, Inc., 1974.

Kintsch, W. *The representation of meaning in memory.* Hillsdale, N.J.: Erlbaum, 1974.

Klare, G.R. *The measurement of readability.* Ames, Iowa: Iowa State University Press, 1963.

Klare, G.R. Assessing readability. *Reading Research Quarterly,* 1974–5, 10, 62–102.

Kohlberg, L. Stage and sequence: The cognitive-developmental approach to socialization. In D.A. Goslin (ed.) *Handbook of socialization theory and research.* Chicago: Rand McNally, 1969.

Kraus, P.E. *Yesterday's children: A longitudinal study of children from kindergarten into the adult years.* New York: John Wiley & Sons, 1973.

Kurzweil Computer Products. *The Kurzweil Report, 1* (1), 1978.

LaBerge, D. & Samuels, S.J. Toward a theory of automatic information processing in reading. In Singer and Ruddell, *Theoretical models and processes of reading.* Newark, Del.: I.R.A., 1976.

Lambert, W.F. The effects of bilingualism on the individual: Cognitive and sociocultural implications. In Hornsby, P. (Ed.), *Bilingualism: Psychological, social and educational implications.* New York: Academic Press, 1977.

Larrick, N. *A parent's guide to children's reading,* 4th ed. New York: Doubleday, 1975.

Lavine, L.O. The development of perception of writing in pre-reading children: A cross-cultural study. Unpublished doctoral dissertation. Department of Human Development, Cornell University, 1972, cited in Gibson, E. and Levin, H. *Psychology of reading,* p. 233.

Leroy-Boussion, A. La fusion auditivophonétique d'un son consonne et d'un son voyelle en unité syllabique au début de l'apprentissage de la lecture chez l'enfant. *Psychologie Français.* 1963, *8,* 259–278.

Levin, H. *The eye-voice span.* Cambridge, Ma.: M.I.T. Press, 1979.

Levin, H. & Cohn, J.A. Studies of oral reading XII. Effects of instructions on the eye-voice span, in Levin, H., Gibson, E.J., & Gibson, J.J. (Eds.), *The analysis of reading skill.* Final report, Project No. 5-1213, Contract No. OE6-10-156, Cornell University and the U.S. Office of Education, 1968.

Levin, H. & Turner, A. Sentence structure and the eye-voice span, in Levin, H., Gibson, E.J., & Gibson, J.J. (Eds.), *The analysis of reading skill.* Final Report Project No. 5-1213 from Cornell University to U.S. Office of Education, December, 1968.

Liberman, A.M., Cooper, F.S., Shankweiler, D.P. & Studdert-Kennedy, M. Perception of the speech code. *Psychological Review,* 1967, *74,* 431–461.

Liberman, I.Y. & Shankweiler, D. Speech, the alphabet, and learning to read. In L.B. Resnick, and P.A. Weaver, (eds.), *Theory and practice of early reading,* Vol. 2. Hillsdale, N.J.: Erlbaum, 1979.

Lloyd, D.N. Concurrent prediction of dropout and grade of withdrawal. *Educational and Psychological Measurement,* 1976, 36, 983–991.

Loban, W. *The language of elementary school children.* National Council of Teachers of English, Research Report No. 1, 1963.

Lorge, I. Predicting reading difficulty of selections for children. *Elementary English Review,* 1939, *16,* 229–233.

Lorge, I. Predicting readability. *Teacher's College Record,* 1944, 45, 404–419.

Lorge, I. and Chall, J.S. Estimating the size of vocabularies of children and adults: An analysis of methodological issues. *Journal of Experimental Education,* 1963, *32,* 147–157.

MacDonald, F.J. Report on phase II of the beginning teacher evaluation study. *Journal of Teacher Education,* 1976, *27,* 39–42.

Mackworth, N. & Bruner, J. How children and adults search and recognize pictures. *Human Development,* 1970, *13,* 149–177.

Maraini, F. *The persistence of the ideographic script in the Far East: Its competitive values versus the alphabet.* Paper presented at the meeting of the International Congress of Anthropological and Ethnographical Sciences, Chicago, August–September, 1973.

Marston, Emily. *An analysis of selected studies of reading interests and preferences of children, adolescents, and young adults.* Unpublished qualifying paper, Harvard University, 1976.

Marston, E. *An investigation of variables relating to the v￼ ￼ntary reading habits of eighth graders,* unpublished Ed.￼ thesis, Harvard University, Graduate School of Education, 19￼ ￼.

Mattis, S., French, J.H. and Rapin, I. Dyslexia in children and young adults: Three independent neuropsychological syndromes. *Developmental Medicine and Child Neurology,* 1975, *17,* 150–163.

McCarthy, D. Language development in children. In L. Carmichael (ed.), *Manual of Child Psychology* (2nd ed.). New York: John Wiley, 1954.

McDade, J.E. A hypothesis for non-oral reading: Argument, experiment, and results. *Journal of Educational Research,* 1937, *30,* 489–503.

McKee, P. Vocabulary development. In Whipple, G.M. (Ed.), *The thirty-sixth yearbook of the National Society for the Study of Education,* part I. Bloomington, Ill.: Public School Publishing Company, 1937.

Meyer, A. *Reading disability: A developmental crisis in the elementary school years.* Harvard Graduate School of Education, special qualifying paper, 1977.

Meyer, L.A. A closer look at the Englemann DISTAR and Palo Alto programs. Paper presented at the Association of Behavior Analysis, Dearborn, Michigan, May 24, 1980.

Moore, P.J. *Children's Reading Strategies: A Developmental Perspective.* University of Newcastle, June 1980. A Report to Educational Research and Development Committee (ERDC), Australian Government.

Morphett, M.V. & Washburne, C. When should children begin to read? *Elementary School Journal,* 1931, *31,* 496–503.

Morse, W.C. A comparison of the eye-movements of average fifth and seventh grade pupils reading materials of corresponding difficulty. In W.S. Morse, F.A. Ballantine & W.R. Dixon (eds.), *Studies in the psychology of reading.* New York: Greenwood Press, 1951, reprinted 1968.

National Advisory Committee on Dyslexia and Reading Disorders. *Reading disorders in the United States.* Chicago, Ill.: Development Learning Materials, 1970.

National Assessment of Educational Progress. *NAEP Newsletter,* 1981, *14* (1), 1–2.

Neisser, U. *Cognitive psychology.* New York: Appleton-Century-Crofts, 1967.

Nodine, C.F. & Evans, J.E. Eye movements of pre-readers containing letters of high and low confusability. *Perception and Psychophysics,* 1969, *6,* 39–41.

Nodine, C.F. & Lang, N.J. The development of visual scanning strategies of differentiating words. *Developmental Psychology,* 1971, *5,* 221–232.

Nodine, C.F. and Simmons, Processing distinctive features in the differentiation of letter-like symbols. *Journal of Experimental Psychology,* 1973.

Nodine, C.F. & Stuerle, N.C. Development of perceptual and cognitive strategies for differentiating graphemes. *Journal of Experimental Psychology,* 1973.

Olson, W.C. *Child Development* (2nd ed.), Boston: D.C. Heath, 1959, cited in Harris, A.J. Reading and human development, in N.B. Henry (ed.) *Development in and through reading,* 60th yearbook of the National Society for the Study of Education, Pt. 1. Chicago, Ill.: NSSE, 1961.

Orton, S.T. *Reading, writing and speech problems in children.* New York: W.W. Norton, 1937. (1964 Reprint).

Perfetti, C.A. Language comprehension and fast decoding: Some prerequisites for skilled reading comprehension. In J.T. Guthrie (ed.) *Cognition, curriculum and comprehension.* Newark, Del.: International Reading Association, 1977.

Perfetti, C. & Lesgold, A.M. Coding and comprehension in skilled reading and implications for reading instruction, in Resnick & Weaver (eds.), *Theory and practice of early reading,* Vol. 1. Hillsdale, N.J.: Erlbaum, 1979.

Perry, W. *Forms of intellectual and ethical development in the college years: A scheme.* New York: Holt, Rinehart & Winston, 1970.

Pflaum, S., Walberg, H.J., Kargianes, M.L., Rasher, S.P. Reading instruction: A quantitative analysis. *Educational Researcher,* 1980, *9,* (July–August), 12–18.

Pflaum-Connor, S. Language and reading acquisition for the English-speaking minority student, in Pflaum-Connor (Ed.), *Aspects of reading education.* Berkeley, Cal.: McCutcheon, 1978.

Piaget, J. *Structuralism.* New York: Basic Books, 1970.

Popp, H.M. Current practices in the teaching of beginning reading, in Carroll & Chall (eds.), *Toward a literate society.* N.Y.: McGraw-Hill, 1975.

Popp, H.M. Selecting reading instruction for high-risk children: A theoretical approach. *Bulletin of the Orton Society,* 1978, *28,* 15–42.

Popp, H.M. & Lieberman, M. *A study of the relationship of student achievement to components of reading programs and environmental characteristics,* Final Report, Contract no. 400-75-0064, Harvard Graduate School of Education, May, 1977.

Postman, N. *Teaching as a conserving activity.* New York: Delacorte Press, 1979.

Pray, R.T. *Home-school language switching: Bilingualism and the acquisition of reading.* Qualifying paper, Harvard Graduate School of Education, 1979.

Preston, R.C. Reading achievement of German and American children. *School and Society,* 1962, *90,* 350–354.

Read, C. Preschool children's knowledge of English phonology. *Harvard Educational Review,* 1971, *41,* 1–34.

Reid, E.R. Another approach to mastery learning. *Educational Leadership,* 1980, *38* (2), 170–172.

Resnick, L.B. & Weaver, P.A. (eds.) *Theory and practice of early reading,* 3 Vols. Hillsdale, N.J.: Erlbaum, 1979.

Roberts, T. Auditory blending in the early stages of reading. *Educational Research* (Gr. Brit.), 1979, *22,* 49–53.

Rode, S.S. Development of phrase and clause boundary reading in children. *Reading Research Quarterly,* 1974, *10,* 124–142.

Roit, M.L. *A re-examination of a multiple-syndrome theory of dyslexia,* Special Qualifying Paper, Harvard Graduate School of Education, 1977.

Rosenshine, B. Recent research on teaching behaviors and student achievement. *Journal of Teacher Education,* 1976, *27,* 61–64.

Rosenshine, B. Content, time, and direct instruction, in P. Peterson, & H. Walberg (eds.), *Research on teaching: Concepts, findings and implications.* Berkeley, Cal.: McCutcheon, 1979.

Rosner, J. *Phonic analysis training and beginning reading skills.* Pittsburgh, Pa.: Learning Research and Development Center, University of Pittsburgh, 1971.

Rosner, J. Auditory analysis training with pre-schoolers. *Reading Teacher,* 1974, *24,* 379–384.

Roswell, F. & Natchez, G. *Reading disability: A humanistic approach* (3rd ed.). New York: Basic Books, 1978.

Rozin, P. & Gleitman, L. The structure and acquisition of reading, II, in A.S. Reber & D.L. Scarborough (eds.), *Toward a psychology of reading.* Hillsdale, N.J.: Erlbaum, 1977.

Rubin, R.A. Reading ability and assigned materials: Accommodation for the slow but not the accelerated. *The Elementary School Journal,* March, 1975, Vol. *75,* No. 6, pps. 373–377.

Ruddell, R.B. *Reading-language instruction: Innovative practices.* Englewood Cliffs, N.J.: Prentice-Hall, 1974.

Russell, D.H. *48th Yearbook of the NSSE, Part II—Reading in the elementary school.* Chicago, Ill.: University of Chicago Press, 1949.

Russell, D.H. Continuity in the reading program, in N.S. Henry (ed.), *Development in and through reading,* 60th yearbook of the National Society for the Study of Education, Part I. Chicago, Ill.: NSSE, 1961.

Rutter, M. et al. *Fifteen thousand hours: Secondary school and their effects on children.* Cambridge, Mass.: Harvard University Press, 1979.

Samuels, S.J. Hierarchical subskills in the reading acquisition process, in Guthrie (ed.), *Aspects of reading acquisition.* Baltimore, Md.: The Johns Hopkins University Press, 1976.

Samuels, S.J., Dahl, P. & Archwanety, T. The effects of hypothesis/ test training on reading skill. *Journal of Educational Psychology,* 1974, *66,* 835–844.

Sartre, J.P. *The words.* New York: George Braziller, 1964.

Satz, P., Friel, J. & Rudegair, F. Some predictive antecedents of specific reading disability: A two-, three-, and four-year followup, in J.T. Guthrie (ed.), *Aspects of reading acquisition.* Baltimore, Md.: Johns Hopkins University Press, 1976.

Satz, P., Rardon, D., & Ross, J. An evaluation of a theory of specific developmental dyslexia. *Child Development,* 1971, *42,* 2009–2021.

Schmidt, W.A. *An experimental study in the psychology of reading.* Supplemental Educational Monograph, No. 2., Chicago, Ill.: University of Chicago Press, 1917.

Schram, W. *Television and the test scores.* New York: College Entrance Examination Board, 1977.

Shankweiler, D. & Liberman, I.Y. Misreading: A search for causes, in Kavanaugh & Mattlingly (eds.), *Language by ear and by eye.* Cambridge, Mass.: M.I.T. Press, 1972.

Simons, H. Reading comprehension: The need for a new perspective. *Reading Research Quarterly, VI, 2,* 1971, 338–363.

Simons, H.D. Black dialect, reading interference, and classroom interaction, in L.B. Resnick & P.A. Weaver (eds.), *Theory and practice of early reading,* Vol. 3. Hillsdale, N.J.: Erlbaum, 1979.

Slobin, D.I. *Psycholinguistics.* Glenview, Ill.: Scott-Foresman, 1971.

Smethurst, W. *Teaching young children to read at home.* New York: McGraw-Hill, 1975.

Smith, F. *Understanding reading.* New York: Holt, Rinehart, Winston, 1971.

Smith, F. *Reading and nonsense.* New York: Teachers College Press, 1978.

Smith, F. Conflicting approaches to reading research and instruction, in L.B. Resnick & P.A. Weaver (eds.), *Theory and practice of early reading,* vol. 2. Hillsdale, N.J.: Erlbaum, 1979.

Smith, L. An analysis of the effectiveness of remedial reading programs. Qualifying paper, Harvard Graduate School of Education, 1972.

Soderbergh, R. *A linguistic study of a Swedish preschool child's gradual acquisition of reading ability.* Stockholm: Almqvist & Wiksell, 1971.

Southwest Regional Laboratory for Educational Research and Development. *Beginning reading program.* New York: Ginn, 1972.

Spache, G.D. & Spache, E.B. *Reading in the elementary school,* 4th edition. Boston, Mass.: Allyn and Bacon, 1977.

Stallings, J. *Implementation and child effects of teaching practices in follow-through classrooms.* Monographs of the Society for Research in Child Development, Serial No. 163, Vol.40, No. 7–8, 1975.

Sticht, T.G. (ed.). *Reading for working.* Alexandria, Va.: Human Resources Research Organization, 1975.

Sticht, T.G., Beck, L.J., Hauke, R.N., Kleiman, G.M., & James, J.H. *Auding and reading.* Alexandria, Va.: Human Resources Research Organization, 1974.

Strang, R.M., McCullough, C.M. & Traxler, A.E. *Problems in the improvement of reading.* New York: McGraw-Hill, 1945.

Strickland, R.G. The language of elementary school children: Its relationship to the language of reading textbooks and the quality of reading of selected children. *Bulletin of the School of Education,* Indiana University, 1962, *38,* 1–131.

Taylor, E.A. *Controlled reading.* Chicago, Ill.: University of Chicago Press, 1937.

Taylor, E.A. The spans, perception, apprehension, and recognition as related to reading and speed reading. *American Journal of Ophthalmology,* 1957, *44,* 501–507.

Taylor, H.G., Satz, P. and Friel, J. Developmental dyslexia in relation to other childhood reading disorders: Significance and utility. *Reading Research Quarterly,* 1979, *15,* 84–101.

Taylor, I. Writing systems and reading, in G. Mackinnon & T.G. Waller (eds.). *Reading research: Advances in theory and practice,* Vol. 2. New York: Academic Press, 1981.

Taylor, S., Frankenpohl, H., & Pettee, J. Grade level norms for the components of the fundamental reading skill. *Educational Development Laboratories Research and Information Bulletin,* No. 3, 1960.

Templin, M.C. *Certain language skills: Their development and interrelationships.* Minnrelat University of Minnesota Press, 1957.

Terman, L.M. *Genetic studies of genius Vol. 1, Mental and physical traits of a thousand gifted children.* Stanford: Stanford University Press, 1925.

Thorndike, E.L. Reading as reasoning: A study of mistakes in paragraph reading. *Journal of Educational Psychology,* 1917, *8,* 323–332.

Thorndike, R.L. *Reading comprehension in education in fifteen countries.* International Studies in Evaluation III, Stockholm: Almqvist and Wiksell, 1973.

Thorndike, R.L. Reading as reasoning. *Reading Research Quarterly,* 1973–74, *9,* 137–147.

Tinker, M.A. *Bases for effective reading.* Minneapolis, Minn.: University of Minnesota Press, 1965.

Tinker, M.A. & McCullough, C.M. *Teaching elementary reading,* 4th edition. Englewood Cliffs, N.J.: Prentice-Hall, 1975.

Toffler, A. *The third wave.* New York: Morrow, 1980.

Torrey, J. Learning to read without a teacher: A case study, in F. Smith (ed.), *Psycholinguistics and reading,* New York: Holt, Rinehart, and Winston, 1973.

Vellutino, F.R. *Dyslexia: Theory and research.* Cambridge, Mass.: M.I.T. Press, 1979.

Venezky, R. Two approaches to reading assessment: A comparison of apples and oranges, in Pflaum-Connor (ed.), *Aspects of reading instruction.* Berkeley, Cal.: McCutcheon, 1978.

Venezky, R.L. The origins of the present-day chasm between adult literacy needs and school literacy instruction, paper presented at Harvard Graduate School of Education Conference on Literacy and Competency, Cambridge, Mass., April 15, 1981.

Vernon, M.D. *Reading and its difficulties.* London: Cambridge University Press, 1971.

Vernon, M.D. Varieties of deficiency in the reading processes. *Harvard Educational Review,* 1977, *47,* 396–410.

Vogel, S.A. Syntactic abilities in normal and dyslexic children. *Journal of Learning Disabilities,* 1974, *7,* 103–109.

Vurpillot, E. The development of scanning strategies and their relation to visual differentiation. *Journal of Experimental Child Psychology,* 1968, *6,* 622–650.

Vygotsky, L.S. *Thought and language,* edited and translated by E. Hanfmann, and G. Vakar. Cambridge, Mass.: M.I.T. Press, 1962.

Wagner, D.A. & Lofti, A. Traditional Islamic education in Morocco: Socio-historical and psychological perspectives. *Comparative Education Review,* 1980, *24,* 238–251.

Walker, R.Y. A qualitative study of the eye movements of good readers. *American Journal of Psychology,* 1938, *51,* 472–481.

Wallach, M.A. & Wallach, L. *Teaching all children to read.* Chicago, Ill.: University of Chicago Press, 1976.

Wallach, M.A. & Wallach, L. Helping disadvantaged children learn to read by teaching them phoneme identification skills, in L.B. Resnick & P.A. Weaver (eds.), *Theory and practice of early reading,* Vol. 3. Hillsdale, N.J.: Erlbaum, 1979.

Walmsley, S.A. *The criterion-referenced measurement of an early reading behavior,* unpublished Ed.D. dissertation, Harvard Graduate School of Education, 1975, *Dissertation Abstracts International,* 1976, 36, 7193A–7194A (University Microfilms No. 76-10, 570, 190).

Weaver, P.A. *Research within reach.* St. Louis, Mo.: CEMREL, 1978.

Weber, G. *Inner-city children can be taught to read.* Washington, D.C.: Council for Basic Education, 1971.

Weber, R.M. First graders' use of grammatical context in reading, in Levin & Williams (eds.), *Basic studies in reading.* New York: Basic Books, 1970.

Wells, G. (ed.). *Learning through interaction.* New York: Cambridge University Press, 1981.

Werner, H. & Kaplan, E. *The acquisition of word meanings: A developmental study.* Monographs for the Society for Research in Child Development, Vol. 15, Serial No. 1, 1952.

Westport, (Conn.) Public Schools, Reading survey, unpublished, 1964.

White, S., Day, M.C., Freeman, P.K., Hantman, S.A., & Messenger, K.P. *Federal programs for young children: Review and recommendations Vol. 1: Goals and standards of public programs for children.* (AEW Rep. No. DHEW-05-74-101) Washington, D.C.: U.S. Government Printing Office, 1973 (ERIC Document Reproduction Service No. ID 092 230).

Wiig, E.H. & Samel, E.M. *Language disabilities in children and adolescents.* Columbus, Ohio: Chas. Merrill, 1976.

Wirtz, W. *On further examination: Report of the advisory panel on the Scholastic Aptitude Test Score decline.* Princeton: College Board Publications, 1977.

Wolf, M. *The relationship of disorders of word-finding and reading in children and aphasics.* Unpublished Ed.D. thesis, Harvard Graduate School of Education, 1979.

Wolff, P.H. *The developmental psychologies of Jean Piaget and psychoanalysis.* New York: International Universities Press, Inc., 1960.

Zinchenko et al. The formation and development of perceptual activity. *Soviet Psychology and Psychiatry,* 1963, *2,* 3–12.

Zorfass, J. Stage struck: Reasons why the deaf can't read, unpublished paper, Harvard Graduate School of Education, 1980.

INDEX

About the Author

JEANNE S. CHALL, Ph.D., is Director of the Reading Laboratory and Professor of Education at Harvard University. She is the author of the classic study, *Learning to Read: The Great Debate* (McGraw-Hill, 1967; updated edition, 1983), and numerous other publications including the famous Dale-Chall readability formula. A member of the National Academy of Education, Dr. Chall lives in Cambridge, Massachusetts.

Credits

Excerpt from *Building Dreams,* Teacher's Edition, Book 3-1. Copyright © 1980 by American Book Publishers.

Fink, Rosalie. "The Stages and Adult Dyslexics," from *Successful Dyslexic Alternative Pathways to Reading: A Developmental Study* by Rosalie Fink. Copyright © 1992 by Rosalie Fink Reprinted by permission.

Gates, Arthur. Excerpt from *The Improvement of Reading* by Arthur Gates. Copyright © 1947 by Arthur Gates. Reprinted by permission of Macmillan/McGraw-Hill School Publishers.

Gessell, A. L., F. L. Ilg, and L. B. Ames. Excerpt from *Youth the Years from Ten to Sixteen* by A. L. Gessell, F. L. Ilg, and L. B. Ames. Copyright © 1950, 1956 by A. L. Gessell, F. L. Ilg, and L. B. Ames. Reprinted by permssion of The Gessell Institute of Child Development.

Geva, Esther. "Discussion of J. S. Chall's 'The Reading Crisis: Why Poor Children Fall Behind.'" Reprinted by permission.

Knox, Warren, et al. Excerpt from *The Wonderful World of Science,* Revised Book 6 by Warren Know, et al. Copyright © 1957 by Warren Knox, et al. Reprinted by permission of Macmillan Publishing Company.

Levin, Harry. Excerpt from *The Eye-Voice Span,* by Harry Levin. Copyright © 1979 by Harry Levin. Reprinted by permission of MIT Press.

Excerpt from *Moving On,* Teachers Edition, Book 1. Copyright © 1980 by American Book Publishers. Reprinted by permission.

Perry, W. Excerpt from *Forms of Intellectual and Ethical Development in the College Years,* by W. Perry, copyright © 1970 by Harcourt Brace and Company, reprinted by permission of the publisher.